William C. Bullitt AND THE SOVIET UNION

Indiana University International Studies

William C. Bullitt AND

THE SOVIET UNION

by Beatrice Farnsworth

INDIANA UNIVERSITY PRESS
BLOOMINGTON AND LONDON

TO MY MOTHER AND FATHER
AND TO JOHN

CONTENTS

ACKNOWLEDGMENTS

My sincere thanks to the late Mr. William C. Bullitt, who, without inquiring into my interpretations, kindly permitted me to use his unpublished papers at Yale University. At a last interview, in August, 1966, only six months before his death, Bullitt was in gay spirits; and as always vociferous in his views. I am grateful to Mr. Bullitt for his readiness to sit with me, recall the past, and freely answer all questions. My book was already in the Press at the time of Bullitt's death from leukemia in February, 1967.

While this essay was originally written as a dissertation for the degree of Doctor of Philosophy at Yale, I had first embarked on the topic of Bullitt's diplomacy with the aid of Professors Jesse D. Clarkson and Robert H. Ferrell, who introduced me to historical research under the auspices of what was then the Social Science Research Council undergraduate research training program. I am indebted to the Social Science Research Council, to Yale University, and to the Edwin S. Reid Foundation for considerable support given in the early part of this project.

I feel unusually fortunate to have been guided by dedicated and distinguished scholars. Professor Robert H. Ferrell, who continued to be my teacher long after undergraduate days, has always been willing to read chapters and make valuable suggestions. It is impossible for me to describe fully the amount of help given by Professor Samuel Flagg Bemis; perhaps only those students who have had the benefit of his aid can appreciate the time and thought Professor Bemis has given each of us. I am grateful for his careful search for errors in style and organization—even from a room in Grace-New Haven Hospital—several years ago.

This essay has been completed under the auspices of the Radcliffe Institute for Independent Study. I wish to thank the Institute for its invaluable support over the two-year period during which I have been a fellow, and especially to thank Miss Constance E. Smith, Dean of the Radcliffe Institute, for her sympathetic help. My husband, John, has given good-natured aid at all points; my work has benefited from his suggestions as to style.

Research was made easier thanks to the helpfulness of the staff members of the Yale University library, the Harvard and Cornell University libraries, the Roosevelt library at Hyde Park, the Historical Manuscripts Division of the Department of State, the Foreign Affairs section of the National Archives, the Manuscript Division of the Library of Congress, and the Massachusetts Historical Society. I am indebted to the librarians in each of these centers who guided me to the necessary materials.

Mr. Henry Cabot Lodge, Jr. kindly granted me permission to use the Lodge papers at the Massachusetts Historical Society.

I owe thanks to Mrs. Jane Corcoran, who typed my manuscript in her "spare" time and rushed to meet a deadline.

B. F.

William C. Bullitt AND THE SOVIET UNION

I

William C. Bullitt and World War I

" 'Bill, I don't dispute your facts, they are accurate.' " Franklin D. Roosevelt continued, " 'I don't dispute the logic of your reasoning. I just have a hunch that Stalin is not that kind of man. Harry says he's not. . . and I think that if I give him everything I possibly can and ask nothing from him in return, *noblesse oblige*, he won't try to annex anything and will work with me for a world of democracy and peace.' "

William C. Bullitt jerked forward, his light-colored eyes very bright, his voice agitated. He reminded the President that "when he talked of *noblesse oblige* he was not speaking of the Duke of Norfolk but of a Caucasian bandit whose only thought when he got something for nothing was that the other fellow was an ass. . . ." The President showed a trace of irritation: " 'It's my responsibility and not yours; and I'm going to play my hunch.' "[1]

Events proved the President wrong, his former adviser correct. Stalin did not cooperate. In 1941 Bullitt's ability to forecast Soviet policy exceeded Roosevelt's. Still, it had taken William C. Bullitt nearly twenty years to achieve insight to the Soviet regime and to complete his education as a diplomat. The fitful development of Bullitt's education, and his efforts to influence American foreign policy in accordance with its evolution, will be the subjects of this study.

I

At birth in 1891 Bullitt fell heir to the advantages that come with established wealth and a three-hundred-year-old American name: security, culture, social position. Like other junior aristocrats of his Philadelphia circle, he was photographed in the family album wearing long curls, buttoned boots, and a little Lord Fauntleroy suit. He spoke French at dinner table. He enrolled in a fashionable school to prepare for Yale. He attended the dancing class where for over half a century young Philadelphia society had learned to waltz. Easter cotillions with boys in blue suits and girls in pastel chiffon; summer visiting his aunt, a duchess, in Europe; hours spent listening to proud tales of the dissenters in his ancestry —Captain William Christian, who was hanged, drawn, and quartered for opposition to Cromwell; Fletcher Christian, who led the mutiny against the tyrannous Captain Bligh; and most impressive of all the fiery Patrick Henry, who cried "Give me liberty or give me death." Family dinners with "silver plates on heavy linen, mountains of fruit and trees of roses, forests of candles, deep-cut glass. Twenty-dollar gold pieces under children's napkins."[2] Such was the future ambassador's childhood.

From the secure world of Rittenhouse Square, Bullitt derived an imperiousness, an amazing assurance, a belief that he might act as he pleased and probably not suffer the consequences. One sees this side of Bullitt's personality in his career at Yale. Bullitt—class of '12 —was intent on being a Yaleman distinguished for importance and leadership. He did become an outstanding campus figure—president of the Dramatic Association and Debating Society, an editor of the *News*, a significant man in Scroll and Key, and member of Phi Beta Kappa. His class voted him "most brilliant senior." In the contest for most versatile, he finished second. But one suspects that the combination of abilities was not always pleasing. A yearbook comment is uncomfortably suggestive: "Bill Bullitt," a classmate wrote, "is still holding forth at the Elizabethan Club electing to membership whom he pleases and setting the pace of undergraduate thought in general."[3]

Still, there was more to Bullitt than ebullient "big man on campus"—something sincere occasionally hidden by the glow of Rittenhouse sophistication and undergraduate success. Following family tradition, Bullitt began to study law at Harvard, but soon he became shocked at legal ethics.[4] Some years later, explaining his early reactions, he recalled a teacher putting cases to a class in criminal law. When a student, probably Bullitt, objected that the teacher's solution was unjust, he was coolly informed he would find "the Divinity School three blocks to the left." As Bullitt remembered, the class guffawed, but he became convinced that law was no job for anyone who cared about making life fuller and finer; that, in fact, law was no job for anyone but a crook. Bullitt's imagination and nervous energy were also uncomfortable within the confines of legal thought. He left Harvard before the year ended.

Though his influential family could have secured him an important position, Bullitt was eager to make his way in a new field. He returned to Rittenhouse Square and joined the staff of the Philadelphia *Public Ledger* as a ten-dollar-a-week beat reporter. The young man, Yale '12, worked a twelve-hour day on a night shift in a callous world of ambulance drivers and tough policemen. But Bullitt was not long on a beat. Europe was at war. Bullitt, in Europe the summer of 1914, had witnessed its outbreak. He could not forget exuberant, singing mobs in England, in Germany, in France, all certain as they marched to battle that God was on their side. The relative guilt of the participants, the probable outcome of the fighting, the secret aims of each side, all fascinated the new journalist. He started to submit to the editorial page analyses of the European situation. When the associate editor went to another paper, Bullitt got his job—just six months after he joined the staff. He began then to establish a reputation in journalism.

When Henry Ford dispatched his quixotic peace ship to Europe late in 1915, the *Ledger* sent Bullitt to cover the "ark." The young journalist wrote a series of clever articles ridiculing the pilgrims and delighting his colleagues. He began his first report:

> What is so rare as a day on which pacifists are pacific? The pilgrims had every reason to be calm today. They were filled with turkey and surrounded by beauty. The hills of snow and pine leaping out of the blue Christiansand Fjord under the pink fingers of the sunset would have made a dinosaur a household pet. But the pacifists were spoiling for their daily battle. . . . A meeting called by Judge Lindsey, after dinner, unanimously adopted a new peace platform. Speeches redolent with the fatherhood of God and the brotherhood of man soared upward. A general embrace seemed imminent. But there was just a tinge of disappointment on the faces of the pacifists. They all seemed to feel that something had been forgotten. What was it? Of course! They had overlooked the evening fight; and to be a pacifist and to forget one's evening fight is more serious than to be a baseball fan and miss the world series. Col. S. S. McClure leaped into the breach. The Colonel is a trifle disgusted with the pilgrims. Earlier in the evening he had exclaimed: "There is one word in the world I hate—pacifist. I came on this boat a pacifist, but I have become a militarist. If I wanted to raise soldiers in the United States, I would just parade this shipload of pacifists across the nation. They would insure enlistments by the million."

As the ark headed home in January, Bullitt cabled: "I swear that I've been nuts for weeks."

When Bullitt married Ernesta Drinker of Philadelphia in March, 1916, he persuaded the *Ledger* to send him abroad—at his own expense—as war correspondent to the Central Empires. The blithe young journalist, on his wedding trip, found that wartime Europe could be as amusing as Ford's peace ship. The *Ledger* featured articles for its Sunday readers hilariously entitled: "Spare us from efficiency! Cry of traveler in Germany!" recounting the horrors of German frontier inspection. Books, pencils, writing paper, and visiting cards all fell under the embargo. This he bore bravely,

Bullitt informed his readers, but when guards dared confiscate the eleven tubes of hair tonic brought along for his prematurely balding head, "his manhood was undone"; they led him away, "bleating helplessly."[5]

Even from this gay youth, there were articles of a more serious nature. Imagining that he might extend his activities beyond those of ordinary correspondent, Bullitt had entered Germany and Austria equipped with eighty-seven letters of introduction and a special letter of identification from the State Department. These he hoped would enable him to speak with top military and civilian leaders. The letters were met with clicking heels and salutes. Bullitt conferred with important figures and asked them significant questions. Would you look with favor now upon a move for peace by Woodrow Wilson, he inquired of Count Tiza of Austria. When Tiza replied that the present time—September 3, 1916—was inopportune for such a step but that he hoped Wilson might make the overture in a few weeks, Bullitt told the Count he would repeat their conversation to the State Department.[6] In Germany, Bullitt offered to take a confidential communication from Von Jagow to the American government.[7] Bullitt had many interviews of this sort. "Every time Billy has a new idea about the war," Mrs. Bullitt noted in her diary, "he gets a German and inflicts it on him."[8]

Bullitt returned to his Philadelphia newspaper office in the autumn of 1916. His articles on the Central Empires had made him something of an authority on foreign affairs. In May, 1917, a month after American entry into World War I, Bullitt was therefore invited to work with George Creel's Committee on Public Information. His job consisted of preparing weekly news articles from confidential telegrams to the Department of State. Three months of this work convinced Bullitt that the material he was allowed to use was insufficient for the articles he wanted to write. He decided to rejoin his newspaper.

The United States now at war, the *Public Ledger* opened a

Washington bureau in September, 1917; twenty-six-year-old Bullitt, already in the capital, was chosen to head it. As chief of a news bureau, the young journalist repeated a pattern of rapid successes. Aided by three assistants, who covered routine work, he was left free to make contacts and develop special stories. Bullitt had met previously some members of Washington officialdom at resorts and social functions. One of these former acquaintances was Colonel Edward M. House, President Wilson's chief adviser. The urbane, kindly Texan soon developed a high opinion of Bullitt's ability and showed him special favors. From highly-placed friends like the Colonel, Bullitt began to get hold of exclusive stories which aroused the envy of rival reporters. Soon newspapers around the country were telegraphing the *Ledger* for its Washington daily news schedule.[9]

Still, writing "editorials no one ever read" no longer satisfied Bullitt. He turned now to Colonel House with a request. Apologizing for what might appear as "insufferable cockiness," Bullitt explained that he was still searching for some service to which he could give everything in him for twenty-four hours a day. Would Wilson perhaps need another personal secretary, a young man "who is used to keeping his mouth shut."[10] There is no reply to Bullitt's request in the House papers at Yale. Presumably it was the Colonel who underlined the words "keeping his mouth shut" and drew a question mark beside the phrase. Bullitt did not receive the position.

Not through the aid of Colonel House, but in a peculiarly unfortunate way, the young newsman soon came to Wilson's attention. Bullitt got himself into a good deal of trouble in October, 1917, by publishing in the *Ledger* a story concerning the personnel of a proposed interallied war conference, a story which the Department of State had requested not be printed. The matter was grave enough for the President to take a personal interest in it. Although Bullitt explained that since he had not been present at the news conferences in which the Department had requested secrecy, he knew nothing of the restriction, Wilson remained convinced that Bullitt's behavior had been deliberate. The President went so far as to write personally to H. B. Brougham, of the *Ledger*, insisting that a man who "would do what Mr. Bullitt did" should not be trusted with as responsible a position as he occupied in Washington. We can "never trust to his discretion again," the President concluded. He demanded Bullitt's immediate removal from his Washington post.[11]

The eagerness with which prominent men came to Bullitt's defense tells us much of the regard in which he was held. In reply to the irate President, the editor of the *Ledger* maintained that he considered Bullitt innocent, that the responsibility for the story lay with the *Ledger*'s night editors, who had been aware of the Department's restriction when they allowed the story to go to press. Even Secretary of State Robert Lansing, who had demanded the secrecy, defended Bullitt on the same grounds. Lansing declared himself personally convinced of Bullitt's innocence: Bullitt was a "man of integrity who would not knowingly violate a confidence." Indeed, Bullitt was "the safest representative of the *Public Ledger* we could have in the State Department."[12] Apparently no one—least of all the Secretary—wondered why Bullitt was not present at the news conference. Bullitt has himself explained: he avoided Lansing's meetings with the press because he felt that the Secretary of State never had anything significant to say.[13]

Although Wilson consented finally to withdraw his demand that Bullitt leave the capital, Bullitt was no longer interested in heading the *Ledger*'s Washington bureau. Knowing that he would soon be called to military service, Bullitt began efforts in December, 1917, to obtain a commission in the Signal Officer's Reserve Corps. Again, in letters regarding Bullitt's personal character and qualifications, older men expressed their esteem. "Few men of his age have so clear a knowledge of world politics and the conditions that this war has brought about as Mr. Bullitt," wrote John Sturgis, editor of the *Public Ledger.* "His enthusiasm is unbounded," Sturgis continued, "but is tempered by keen logic and well ordered judgment. I know of no man whose personal character and habits are of a higher standard than his."[14] Professor Chauncey B. Tinker of Yale described Bullitt as "one of the most brilliant graduates of this University, a man of keen intellect, wide experience and tireless will." Tinker indicated regret that the government had not long since availed itself of Mr. Bullitt's "unusual gifts."[15]

Although Bullitt was offered a commission in the army and an assignment to the war college in connection with gathering political information, he did not enter the armed services, for he was able instead to secure a position as an assistant in the Department of State. In December, 1917, Bullitt moved from the offices of the *Public Ledger* into the somber State, War, and Navy Building overlooking the White House lawns. The State Department presented a very congenial group. Bullitt's desk was in a "big splendid room" filled with eager young men—chiefly recent graduates of Yale, Harvard, and Princeton— each seated behind a large desk covered with yellow telegrams and pink envelopes in stacks that grew higher through the day. Bullitt worked in the West European Division under the immediate supervision of Joseph Grew, a young career diplomat. Kindly William Phillips, Undersecretary of State, had his office next door. A few doors down the hall was the Assistant Secretary of the Navy, Franklin D. Roosevelt. Although Bullitt did not care for his chief, Secretary of State Robert Lansing, whom he judged too ponderous (and who he sensed was often in a position subordinate to Presidential adviser Colonel House), he took an immediate liking to the Counselor of the Department, Frank Polk.

Thus Bullitt began his diplomatic career. Bullitt has explained why he left a promising future in journalism for a government position. He "planned to end the war—" not by military service but from behind an influential desk in Washington.[16] An explanation of this sort elicits smiles, yet it is almost understandable coming from an energetic twenty-six-year-old who had behind him the plaudits of Yale and the friendship and admiration of the influential.

It appears not to have taken long for his superiors to agree with Bullitt's own estimation of his ability. Bullitt, who read German as well as English and French, had as his particular task analyzing the press of the Central Powers. Hoping to alienate the German Socialists from their government, Wilson utilized Bullitt's analyses to incorporate in his speeches the Socialists' own criticism of the German leaders.[17] Both the President and Colonel House were impressed by Bullitt's work. "I enjoy reading your reports," the Colonel wrote Bullitt, "there is always something in them that I have not seen elsewhere which gives one food for thought."[18] Presumably in reply to a question from the Secretary of State as to whether Bullitt's services were of such a nature to preclude his entry into the armed forces, William Phillips described Bullitt as "peculiarly well qualified for this work, not only because of his experience as a newspaper man, but also because of his knowledge of Germany and Austria and his personal acquaintance with many of the officials." "I have no hesitancy in saying," Phillips concluded, "that in my opinion he is necessary to the adequate and effective operation of the Department and cannot be replaced without substantial material loss."[19]

II

Professor Charles Seymour of Yale, who worked alongside Bullitt in wartime Washington, was also impressed by his former student's analytic mind. But, Professor Seymour has recalled, "Bullitt was always on the *qui vive* to follow up a new idea regardless of its direction."[20]

Although Bullitt's province was internal politics of the Central Powers, it took but a short time for the deteriorating Russian situation to absorb his thoughts. By the beginning of 1918, the Bolshevik seizure of power and its implication for the Allied war effort had become the chief topic of discussion among men old and young in the Department of State. But it was more than the excitement of a political overthrow, more than the anxiety as to whether Russia would formally remove herself from the war, that caused Bullitt's fascination with the revolution. Sometime early in 1918 Bullitt set down random thoughts on what the war and events in Russia might mean in the life of a young man. These notes—perhaps sketches for a character in a projected novel or play—illustrate the emotional impact of Russia's revolution. Bullitt wrote:

> What am I going to get killed for? I am going to get killed. I have no doubt of that. For years I have been sure that I should die in an aeroplane, and when we entered the war I said to myself "Here it is" and began to fly. I have counted myself out as a casualty already and don't worry about it anymore. . . . But I am naturally a coward. I shrink from unpleasantness. So I have had to force myself to do the hardest things always. And flying was the hardest thing. So I had to do it. . . . But what do I want to come out of the war. If I am going to die I would like something worth while to come out of it. What do I want to come? I do not want particularly to kill Germans. And I do not want a great lot of Germans to be killed. I would like to finish off the Kaiser and some of the officers whose pictures I have seen. But you never get a crack at those people. The Germans you get a chance to kill are young fellows who look like your own friends. There was a picture in Leslies last week of a boy in a machine gun crew who looked like my roommate at college. I know I would like him if I knew him. I don't want particularly to kill Germans.
>
> And there isn't anything that I want especially to die for in the President's list of fourteen peace terms or in the elaborate war aims of the Inter-Allied Labor and Socialist Conference.

Those two statements of aims seem to me to be the fairest I have seen and to be the blue prints of the good machinery for building and repairing the peace of the world. But there is nothing in political machinery that warms me enough to make me want to die for it.

Still there is something in the possibilities of this war that makes me glad to have a chance to serve. I suppose it is the sort of feeling that Wordsworth talks about in his poems on the French Revolution in which he says "Bliss was it in that dawn to be alive but to be young was very heaven" or something of the kind. I haven't got Wordsworth handy. I feel as if there might be a dawn after this war. Not a dawn of new international political machinery; but a new dawn in men's hearts. I feel as if there might be after this war, if it comes out right, a sort of spiritual conversion in the hearts of Americans and Englishmen and Frenchmen and Italians and Russians and Germans and all the worried peoples of Austria Hungary. . . . No machinery for bringing peace on earth can bring good will to men unless the hearts of the people of the world are changed. What's to prevent the Germans and the Japanese from using a League to enforce Peace as a cloak behind which they may prepare to dominate the world by force. What's to prevent sweat shops and factory towns. No machinery will do the trick. There has got to be a spirit and conversion. . . . I know a lot of men who have been in Russia since the Revolution began and they have all suffered conversion. They are done with Emperors, political emperors, financial emperors and moral emperors. They have exiled the Czar. Taken over the banks and buried Mrs. Grundy. As a nation they have become brotherly, open hearted, free from convention and unafraid of life. Is it impossible that the war may end in a similar state of grace in the rest of Europe and America? I believe it may end that way and that is the thing I am ready to die for.[21]

Not only for his fictional young hero, but for himself, as for John Reed, and for many other young and restless people, Russia represented brotherhood, a spiritual conversion, indeed a state of grace. Had he too not been seeking a spirit to live and die for, Bullitt might have regarded Bolshevik Russia as less glorious. As it was —as it is in fact with all men—Bullitt's intensity of feeling caused him occasionally to distort actualities in order to satisfy his emotional needs.

If Bullitt had kept his enthusiasm for the Bolsheviks to himself, his attitude would have been of minor significance. Once engrossed in the activities of Lenin and Trotsky, however, Bullitt became increasingly attentive to American relations with Russia. The roots of a policy which Bullitt was to pursue for twenty years were revealed in his early reactions to the revolution.

The Bolsheviks, seeking to take Russia officially out of the war, had begun negotiations on December 3 for a separate peace. Twelve days later Russia and the Central Powers signed a truce. When the formal peace conference convened at Brest-Litovsk on December 22, however, the negotiators found a major obstacle to agreement: treatment of the Russian territory occupied by troops of the Central Powers. Although the German delegation on December 25 conveyed to the Soviet representatives the impression that they would be prepared upon ratification of a separate peace to withdraw their forces from the Baltic countries and Poland, it soon became clear that Germany would do nothing of the kind. The Bolsheviks insisted, however, that the forces of the Central Powers should evacuate the Baltic areas. The German counterproposal required the Bolsheviks to recognize that the inhabitants of these territories had already demanded independence and separation from the Russian federation. Complete deadlock resulted. The conference adjourned temporarily (to be resumed on January 9) not only because of the stalemate but to give Russia's allies a last opportunity to enter the Brest-Litovsk negotiations. On December 29 Trotsky issued a final "Appeal to the Peoples and Governments of the Allied countries," urging them to join the peace conference.

On January 3, 1918, despite Trotsky's declaration, the *New York Times* carried a misleading front-page headline: "Negotiations Said To Be Broken Off." That same day William C. Bullitt, whose official assignment was to analyze the press of the Central Powers, assumed for himself an additional task. Prompted by the adjournment of negotiations at Brest, which he, like the *New York Times*, accepted as a break in the peace talks, Bullitt began to write a series of unsolicited memoranda to Colonel House, to William Phillips, even to President Wilson, suggesting a means by which Russia, now presumably turned from Germany, might be swung back to fighting with the Allies.

In the first of these missives, a lengthy memorandum of January 3 to William Phillips, Bullitt announced, "Today the iron it hot." The Bolsheviks, because of German refusal to withdraw from Poland and the Baltic regions, were "bitterly disillusioned" in regard to the sincerity and war aims of the German government. In view of their "momentary hostility" to Germany, a unique opportunity existed for the President. Bullitt then listed steps Wilson should take to prevent Russia from making a separate peace with Germany. By a specific statement of the liberal war aims of the United States and the Allies, the President might be able to unite Russia against the German government. Bullitt urged that Wilson announce American adherence to the six Bolshevik proposals put forth on December 22 at Brest as a basis for peace negotiations.[22] The President should further declare that the United States would be ready and joyful to discuss peace on the basis of those terms when Germany would send to a peace conference men "who sincerely in their hearts desire to create a more decent international order."[23] Only in the first draft of his memorandum did Bullitt go so far as to advise that Wilson recognize Soviet Russia. Still, in a later memorandum, this time to Colonel House, Bullitt declared it obvious that nothing could so stamp the President's words with "uncompromising liberalism as would the act of recognizing the Bolsheviki."[24] "Every principle of liberalism," he added a few days later, "impels toward the recognition of the Sovjet [*sic*]."[25]

In his January 3 message, Bullitt devoted considerable attention to Trotsky's "Appeal to the Peoples and Governments of the Allied Countries." He suggested that the President address Congress on the international situation, drawing attention at that time to the "close spiritual kinship" between his Senate address of January 22, 1917, and the appeal of Trotsky. A comparison of these two documents affords further insight to Bullitt's interpretation of the Russian situation. In his statement of January 22 the President had outlined the kind of peace the United States would wish to guarantee, stressing the principles of governments based upon the consent of the governed, of free access to and freedom of the seas, and of reduction of armaments. It should not be a punitive peace, Wilson had declared, not a victor's terms forced upon the vanquished, but a peace without victory secured by the organized force of mankind. Beyond the fact that Trotsky also urged the principle of self-determination and called for peace, one can find little in common between the two messages. Indeed, it was in the realm of "spiritual" impact that they differed most. Couching his words in Wilsonian loftiness, the President called for a covenant, a universal peace based on American political faith and the principles of mankind. He spoke, Wilson said, "for liberals and friends of humanity in every nation and of every program of liberty." Trotsky, on the other hand, directed himself to the "conscious proletariat" of the Allied countries, declaring that the success of Russia's peace program depended on the extent to which the will of the Allied imperialistic classes would be paralyzed by the will of the revolutionary proletariat in each country.[26] While addressing to the governments a last invitation to take part in the peace negotiations, Trotsky concluded with a promise of entire support to the working classes of each country which would, he predicted, "rise up against its national imperialists, against the jingoes, against the militarists, under the banner of peace, of the brotherhood of nations and of the socialistic reconstruction of society."[27]

How then could Bullitt have divined a kinship between the two messages? A subsequent memorandum to Colonel House tells us much: "I cannot pretend," Bullitt admitted, "to know the Russian situation intimately enough. . . . But I do feel sure that Trotzky [*sic*] is the sort of man we need to have in power in Russia and I think that we should do everything possible to strengthen his hands." At the present time, in dealing with a situation as confused as that in Russia, Bullitt contended, "it seems to be necessary to make decisions in accordance with broad principles without waiting to be sure of all the facts; because after all we cannot possibly get nearly all the facts. . . . Trotzky is a good deal ahead of us in the march toward world liberalism, but he is marching in our direction, and we must support him or Nihilism will follow."[28] Certain that the Bolsheviks were leading the way, impressed by their call for a really democratic peace, Bullitt could find in Trotsky's references to the laboring masses and the revolutionary proletariat, a kinship to Wilson's assertion that he would fain believe that he spoke for the "silent mass of mankind everywhere. . . ."

Neither Wilson nor Lansing shared Bullitt's views. Recognition had already been discounted by both men. Colonel House, although he believed that America should proffer financial, industrial, and moral support to Russia, did not recommend the move.[29] Trotsky's appeal did not excite Wilson's and Lansing's interest, but their reaction remained far different from Bullitt's. Even as Bullitt was expressing his sympathy with Trotsky's declaration, Lansing wrote a careful analysis of the same message. The Secretary began his memorandum to the President by pointing out that from beginning to end Trotsky appealed to a class and not to all classes of society. This Lansing interpeted as a direct threat to existing social order. Shrewdly, he noted the contradiction of appealing to a particular class—indeed making class superior to nationality—while at the same time demanding recognition of the rights of nationalities which comprised several classes. Trotsky had stressed the principle of self-determination in his appeal, calling for its application to the peoples of Ireland, Egypt, India, Indo-China, etc., as well as to Alsace-Lorraine, Bohemia, and the South Slav provinces. Lansing emphasized the dangerous implications such an interpretation could have, for there were enormous differences in applying self-determination to regions lying between two nations and to territories already within the sovereignty of a well-established state. A theory involving the latter seemed to Lansing "utterly destructive of the political fabric of society"; he feared it would result in constant turmoil and change. The Secretary went on to question the authority by which the Bolsheviks assumed the right to speak for the Russian people: "they seized the Government at Petrograd by force, they broke up opposition in the army by disorganizing it, they prevented the meeting of the Constituent Assembly . . . they have acted arbitrarily without pretense of legality. . . ." In view of this situation, Lansing advised against replying to Trotsky's "insidious address."[30]

The President also reacted unfavorably to Trotsky's appeal. The Bolshevik interpretation of self-determination seemed to Wilson particularly significant. In point of pure logic, the President told British Ambassador Sir Cecil Spring Rice on January 3, this principle, which Wilson considered good in itself, "would lead to the complete independence of various small nationalities now forming part of various Empires. Pushed to its extreme, the principle would mean the disruption of existing governments, to an undefinable extent."[31] While not liking the appeal any more than did his Secretary of State, Wilson did believe that if Trotsky's words were allowed to remain unanswered, if nothing were done to counteract them, their effect would be increased.[32]

Wilson saw one way in which he might influence the course of events in Russia—not by recognizing the Bolsheviki, not by adhering to Trotsky's appeal, but by issuing a vigorous statement of liberal American war aims.[33] Like others, Wilson labored under the impression that the Brest negotiations had been broken off. Perhaps this misconception accounted for the unqualified friendliness and sympathy with which his words abounded: cordiality for Russia could not have been more eloquently expressed than in point six of the Fourteen Points.[34]

Wilson's speech of January 8 delighted Bullitt, for he believed that the President was here echoing his own feelings. Yet in his Fourteen Points, Wilson refrained from endorsing the Bolsheviki or hinting at possible recognition. Nor did he declare adherence to the Bolshevik six-point peace program. Rather than the measure in support of Lenin and Trotsky which Bullitt urged on the administration, the references to Russia were simply calculated to bring that nation back to the war.

Bullitt's carefully prepared memorandum of January 3 did not wield the influence for which its youthful author hoped. Its significance lay in what it told of Bullitt's earliest Russian policy. Throughout the spring and summer of 1918, as the Soviet problem grew more acute, as Woodrow Wilson groped toward a policy of his own, William C. Bullitt was to continue his gratuitous suggestions. In months to come his efforts to influence decisions were occasionally to stimulate action.

III

Wilson's Fourteen Points did not prevent the Bolsheviki from reassembling at Brest-Litovsk. As a result of the resumption of peace negotiations, an issue which had absorbed the Allies in December now reasserted itself. Fearful that German influence and power would spread across Russia should a separate peace occur, the Allies spoke again of intervening in the Russian Far East. The British informed Wilson of their desire to see landed at Vladivostok an Allied force sufficient to protect the valuable military supplies stored there, for these supplies might fall into the hands of the Bolsheviki, thence to be sold to the Germans. On January 10

France added its voice to the call for military intervention in Siberia.[35]

The Allies had become similarly apprehensive about possible German moves against north Russia. The result of these fears was to be the arrival in March, 1918, of British and French ships, and a small contingent of British marines, at Murmansk—at the invitation of the local Soviet. The Soviet welcome to the Allies in north Russia proved only temporary. Soviet authorities resisted the intervention as soon as the German danger decreased, and as a larger purpose developed in Allied plans: the linking of intervention in north Russia with simultaneous intervention in eastern Siberia. The aim of intervention would come to be assistance to the counter-revolution. Although in April, 1918, the American government was willing to have one of its warships, with a complement of marines on board, proceed to Murmansk,[36] Washington was opposed to movement into the Far East. Lansing's answer to intervention suggestions indicated his government's belief that existing affairs in Siberia did not require an Allied military mission. The Secretary based his refusal on the assumption that intervention would be likely to offend Russians in sympathy with Allied war aims and might therefore result in uniting all factions in Siberia against the Allies.[37]

The Japanese in the beginning of 1918 were causing the State Department particular concern. Their government had made clear its opposition to joint intervention; it wished rather to intervene alone in Russia. Indeed, Japan had already sent war vessels to Vladivostok and had made plans for landing troops. Wilson, on January 20, indicated his apprehension over Japanese requests for a free hand: "It seems to me clear," the President wrote to Lansing, "that we should show very clearly in our reply that we should look upon military action in that quarter with distinct disapproval."[38]

The President and his Secretary of State had expressed unequivocal opposition to intervention. Yet how long could America hold out against Allied pressure? In official Washington, Secretary Lansing was first to be swung to the Allied view—his conversion took but a month. After reading a message from the French ambassador on February 27 which indicated Japanese willingness to confine their activities east of the Ural Mountains, Lansing suggested that it might after all be wisest if Japan were made a mandatory of the Allies. To the Secretary it seemed inevitable that the Japanese were going to act regardless of American protests. Swayed to Lansing's position, Wilson decided that while he could not sanction intervention, neither could he continue opposing the Allies. On March 1, the President regretfully gave Lansing a message for the Japanese indicating that the United States would have no objection if the governments of the Entente asked Japan to act in Siberia. The President assumed that Japan would proceed as an ally of Russia, with no purpose but to save Siberia from German invasion and intrigue.[39] Wilson was not pleased with his decision; still, he was relieved to have taken action. He instructed Lansing to show his communication to the British, French, and Italians, and then transmit it to the Japanese.

The Secretary of State was leaving for a vacation and therefore charged Counselor of the Department Frank Polk with carrying out the formalities. Had Lansing not now taken his vacation, perhaps the succeeding events would never have occurred. Frank Polk happened to be friendly with William C. Bullitt. And Bullitt chanced to be in the Counselor's office on March 1, as the latter awaited the arrival of the French ambassador, the first Allied representative to read Wilson's note. Knowing Bullitt's preoccupation with Russian affairs, Polk casually handed him the President's message. Bullitt's horror grew as he perused Wilson's endorsement of intervention. Hurriedly he informed Polk that he had discussed the Siberian problem with Colonel House and knew with certainty that this did not represent House's actual view. The Colonel was in New York at the moment, but Bullitt predicted that the note would be changed if House were only given the opportunity to reconsider the matter. Therefore he urged Polk to keep Wilson's message secret, assuring him that it would soon be reversed. Polk could hardly take orders from his young friend, an assistant in the West European Division. "Now get out, Bill, and forget about it," the Counselor said good-naturedly as the French ambassador was announced. That afternoon, Polk, following Presidential instruction, showed the message to the French, and British, and the next morning to the Italians.

Bullitt, of course, did not forget about it. Leaving Polk's office, he rushed down the dark corridor of the State, War, and Navy Building, an idea forming in his mind. At his own desk, he penned a passionate memorandum warning against the step about to be taken:

> If we stand aside while Japan invades Siberia with the assent of the Government of England and France, the President's moral position as leader of the common people of the world will be fatally compromised. . . . The President must oppose invasion of Siberia by Japan in the name of democracy and liberalism. He must act, or his position as moral leader of the liberals of the world will be lost. We cannot wash our hands of this matter. Unless we oppose, we assent. Pontius Pilate washed his hands. The world has never forgiven him.[40]

Hastily Bullitt phoned the Colonel in New York. House had discussed the reversal of America's position with the President, but he had developed his own misgivings about the decision: "I was not well while in Washington," he later noted in his diary, "and was not able to give the matter as clear thought as its importance deserved. The President, too, was tired. . . . Neither of us, I think was altogether fit last week to properly solve the problems which confronted us. There was never a more critical week in our history and the fact that it found us both at rather low ebb was unfortunate to say the least." Now, as Bullitt told him of the message

and read his own memorandum aloud, House grew more per-
turbed. When Bullitt suggested he leave his statement at the
White House, the Colonel approved. He had not known Wilson
was going to act so quickly, House afterward observed.[41]

The Colonel became increasingly uneasy. The next day, March
2, he spoke with Bakhmeteff, the Russian ambassador, and the day
following with Senator Elihu Root, both of whom shared Bullitt's
apprehensions regarding Japanese intervention. On March 3 House
wrote to the President. Like Bullitt he stressed the moral implications of the impending move. "I cannot understand the . . . determination of the British and French," he concluded, "to urge the
Japanese to take such a step. Leaving out the loss of moral advantage, it is doubtful whether there will be any material gain. . . ."[42]

House's message came to Wilson on March 4. "I have been sweat-
ing blood over the question what is right and feasible to do in
Russia," Wilson was to say. "It goes to pieces like quicksilver under
my touch. . . ."[43] Wilson's resolve again fell apart. The President,
swayed first by Lansing, was convinced now by House and Bullitt.[44] He phoned Polk and told him to hold up transmission of the
message to Tokyo. Meanwhile Wilson prepared a substitute note,
which he gave to Polk the next day, March 5.[45] In his revision
Wilson omitted the crucial statement that the United States had no
objection to intervention and instead made clear his continuing
opposition to the move, which he feared might play into Germany's hands as well as seriously impair America's moral position.

Almost immediately following the March 5 note, a new factor
impinged on the Siberian question: the Soviet delegation at Brest-
Litovsk signed a peace treaty with Germany. The immediate problem now became how to persuade the Soviet Congress to withhold its ratification of the separate peace. Buoyed by his success in
influencing House and Wilson—at least against endorsing Japanese
intervention—Bullitt evolved a new plan. Still assuming that the
"iron was hot," he conceived a friendly message from Wilson to

the Soviet ratifying Congress; such a note, he hoped, might halt adoption of the treaty. In a last effort to keep the Russians in the war Bullitt prepared the draft of such a note on March 9 and sent it to the President. Probably Bullitt had discussed his plan with House; for the Colonel, the next day, March 10, sent Wilson a communication from New York suggesting "a reassuring message to Russia when the Soviet meets at Moscow. . . . Our proverbial friendship for Russia could be reaffirmed," House continued, "and you could declare our purpose to help in her efforts to weld herself into a democracy."[46]

The idea of sending a message to the Russian people through the Soviet Congress appealed to the President. The Wilson-Bullitt message went to Russia; but it was no more successful in keeping the Soviets in the war than were the Fourteen Points.[47] The Treaty of Brest-Litovsk was ratified on March 16, 1918.

During the late spring of 1918 the Allies accordingly increased their pressure for a joint Siberian intervention. Growing more and more fearful that Wilson would acquiesce, Bullitt continued vigorous efforts to convince House and Wilson that American action in Russia would be disastrous. When John Reed, the young American Communist serving as Director of Revolutionary Propaganda for the Bolsheviks, sent Bullitt a memorandum on Russia, Bullitt forwarded it to the Colonel. To Reed's memorandum, which attacked the proposed Allied intervention as an ill-disguised move to overthrow the Soviet Republic, Bullitt added a suggestion. The President should create at once a Russian board to gather all information and to plan America's Russian policy—political, commercial, and military. This, Bullitt thought, might end the "wobbling" of United States policy.[48] House was so politely encouraging—"Your suggestions towards solving the problem seem very good and I am sending a copy of part of your letter to the President . . ."[49]—that Bullitt continued his appeals and advice. In late June, when Allied intervention in Siberia seemed imminent, Bullitt wrote: "I am so sick at heart because I feel that we are about to make one of the most tragic blunders in the history of mankind." "How," he asked the Colonel, "can we be so blind to the probability that the day troops of the Allies land at Vladivostok, the Soviets will begin a massacre of the counter-revolutionary upper classes; that these upper classes will appeal to the Germans to save them; and the German army will advance and set up a Government in Russia supported by German bayonets." "The Russian upper classes," Bullitt continued, "are about to appeal to Germany to overthrow the Soviets. Let them appeal. Let them overthrow the Soviets. Let us join the Soviets. And Germany will find in Russia what Napoleon found in Spain." "How," Bullitt pleaded, "shall we stand before the common people of the world if we join hands with the upper classes of Russia?" He was praying that the President would not allow an invasion of Siberia; to do so was as "wrong strategically and politically" as it was "wrong morally."[50] To this plea, House was politely noncommittal: "again let me urge you," he wrote from his summer home in Magnolia, Massachusetts, "to keep in touch with me and give me your point of view on pending questions, for I greatly value it."[51]

By the early summer of 1918 Allied insistence that Wilson approve intervention in Siberia had a new basis. Japan now refused to undertake a military expedition as an Allied mandate unless the United States gave approval and support. Unwilling to abandon the idea of Siberian intervention, the Allies addressed an eloquent appeal to Wilson on July 2. Once more they stressed the reasons for intervention: they felt obliged to take immediate action to save the Czech soldiers, prisoners of war in Russia, who had started for Vladivostok on their way to France; Allied intervention was essential to save the Russian people from domination by German autocracy; finally, Allied intervention was necessary to re-create an eastern front which, by preventing Germany from strengthening the western front, would result in a shortening of the war."[52]

Ultimately, reports concerning the Czechoslovaks tilted the balance to intervention. When official news of the Czech seizure of Vladivostok reached the State Department on July 2, Lansing began to outline what would prove to be a decisive memorandum. Capture of Vladivostok by the Czechs, Lansing claimed, had materially changed the situation. The Secretary stressed now an American responsibility to aid an Allied force in control of the port and eager for such help. Therefore he proposed that troops be sent to assist the Czechs in policing the railroad and in disarming and dispersing the German and Austrian prisoners-of-war who (in greatly exaggerated, inaccurate reports) were said to be opposing them.[53] The President, agreeing, determined now to intervene.[54] Wilson's decision was published to the world on August 3: the purpose of the military action in Siberia, the public was told, was "to render such protection and help as is possible to the Czecho-Slovaks against the armed Austrian and German prisoners who are attacking them. . . ."[55]

In view of their hostility to the Bolshevik regime, it is likely, however, that both President and Secretary seized on the Czechs as a convenient reason for an intervention which they privately hoped might stimulate "the Russian people" to support a pro-Allied and anti-Bolshevik government. Wilson and Lansing may also have hoped to help the Allies in a scheme to move the Czechs westward from Vladivostok to join with an Allied force coming south from Archangel under British command.[56]

Bullitt, in his sympathy for the Soviets, knew immediately that Russia would interpret intervention as an anti-Bolshevik move. He despaired when he heard of Wilson's decision. House received another message: America's Russian policy, Bullitt wrote, had "failed horribly." The men responsible for the policy did not understand the situation: "this is the only explanation for our turning Russia from a source of strength to the allies to one for Germany." "If we are to avoid driving Russia into military alliance with Germany . . . we must put our Russian policy in the hands of men who can weigh evidence and see Russia as it is." Again Bullitt urged a Russian board to be made up of representatives of the State and War departments, the Shipping Board, War Trade Board, and War Industries Board. To head this group, Bullitt recommended Louis Brandeis, since he was "passionately interested in Russia and the Revolution."[57]

The administration did not create a Russian board, but neither did a Russo-German military alliance result from Allied intervention. Wilson needed more information on Russia; so, too, did William C. Bullitt. In realizing that the Bolsheviki would oppose intervention and become more bitter toward the Allies, Bullitt correctly interpreted the Soviet attitude; yet in expressing fear of a Russo-German military alliance, he betrayed the limits of his understanding of the Russian situation. Not at the time of the Fourteen Points, nor upon the occasion of the Wilson-Bullitt message to the Soviet ratifying Congress, nor in September, 1918, could Russia have been a source of military strength to any nation. Russia could not fight; to do so was physically, spiritually impossible. Her army had disintegrated. Her people were starving. Recognizing this, Lenin had concluded the humiliating peace of Brest-Litovsk. Moreover, Lenin regarded any effort to keep Russia fighting as a selfish Allied stratagem to take pressure off the western armies by reactivating an eastern front. The ultimate Allied hope, he felt certain, was to see Germany destroy the Bolsheviks.[58]

Germany's collapse in October and the rapid end to the war prevented Bullitt from learning not only that there had existed no danger of a Russo-German military alliance, but also that his suggestions on policy throughout 1918 were predicated erroneously on the assumption that the iron had not yet grown cold. Lenin's words and Soviet actions suggest that probably the iron had never been hot. This Bullitt was not to realize.

Wilson, too, had based his decision on a false view of the Siberian situation. He pictured armed detachments of the Central Powers threatening to seize the area and being warded off by heroic Czech soldiers. Actually, there was little danger of such a seizure. The Czechs, moreover, aided by White Russian forces, were fighting the Bolsheviki, their immediate enemies.[59] Not only was Wilson mistaken about conditions in Siberia, he was ambiguous about the Czech action which Americans and Japanese were to support. Lansing wrote on July 4 of assisting the Czechs in policing the railroad and disarming and dispersing the German and Austrian prisoners. Then on July 6 Wilson spoke of assisting the Czechs at Vladivostok to form a junction with their compatriots in western Siberia and of guarding the line of communication of the Czecho-Slovaks proceeding toward Irkutsk. In his later *aide-mémoire* to the Allies he referred to helping the Czechs consolidate their forces and get into successful cooperation with their Slavic kinsmen. But to what end were the Czech forces to be aided: were they to be enabled to make their way to France? Or would they be helped to participate in a Russian civil war (which they were already doing)? The official documents remain unclear.

Wilson *did* say on July 6 that American forces would not be used to interfere in Russia.[60] Yet he was unable to prevent American units from being used for precisely this purpose. Neither did he withdraw the troops, as he said he would, when they were thus used, nor did he give the American forces any proper understanding of why they were in Siberia.

Not only did Wilson commit the United States government to a futile action—less than a month after troops arrived World War I ended, thus removing the chief rationale for intervention—but he achieved the opposite of his intentions regarding relations with the Western Allies. One reason compelling Wilson to intervene had been the pressure of Britain and France; the President had not wanted to alienate his associates. Yet when the President did make his decision, neither Britain nor France was given forewarning of his plans. The British, in particular, were outraged because Wilson envisioned no role for Britain or France in Siberia. As a result, the British had simply matched the American step by taking independent action of their own: they ordered troops to Vladivostok. Wilson's unilateral action not only antagonized the Allies, but brought them precipitously into the chaotic Siberian situation without the coordination which would have resulted from prior discussion.[61]

Moreover, Wilson sacrificed to a dubious venture the slight communication which had existed with the Soviet government in the official and semiofficial staffs left on Russian soil after the revolution. With intervention, these liaisons were withdrawn. Whether American-Soviet relations would have developed as they did had intervention not occurred is impossible to say. Certainly the Soviet attitude toward the United States was further poisoned; Soviet propagandists would long exploit the charge that in 1918 America had intervened in Soviet internal affairs with armed force.

Thus, although the result of American policy in 1918 had not taken the shape Bullitt dreaded—a Russo-German military alliance —the outcome was no less grievous. Despite the emotional basis of his advice, Bullitt's preview of the aftermath to intervention proved essentially accurate. He knew in 1918 what both Wilson and Lansing did not appreciate: America's Russian policy *had* to fail horribly.

IV

"What do I want to come out of the war?" William C. Bullitt had written early in 1918. That summer, Bullitt, disheartened and frustrated by the Siberian situation, became convinced that the government he served was not working for a new, more inspiring world. Woodrow Wilson was failing. Then, in late September, as the German army grew weaker, and as Germany's allies were breaking, Wilson turned from problems of Russian intervention to stating once more what he hoped to bring forth from the chaos of the past four years. William C. Bullitt was one of the thousands who listened when, on the night of September 27, President Wilson opened the Liberty Loan drive with a speech second in significance only to his Fourteen Points. The President began by insisting upon a "full and unequivocal acceptance of the principle that the interest of the weakest is as sacred as the interest of the strongest." There could be no bargain with the governments of the Central Empires, Wilson acknowledged, but the Allies must also realize their obligations. The price of a secure and lasting peace was "impartial justice in every item of the settlement, no matter whose interest is crossed; and not only impartial justice, but also the satisfaction of the several peoples whose fortunes are dealt with." It must be a just peace "that plays no favorites and knows no standard but the equal rights of the several peoples concerned . . . no separate interest of any single nation or any group of nations can be made the basis of any part of the settlement which is not consistent with the common interest of all." There could be "no special, selfish economic combinations," and "all international agreements and treaties of every kind must be made known in their entirety to the rest of the world." These were the things for which Wilson would work.

Bullitt thrilled to the President's words. Almost on the heels of his unhappy charge that American foreign policy had "failed horribly" his mood changed from despair to exaltation. As Wilson concluded his ringing words the night of September 27, Bullitt sat down and wrote a fervent note thanking the President for his speech. "Never have you voiced more clearly or more simply the hopes which are in the hearts of the millions in every nation who care about the same things for which you care. More and more," Bullitt continued, "the political and moral leadership of the world is coming into your hands: more and more you are making us

thank God that this is so."[62] That same night Bullitt wrote House
telling him of his gratification that in these troubled times the
United States had as its leader "a man so clean-hearted and so wise
as Mr. Wilson." The President's address had given the dejected
young man "new confidence and inspiration."[63]

As the armistice approached, Bullitt turned his attention from
the Siberian failure to the forthcoming negotiations. Wilson would
vindicate past errors with a peace settlement unique in history.
And Bullitt was determined to participate.[64] He went again to
Colonel House with a request: could the Colonel arrange to have
him included in the delegation? House was agreeable.[65] In December, 1918, the mercurial William C. Bullitt became an enthusiastic
member of the group who, with Woodrow Wilson, sailed to Paris
and the Peace Conference.

II

The Bullitt Mission
of 1919

Harold Nicolson has recalled the mood in which the young men of the British delegation sailed to the Peace Conference in 1919. "We were journeying to Paris," he wrote, "not merely to liquidate the war, but to found a new order in Europe. . . . There was about us the halo of some divine mission . . . we were bent on doing great, permanent and noble things."[1]

William C. Bullitt of the American delegation shared Nicolson's hopes. Early in 1918 Bullitt had written that there "might be a dawn after this war . . . a new dawn in men's hearts."[2] But while the sophisticated Englishman expected success in 1919, the presumably sanguine American, despite his initial enthusiasm, grew fearful. He began to sense a certain confusion aboard the *George Washington* going to Paris: no one knew quite what the President would do when he arrived; no one knew if the President had any plans. Bullitt recalled that three years earlier he had sailed to Europe with another gentleman who had expected to bring eternal peace to the world; he wondered now if Wilson would be much more successful than Henry Ford.[3]

It was difficult for young Bullitt to stand by quietly. One evening when the ship's passengers were assembled to watch a moving picture, he sat down beside Woodrow Wilson. One can see him now—slender, dark-haired, handsome; a somewhat lordly air. Everyone on board, he told the President, was in a "thoroughly cynical mood." "Call together a group including the members of the Inquiry," he urged, "and explain to them the policies you intend to pursue." If Wilson thought the twenty-eight-year-old presumptuous, he did not reveal his irritation. Instead he replied that he would do as Bullitt suggested, that he was "greatly obliged" for the advice; it simply had not occurred to him that such a conference would be necessary. Bullitt attended that meeting between Wilson and the Inquiry and for the first time he felt encouraged: Wilson would be receptive to advice. If he were convinced of the justice of a position, he promised, he would fight for it to the end —" 'politely if possibly, rudely if necessary.' "[4]

Yet after a few days of thought Bullitt was again convinced that what the President had in mind was desperately inadequate. "The President talks about a new world order. Then he outlines it until I feel as if the world were going to be a well regulated association of Presbyterian Sunday Schools."[5] With these apprehensive thoughts William C. Bullitt arrived in Paris.

During the trip over, the young man's position had been anomalous. Although he had hoped to receive an official title, the name-card on Bullitt's cabin door simply read—"attached to the American delegation." Even after he altered the word "attached" with pencil and eraser to read "attaché," the improvement was slight. In Paris, however, Bullitt was given a position of some importance. First, Colonel House asked him to be one of his secretaries for the Conference. A few days later Bullitt received what he described as a "new and curious job in addition to my work for House."[6] As Chief of the Current Intelligence Section, Bullitt received all information—military and political—and kept in daily touch with the American delegation. Each morning he would move from commissioner to commissioner presenting information: to some he spoke while seated on the edge of a bed, to others as they shaved in their bathrooms or lingered at their breakfast in coffee shops. So passed Bullitt's first weeks at Paris. But his routine was soon interrupted.

Shortly after the Peace Conference began, both Wilson and Lloyd George had stressed to their colleagues the necessity of making a decision regarding Russia, where civil war raged and Allied troops lingered in an anomalous position. With the war's end, the Russion situation had become acutely embarrassing for the Allies; many of the reasons which had originally been given to justify intervention in Siberia and north Russia could no longer be used. The time had come to decide on a new policy or new reasons for the old policy. The Russian question was therefore almost the first major problem to come before the delegates. From the first, the British Prime Minister appeared particularly anxious for a settlement. I hope, Lloyd George declared to the Supreme Council on January 12, that the Allies will not announce they have made peace if Russia, which forms half of Europe, is still at war.[7] As early as January 3, 1919, the British government had suggested a Russian truce to be followed by a meeting in Paris of representatives of the several Russian factions. Then on January 16, Lloyd George, Celtic eyes snapping, asked which Allied government was prepared to send a million men into Russia to crush Bolshevism. No one was. Lloyd George again suggested a meeting in Paris of the Russian governments.

The French delegate—squat, round-shouldered Clemenceau—and the Italian—Sonnino with his aged crew cut and jutting chin—were unenthusiastic. But the worried Wilson completely agreed: Lloyd George's idea seemed to him the only one that "led anywhere." In deference, however, to Clemenceau, who was appalled at the thought of the Bolsheviks coming to Paris, Wilson on January 21 suggested a modification—why not hold the conference at a rather distant place, perhaps near the Black Sea? Recognizing the impossibility of effective military intervention, the Supreme Council thereupon adopted the British-American idea. Clemenceau sat impassive, white mustaches drooping disapproval.

Wilson the next day drafted a proclamation inviting all organized groups in Russia to send representatives by February 15, 1919, to Prinkipo Island in the Sea of Marmora for a conference conditioned on general cessation of hostilities. The anti-Bolshevik groups reacted immediately with indignation; that they should be put on an equal plane with the "Reds" was insulting; that they should be asked to sit down with "criminals" seemed outrageous. The Soviet de facto government itself answered with marked vagueness: in a long, rather insulting reply they suggested terms of peace and offered to stop fighting but did not indicate precisely when.

The Prinkipo Proposal, although not officially dropped, slowly petered out. From the outset the French were opposed to peace with the Bolsheviks and continued to downgrade and even undermine the Prinkipo plan. The Quai d'Orsay went so far as to send word to Ukrainian and other anti-Soviet groups hinting that should they decline the Prinkipo Proposal, France would support their decision to seek to keep the Allies from making peace with the Soviets.[8]

With the Prinkipo scheme floundering, obviously headed for failure, Wilson's trusted adviser, Colonel House, thought of another plan. Since no one knew what conditions were in Russia, why not send in a secret investigating commission? As head of this group, House planned to appoint his young friend "Bill Bullitt."

Whether the idea for this secret mission—to be known only to the Americans and British—originated with the Colonel, or whether it was suggested to him, is not entirely clear. The American journalist Lincoln Steffens claimed to have inspired the scheme; but the idealistic Steffens also took credit for so many plans which obviously did not originate with him that it is not certain we may credit him with this one. According to Bullitt, Lord Northcliffe, the British publisher, first suggested early in January that a fact-finding body be sent to Russia.[9] Both House and Wilson were considering the idea by mid-January; but Bullitt was the only one who worked consistently throughout January and February to convince the Colonel that the scheme be carried out. The two men had discussed the Russian situation on January 19, 1919. Bullitt, who was alarmed over the vacillations of American policy, urged that the Conference send missions as soon as possible from the United States, Britain, and France to examine conditions in Russia with a view to recommending definite action. The make-up of a possible American mission was discussed: Judge Learned Hand, Raymond Fosdick, and William Allen White, all solid citizens, were mentioned as possibilities—"not forgetting Bullitt as general bootblack." Bullitt did not let the matter drop: other memoranda appeared on House's desk urging an immediate armistice offer by the Allies to the Bolsheviki. Then on February 17, 1919, Bullitt and House had another talk about Russia: House asked Bullitt to go to Moscow.[10]

Apparently the Colonel had decided that a small delegation would be more practical than joint groups coming from each nation. At any rate, Bullitt satisfied the Colonel as a shrewd choice: being young and relatively unknown he seemed not likely to attract too much attention.

Quite naturally Bullitt was delighted. He was dissatisfied with the way the conference was going; he was upset over the lack of a Russian policy. Now he assumed that he was to have a hand in formulating plans. He carefully chose his companions: Captain W. W. Pettit, a military intelligence officer and expert on Russian affairs; Lincoln Steffens,[11] a friend of the Bolsheviks, to be a liaison man; and a young naval secretary, R. E. Lynch.

Bullitt contemplated his venture with great seriousness. Unfortunately, however, the limitations of his mission were not made precise to him. Indeed, it is difficult even now, with documentary evidence available, to determine exactly what those limitations were. Afterward, Bullitt claimed that the British and Americans had sent him to Russia to get a statement of terms on which the Bolsheviks would cease fighting, so that if the Allies made another proposal it could be one they knew in advance would be accepted by the Soviets. It is likely that Bullitt derived this impression in the course of casual conversation with House, who did speak on February 17 of the need for " 'keeping in touch with the Bolsheviks with the aim of arranging terms and restoring allied influence and peace.' "[12] Yet Colonel House emphasized in other conversations that there was no need to fear Allied misunderstanding arising from Bullitt's mission; "Bullitt was going for information only."[13]

Apparently, the Colonel saw the projected mission in its various aspects but did not make clear his intentions, perhaps not even to himself. On the other hand, there is no evidence to indicate that Wilson had in mind an offer to Lenin. On the contrary, when the President left for his brief trip to Washington on February 15, 1919, it was with the evident belief that Bullitt would go to Russia simply to gather information. In fact, a day earlier Wilson had remarked to Winston Churchill—over from the War Office seeking an explanation of Allied Russian policy—that the delegates were interested not in a rapprochement with Lenin, but in clear information. Reports from Russia were so conflicting it was impossible to form a coherent picture of the state of the country.[14] While he could not refer to the "secret" mission explicitly, Wilson obviously had it in mind when he told Churchill that he himself would be "quite content" if "informal American representatives should meet representatives of the Bolsheviks."

On his own, Bullitt proceeded to draw up a list of specific proposals, which he presented to Colonel House for approval. House, temporarily in charge of the American delegation and preoccupied with a great many matters during Wilson's absence, added to the confusion by giving Bullitt free rein in organizing his mission.

House listened agreeably as Bullitt asked him whether, if the Bolsheviks proved ready to declare an armistice on all fronts, the United States would be prepared to do likewise. In event of an armistice would the United States insist on establishment of economic relations with Russia subject only to Soviet promise that goods be distributed equally to all classes of the Russian population? Would the United States insist on a joint statement asserting that all Allied troops be withdrawn from Russia on condition that there be no retaliation against persons who had cooperated with the Allied forces? Finally, would the United States insist that the Allies accept such a proposal if offered?[15]

According to Bullitt's own report, the Colonel answered these questions affirmatively—adding that it was not absolutely essential for Bullitt to get explicit assurance regarding payment of the Russian debt.[16]

In order to get an idea of the British view, Bullitt discussed the Russian question with Lloyd George's confidential secretary, Philip Kerr. The two men prepared what they thought might be a basis for peace with Russia. Then Kerr, on February 21, presented Bullitt with a list of points carefully terming them his own proposals, bearing no official significance. The British points (already canvassed between Kerr and Bullitt) were almost identical with those which Bullitt put to House: an armistice on all fronts, economic relations subject to equal distribution of goods, withdrawal of troops but no retaliation against those who had cooperated with the Allies. In addition, Kerr requested that all de facto governments in Russia should remain in control of the territory they then occupied.[17]

In essence the proposals Bullitt took to Russia were his own. They were sanctioned officially by no one. House had given only his casual approval. Kerr's emphasis in stressing that they represented only his private views indicated the Prime Minister's reluctance to commit himself too far regarding the Soviets. Indeed no substantial evidence indicates whether, before Bullitt departed, Lloyd George had seen the proposals.[18] Wilson, who sailed for Washington on February 15, probably did not know of their existence.[19]

Aware as we are now of the unfortunate outcome of Bullitt's mission, it is not difficult to look back and discover from the beginning evidence of vagueness.[20] But Bullitt, who went to Russia in all earnestness, could not be expected to have read the future.

> *"The fineness of the man's enthusiasm made my heart ache when I met him first. It was not my business to disillusion him, but I knew what was ahead of him."*[*]

II

The British made the necessary advance arrangements for the Bullitt mission, which left Paris for Petrograd on February 22. They reserved places on trains and boats, and British consuls speeded the group along its passage through Norway, Sweden, and Finland. In Stockholm, the American minister, Ira Morris, put Bullitt's mission in touch with Bolshevik agents, who then communicated with Russia and arranged for a diplomatic guide to Petrograd—one Kil Baum, a Swedish "Red."

Throughout the trip, Lincoln Steffens afterward recalled, Bullitt and Lynch skylarked, "wrestling and tumbling like a couple of bear cubs."[21] A noisy secret mission. Young Bullitt knew what he was doing; no one could suspect the group of secrecy or importance.

When the Bullitt party reached its destination, it discovered that Lenin had sent his Commissar for Foreign Affairs, Georgi Chicherin, to interview this mysterious special party from Paris, this mission that arrived by night in the deserted, cold, former capital of Imperial Russia. If the Bolsheviks were not sure why the

---

* Ramsay MacDonald on Bullitt. October 23, 1919. N. Y. *Call.*

group had come, the presence of an official of Chicherin's rank would indicate they took it seriously. The bearded, gentle-eyed Steffens explained to the Commissar that it was in the Bolshevik's interest to cooperate with Bullitt so as to enable Wilson and Lloyd George to win over the hostile French. This information Chicherin wired to Lenin, who sent back an invitation for the mission to come on to Moscow.

On they went. Upon arrival in the new Communist capital, Bullitt and Steffens were put up in a confiscated palace, which they found to be heated and plentifully staffed with servants.[22] Food was the principal difficulty in Moscow, 1919, but Bullitt and Steffens, anticipating their needs, had brought along mail pouches filled with canned goods. To this the Russians added plenty of black bread, tea, and "piles of caviar." The two emissaries, well established in their palace, were treated to operas, theater, and concerts; they even sat one evening in the historic box of the Czars.

But Bullitt, who had journeyed to Russia intent on doing important things, had no desire to waste time on trifles. Each day he negotiated with the worldly, cultured Chicherin and his aide Maxim Litvinov, that heavy-set, stolid, and hard-working bureaucrat, who even in 1919 was virtually assistant commissar for foreign affairs. Lenin was always nearby. A very striking man, Bullitt reported, "straightforward and direct, but also genial and with a large humor and serenity."[23]

From Chicherin and Litvinov, Bullitt received on March 14 a response to his careful approaches: a statement of the conditions to which the Soviet government would agree in exchange for peace with the world outside. The deadline for an Allied offer to this effect was April 10, 1919. The Russians accepted, with only a few modifications, the seven points of the Kerr memorandum and the questions answered affirmatively by House. The Soviet government promised that all de facto governments would remain in control of the territory they then occupied. That is, it offered to give up, at least for the time being, all of the Urals, Siberia, the Caucasus, the area around Archangel and Murmansk, Finland, the Baltic states, part of White Russia and most of the Ukraine. Allied troops were, of course, to be withdrawn, and military aid to anti-Soviet governments was to cease. The Soviets offered again to recognize their share of responsibility for the repudiated Russian debt. Finally they asked for a peace conference with the Allies.

Probably we will never know with certainty what was in Lenin's mind when he made this offer, but available evidence suggests sincerity. The Bolsheviks in 1919 were in the throes of civil war, suffering an Allied blockade, uncertain of their future. Above all, they needed an end to Allied support of the White armies, and a return to peace. Lenin seemed, indeed, to be preparing the people for another Brest-Litovsk at Allied hands.[24] On March 13, the eve of making his secret offer to Bullitt, he advised his countrymen, "it would not now be useless to recall this policy [Brest-Litovsk], now that the Entente countries are adopting an analogous position towards us," now that they want to "pillage" and "crush" Russia.[25] It appeared to Lenin that another "onerous" treaty would actually be beneficial: the governments of Denikin and Kolchak could not sustain themselves; with the withdrawal of Allied support, they would collapse. The counterrevolution would then come to an end.[26]

Obviously Lenin had much to gain from peace. How hopeful he was of a favorable outcome of the Bullitt plan is somewhat more difficult to determine. His experience a year earlier, at the time of Brest-Litovsk, with the empty words of the American Red Cross representative, Raymond Robins, must have made him wary of assurances from unofficial American visitors.[27] On the other hand, according to the testimony of Commissar Chicherin, the Bolsheviks took Bullitt's mission seriously.[28]

Another perplexing factor in the Bullitt-Lenin exchange was the continuance of Bolshevik revolutionary propaganda at the same time that the Soviets were calling for peace. Paradoxically, Bullitt reached Russia two days after the founding Congress of the Communist International had ended its sessions. Lenin, however, was aware of the poor impression these meetings would create. He himself gave a peculiarly frank explanation of the contradiction. To the newspaperman Arthur Ransome he revealed his fear that the Allies would ask, "How can we leave them in peace when they set about setting the world on fire?" The short, stocky dictator bluntly set forth his position: " 'We are at war, Messieurs: And just as during your war you tried to make revolution in Germany . . . so we, while we are at war with you, adopt the measures that are open to us. We have told you we are willing to make peace. . . . I am sure we could come to terms, if they want to come to terms at all,' " Lenin added to Ransome.[29]

Bullitt spent only one week in Moscow. Having received what he came for, a definite statement of Soviet terms, he was anxious to bring the plan back to Paris. At Helsingfors, on March 16, he dispatched Lenin's proposals, which in Bullitt's opinion presented an opportunity to make peace with the revolution on a just and reasonable basis—perhaps a "unique opportunity."[30] He added a message: The Russian people still had hope. They had gathered the impression that Wilson was "beginning to see through the lies against them" to the "very simple truth" that a "dull, inexperienced, a young people were trying rudely but conscientiously and at the cost of great suffering to themselves to find a better way to live for the common good than the old way."[31]

Bullitt was aware there would be difficulty in getting his plan across. And he had reason for concern. He had gone to Russia ostensibly to seek information but equipped with a list of questions; he was returning to Paris with a specific plan for settlement. Explanations of the Bullitt plan as a "revived Prinkipo" have been misleading. Bullitt's idea went far beyond that original proposal.

His project called for an Allied offer of peace to be extended to Lenin by April 10,[32] then a short period of armistice, to be followed by a conference between the Allies and the Bolsheviks. Recognition, although not explicitly mentioned, was certainly implied. One wonders if Bullitt, as he made his way out from Russia, had uncomfortable moments envisioning the reactions of Clemenceau, the Tiger, to this latest diplomatic innovation.

Arriving at the Hotel Crillon in Paris the evening of March 25, Bullitt immediately called on House. Together they went over the entire Russian situation. The Colonel, impressed with his emissary's achievement, appeared to Bullitt to be in favor of extending the peace to Russia, if possible on the basis of the Soviet proposal.

While Bullitt spoke, the Colonel had been busy "maturing plans" which he intended to put in execution the next day. Later he noted that at last he could see a way out of "that vexatious problem, that is, if we can get action by the Prime Ministers and the President."[33]

Encouraged by House's optimism, Bullitt anticipated little trouble from Lloyd George when he accepted the Prime Minister's invitation to breakfast at his apartment in the Rue Nitot on March 27. With General Smuts, Sir Maurice Hankey, and Philip Kerr present, the young Philadelphian and the Prime Minister of Great Britain sat down to consider the Russian situation. Lloyd George, having seen the Russian proposal when Bullitt wired from Helsingfors, handed the statement to General Smuts seated across the table. " 'That is the same one I have already read,' " he observed. Then he added, " 'General, this is of the utmost importance and interest, and you ought to read it right away.' "[34] Smuts after perusing the proposal agreed it was indeed important and ought not to be allowed to lapse.

Now the mercurial Welshman, David Lloyd George, revealed his fears! The kind and flattering words, a host's display of politeness—that was all. Unrolling a copy of the *Daily Mail*, Lloyd George pointed to a flaming article attacking Lenin.[35] As long as the British continued to be hysterical over the Russian "menace," how could he, the Prime Minister, be sensible? He shook his shaggy, gray head. Then to ease the American out, Lloyd George smoothly assured him that, of course, all reports from people sent into Russia agreed in general with his; he conjectured amiably that the thing to do now was send somebody to Russia who was known to everyone as a complete conservative so that the whole world would believe the report he brought back. Over coffee cups, the Prime Minister cheerfully ran through the names of people who might go. He thought of Lord Lansdowne, but then concluded that the best man for the job would be the Marquis of Salisbury, who was certainly respectable and well known. All this was idle chatter. Lloyd George knew it. So did Bullitt, respectable enough himself, but young. Although claiming willingness to follow the lead of the United States, the Prime Minister felt compelled, for serious political reasons, to ignore Bullitt's proposals.

Despite his personal reluctance to act, Lloyd George did advise that Bullitt issue a full report on conditions in Russia. The young man subsequently prepared such a statement, submitting it for release to the Commissioners. But Lansing cautiously advised them: "Keep entirely silent" on the Bullitt report.[36] The President concurred. Wilson and Lansing were prudent; they knew Bullitt's conclusions would set off outraged attacks from the anti-Bolshevik press.

Russia today, the report began, is in a condition of acute economic distress. The cause of the distress Bullitt attributed to the land and sea blockade maintained by the Allied powers. In consequence, every man, woman, and child in Moscow and Petrograd was suffering from slow starvation. The daily ration of Lenin and the other commissars, Bullitt observed, was the same as that of a soldier in the army or of a workman at hard labor.

As for social conditions, he reported that the destructive phase of the revolution was over and that all the energy of the government was turned over to constructive work. The terror was over and good order had been established: streets were safe, shooting had ceased, robberies were rare, prostitution had disappeared. Thousands of new schools had been opened in all parts of Russia and the Soviet government seemed to have done more for the education of the Russian people in a year and a half than czardom had in fifty years.

Turning to the political situation, Bullitt declared that the Bolshevik government was firmly established. He observed that perhaps the most striking fact in Russia was the general support given the government by the people in spite of their starvation. Indeed, the people laid the blame for their distress wholly on the blockade and on the governments which maintained it. The Soviet form of government, he thought, had become to the Russian people "the symbol of their revolution . . . it has acquired so great a hold on the imagination of the common people that the women are ready to starve and the young men to die for it."

Above all, Bullitt was impressed with what he described as the belief of the convinced Communists in their cause. This he found to be almost religious. "Never in any religious service," he reported, "have I seen higher emotional unity than prevailed at the meeting of the Petrograd Soviet in celebration of the foundation of the Third Socialist Internationale." He found characteristic the remark of one young man when questioned in regard to his starved appearance. The youth told Bullitt very simply: " 'I am ready to give another year of starvation to our revolution.' "

Lenin made a deep impression. Bullitt told of his visit to the Soviet leader. He was obliged to wait a few minutes before seeing Lenin until a delegation of peasants left his Kremlin office. They had heard in their village that Comrade Lenin was hungry. They had come hundreds of miles carrying 800 poods of bread as the gift of the village to Lenin. Just before them was another delegation of peasants to whom the report had come that Comrade Lenin was working in an unheated room. They came bearing a stove and enough firewood to heat it for three months. Lenin, Bullitt noted, was the only leader who received such gifts, and he turned them into the common fund.[37]

As a member of the Department of State in 1918, Bullitt had expressed similar views on Russia although he had not been there since the revolution. A visit to Moscow had only confirmed his early opinions. Bullitt's report was the product of a one-week sojourn and a preconceived belief that what he would see, he would like. In one short week Bullitt could not have observed all he described. He eagerly accepted as true the rather wishful exaggerations of Soviet leaders. The destructive phase of the revolution and the terror had not ended in February, 1919, but was merely in a temporary lull. Thousands of new schools had not opened anywhere but on paper. The blockade was, indeed, responsible for much of the privation, but so too was the chaos caused by over-rapid nationalization of industry and banks. Bullitt, reporting that the Soviet government had become the symbol of the revolution, conveyed the impression that support for the government was nearly unanimous. Yet in 1919 there was much opposition to the Bolsheviks. Support, although not so rare as others thought, was neither so widespread as Bullitt suggested. Again, in the single week he spent in Russia, Bullitt could not have witnessed enough to determine accurately the feeling of the population toward its government. Within the groups to which he was introduced, and in the meetings he attended—particularly at the celebration of the founding of the Third International—Bullitt would have seen that religious dedication of which he wrote. Still this was only one aspect of the Russian story.

This is not to suggest that Bullitt's impressions were entirely erroneous. There was acute suffering in Russia to which the Allied blockade contributed enormously. The Soviets did have admirable plans in the field of education; the convinced Communists did feel a religious dedication to their cause; and Lenin and his comrades were subsisting on the same meagre diet as the masses. Still, Bullitt reported only what was good, on no bad aspects of the regime did he dwell.[38] Bullitt did a brilliant job in Moscow of achieving a peace settlement with Lenin; this was partly due to his own ability, partly to Lenin's eagerness to have peace with the Allies. But Bullitt did not distinguish himself in reporting the realities of Russia, 1919.

That he went to Soviet Russia in the company of men equally enthusiastic and similarly imbued with idealistic fervor may have contributed to the tone of Bullitt's conclusions. On their return journey, Bullitt, Steffens, and Pettit had discussed their reactions. They were not depressed by the hunger and suffering in Russia as they would have been in New York or London. Captain Pettit, Bullitt's assistant, put their feelings into words: Petrograd, he said, " 'is a temporary condition of evil, which is made tolerable by hope and a plan.' "[39] Steffens exulted, "I have been over into the future, and it works."[40] Bullitt, the youngest of the three, could not understand why it was that having been "so elated by the prospect of Russia," they were still glad to be going back to Paris. Steffens was whimsical in his reply: though they "had been to heaven," they were so accustomed to their own civilization that they "preferred hell." "We were ruined," Lincoln Steffens explained; "we could recognize salvation, but could not be saved."[41]

III

The fate of Bullitt's plan for peace very quickly became apparent. At first, House had appeared to Bullitt completely enthusiastic. In a telegram on March 19, the Colonel had expressed hope that the statement from Lenin would be in "official form" for quick results. House seemed delighted with Lenin's willingness to cooperate. On March 26, the day after Bullitt arrived back, the

Colonel had asked his aide, Gordon Auchincloss, and his legal expert, David Hunter Miller, to work out details of an agreement with the Soviet government along the lines of the Bullitt-Lenin proposals.[42]

Still one wonders, in view of his subsequent actions, if the Colonel ever felt himself entirely committed to the details of Bullitt's controversial plan, or whether, in the delicate matter of achieving peace with Russia, House needed to keep several possibilities in his mind at once. Even while considering Bullitt's idea, was he thinking back to the Prinkipo plan for a conference of all Russian parties? Or was he contemplating still another, newer proposal being suggested now by Vance McCormick, which would not require any peace conference but which would focus instead upon a plan of food-relief for Russia?[43]

Yet, initially, on March 26, House did appear to be going forward with the Bullitt proposals. To the Italian Prime Minister, Orlando, House suggested drawing up a treaty with Russia, "practically on our own terms," and sending it to Moscow for Soviet signatures along with a promise that the Allies would sign it. As a means of creating interest in his idea, the Colonel wisely noted that if the Allies did not make peace with Russia, it was certain that Russia and Germany would draw together. On the other hand, if they did come to terms, Russian dislike for Germany would give the Entente a dominating influence in Moscow. The voluble Orlando, more conciliatory than his stubborn-chinned foreign minister Sonnino, assured House of his cooperation.[44]

The Colonel next had accepted Lloyd George's invitation to lunch on March 28 with the intention of discussing the Russian question and perhaps committing Lloyd George as he had done with Orlando. But he arrived at the Prime Minister's apartment only to be greeted by an agitated description of the "row" Lloyd George had just witnessed at Wilson's house between the President and Clemenceau over the Saar Valley. "We scarcely touched upon the Russian question," House noted in his diary that night.[45] But he did manage to tell Lloyd George what he had in mind—a plan for getting food to Russia. Lloyd George, although unsympathetic to Bullitt's project, which involved a conference, impressed the Colonel as willing to meet him halfway.

The Wilson-Clemenceau row had done its damage—it had diverted the President from the problem of immediate peace with the Bolsheviks. The night Bullitt arrived in Paris from Russia, House had telephoned Wilson informing him "Bill Bullitt" was back with an interesting proposal from Lenin—one that seemed to offer an opportunity to make peace in Russia. Arrangements were quickly made for Wilson to see Bullitt the next evening—March 26—but that evening the President had a headache and did not appear. House had later telephoned Wilson wishing to take his Russian plan up with him before approaching Lloyd George, but the Colonel found that Wilson's "one-track mind" was against considering the question at present—he was too much occupied with Germany to think of Russia.[46]

Wilson did manage to keep Russia in a corner of his thoughts. The next day, March 27, the President in the Council of Four tentatively mentioned the problem, indicating again that he was against intervention and declaring that the sole means of killing Bolshevism was to fix the frontiers and open all the gates to commerce.[47] Perhaps Wilson was groping toward introducing concrete plans based on Bullitt's proposals. That same day he discussed the Russian question again—this time with House, who was trying to think out something "workable." Wilson suggested talking to Hoover and Robinson (of the War Shipping Board) about the possibilities of getting ships and food to Russia.[48] But the following day—March 28—occurred the flare-up with Clemenceau, which erased from Wilson's mind all thoughts of Russia—at least for many weeks to come.

To Wilson, who had sent Bullitt to Russia only to seek information, the young emissary's plan finally became an impossibility. Bullitt had returned to Paris on the eve of a turning point in the conference, the beginning of what Charles Seymour has called the period of "crisis and compromise." The President had himself just returned to Paris from that brief and unhappy trip to Washington in February, 1919, his position considerably weaker than when he had sailed home, the Covenant in his pocket. The days spent in the American capital had revealed to Wilson the strength of senatorial opposition to his idea for a League of Nations. He arrived at Paris angered that because of senatorial insistence he had to approach the Allies as a suppliant obliged to ask them to include in the Covenant an amendment safeguarding the Monroe Doctrine. Certainly the French and British (by March 27 Lloyd George had already expressed unwillingness) would grant this favor only in return for concessions. And the President was already agitated by what he considered House's many compromises and concessions during his absence. Would he himself have to concede still further to get a Russian peace?

Wilson quickly became overwhelmed with problems. By his own admission his was a one-track mind; but the Saar, Reparations, the Rhineland, were all demanding attention. His health began to deteriorate. He became worn out physically and mentally. On April 3 he suffered an attack of influenza.

Was it likely then that Wilson would choose this time to bring up the Bullitt plan—a peace offer to Lenin to be made before April 10?[49] Was it likely that Clemenceau would be inclined to grant other requests if antagonized by the Russian issue? And what of Lloyd George, who for quite genuine political reasons was unwilling to commit himself on Bullitt's program? Acceptance of the Bullitt plan would threaten even his strong majority in Commons and perhaps mean the appearance in Paris of his powerful critic Lord Northcliffe as head of the British delegation—a signal of victory for Clemenceau. In such an eventuality Wilson would stand alone, bereft even of Lloyd George's uncertain support. Surely Wilson saw the risks in pressing either delegation. So the President refused even to see William C. Bullitt—whom he regarded as, after all, simply a clever young schoolboy—for the youth would urge him to act on a plan in every way diplomatically impossible in the immediate circumstances.

Not to be underestimated either is the effect Wilson's negative attitude had on Colonel House. The President's lack of enthusiasm may well have been the most significant factor in causing House, as early as March 28, to abandon the Bullitt plan for the more cautious idea which Wilson preferred of achieving peace through a food-relief program.[50]

A politician as astute as the Colonel knew that in the anti-Bolshevik atmosphere of Paris, Bullitt's plan for direct negotiations with Lenin could not survive unless vigorously supported by Wilson and Lloyd George. With Wilson refusing to act on the Russian matter, and with Lloyd George under continual attack in the Northcliffe press, who was there to support Bullitt's proposals in the Council of Four?

Another, more personal element seems relevant. The Colonel must have been sensitive over Wilson's criticism of his "many compromises." Their close friendship was becoming strained as Wilson, in his distress, blamed House for undoing his previous work. Surely, the Colonel would hesitate to antagonize the President further by pushing too hard on behalf of Bullitt.

To decrease still further Bullitt's chances for success, Bela Kun raised his Communist rebellion in Hungary; radicalism gained ground in other areas in Europe; and French and British press indignation (doubtless inspired by government leaks) reached a height. Finally the one-hundred-mile advance made by Kolchak in east Russia effectively killed all hope. Paris was predicting that Kolchak would be in Moscow in two weeks, and as a result everyone, including members of the American commission, became hesitant about dealing with the Soviet government, a group they assumed would soon be gone.

Looking back a year later, Lenin offered his own bitter explanation for the failure of Bullitt's peace plan. He recalled that he had made the agreement with Bullitt, leaving huge territories to Denikin and to Kolchak, in the belief that the White governments would be unable to maintain themselves if peace were signed. But the "merchant-capitalists" in Paris, who could reason only as merchants, had not understood this; instead they had said, " 'if the Bolsheviks are agreeing to such a peace, it means they are gasping their last breath,' " and "all the bourgeois press was full of delight," and "all the diplomats rubbed their hands," and "millions of pounds of sterling were sent to Kolchak and Denikin." And so, in Lenin's view, his offer to Bullitt had backfired.[51]

No one mentioned the Bullitt mission in the Council of Four, where a rather artificial situation ensued: Wilson and Lloyd George said nothing; nor did Clemenceau refer to the venture undertaken behind his back. But, of course, the shrewd Frenchman knew all about Bullitt: not only were British and French newspapers beginning to spill the story, but the *New York Times* had carried a small Paris item revealing Bullitt's "secret" mission as early as March 22![52]

Although Russia was hardly mentioned in the Council of Four during April, Colonel House continued to work on the Russian question, concentrating now on Vance McCormick's alternate plan for bringing food to Russia. The Colonel talked with Herbert Hoover on March 29 about getting the neutrals to take the lead in a feeding plan, and together they developed a project along the lines of the Belgian Relief Commission, a scheme which would not raise any necessity for political recognition, nor require the Soviets to sit down and make a settlement, but which would be conditioned upon the Bolshevik promise to cease war on all fronts against the Allies.[53] In conjunction with this idea, Hoover and

House's son-in-law, Gordon Auchincloss, approached Fridtjof Nansen, the redoubtable Arctic explorer, and got him to send a letter to Wilson suggesting "a purely humanitarian commission" for the provisioning of Russia.[54]

On April 6, four days before the Soviet deadline would expire, Bullitt began a last effort to get action on his original plan. Recalling that Wilson had once, aboard the *George Washington*, accepted one of his suggestions, Bullitt now drafted an urgent letter to the President. He begged for "fifteen minutes to discuss this matter with you."[55] That same day he prepared a telegram to Chicherin which informed: PROPOSITION RECEIVING SERIOUS CONSIDERATION. IT MAY BE IMPOSSIBLE TO ACHIEVE RESULTS BY APRIL TENTH STOP TEN DAYS EXTENSION VERY DESIRABLE. PRELIMINARY MOVES MAY BE MADE VIA NEUTRALS. BULLITT. The telegram was never dispatched. Perhaps Bullitt finally realized the futility of his efforts.

Bullitt did see to it that his commission sent some explanation to Chicherin. For if Lenin heard nothing by April 10 he would in all likelihood issue orders to his forces to attack on all fronts; to forestall a large Soviet offensive, at least for a week, Bullitt suggested the following telegram: ACTION LEADING TO FOOD RELIEF VIA NEUTRALS LIKELY WITHIN WEEK. BULLITT. The Commissioners revised the message, then sent it, presumably on April 10.[56]

The Paris Peace Conference did not settle the Russian situation. Failure to do so encouraged Soviet hostility and forced upon the Bolsheviks an isolation they did not at first seek.[57] One is tempted to conjecture what the outcome would have been had the Peace Conference at Paris made peace with the Bolsheviks on the basis of Bullitt's plan. Had the blockade been lifted, the Allies probably could have obtained more influence over Russia simply because of Soviet fear that delivery of supplies might again be stopped. There was no other Communist nation in 1919 to which the Soviets could have turned. If Russia from the beginning had been allowed to join the Western nations she might well have modified her Communist program if only out of necessity.

These were Bullitt's thoughts; they were not shared by Wilson or Lloyd George. For Bullitt his mission had been a serious undertaking. Like the Ancient Mariner stopping the wedding guest, he told his story over and over. Bullitt talks about the Bolsheviks, Harold Nicolson noted in his diary, "I blink politely."[58]

Steffens later wrote, "This gay boy did a man's work, soberly, sanely, shrewdly—even wisely, after we got to Moscow. There was no more swank then."[59]

Bullitt had done his best in Russia. He had set his heart and bent his efforts toward acceptance of his plan. But he had failed.

III

Bullitt and Lodge

"I arose at early daylight and went for a walk in the deserted streets. Within a few blocks I met General Smuts and John Maynard Keynes of the British Delegation. We seemed to have come together by some sort of telepathy. It flashed into all our minds why each was walking about at that time of morning. Each was greatly disturbed. We agreed that the consequences of many parts of the proposed Treaty would ultimately bring destruction. We also agreed that we would do what we could among our own nationals to point out the dangers." *

I

Perhaps it was the bitterness of his disappointment that caused Bullitt to resign as a member of the American peace delegation; but it was the Treaty of Versailles that directly prompted his action. Bullitt read the entire treaty in one night. His most dismal apprehensions aboard the *George Washington* were realized. On May 17, 1919, he drafted and redrafted, page after page, a letter of resignation. He addressed it to Woodrow Wilson: "not because he will care what I may think, but because I have expressed the thoughts which are in the minds of many young and old men in the commission. . . ."[1]

Russia, "the acid test of good will," for me as for you, he told

* Herbert Hoover's thoughts on reading the Versailles Treaty. Paris, May 7, 1919. *The Ordeal of Woodrow Wilson* (New York, 1958), p. 234.

55

Wilson, had not even been understood. Unjust decisions of the conference in regard to Shantung, the Tyrol, Thrace, Hungary, East Prussia, Danzig, and the Saar Valley, and the abandonment of the principle of the freedom of the seas made new international conflicts certain. It was Bullitt's conviction that the League of Nations would be powerless to prevent those wars. "I am sorry that you did not fight our fight to the finish," he concluded, "and that you had so little faith in the millions of men, like myself, in every nation who had faith in you."[2]

What is most interesting in Bullitt's letter to Wilson are the parts which never appeared in the brief, final draft. With rare prescience young Bullitt warned the President that the subjection of 36 million Chinese to the domination of Japan would encourage Japanese imperialism and ultimately lead to war between Japan and the United States. Severing East Prussia from Germany and establishing Polish domination over the German city of Danzig would stimulate the spirit of German irredentism and trouble the peace of Europe as Alsace-Lorraine had for so many years. The three million Germans, the over-a-million Magyars, and the half-million Ruthenians in Czechoslovakia would cause new minority stirrings in the heart of Europe.

When he first had heard of Wilson's League of Nations, Bullitt had wondered what would prevent the Germans and the Japanese from using a League to enforce peace as a cloak behind which they might prepare to dominate the world by force.[3] Now with the League formulated, Bullitt predicted that in the new organization cynical imperialism would be able legitimately to ignore the requests of the League Council.[4]

These opinions Bullitt did not keep to himself; he discussed his views with most of the men of the American commission to whom he went with the news of his pending resignation. One member of the peace delegation, however, although sympathetic to his protests, told Bullitt frankly that he could see no need for

so dramatic a gesture. Henry White pointed out that Bullitt occupied no position of responsibility in the organization of the
Peace Conference, was responsible to no one for such action as
the Commissioners might choose to take or not to take—was, after
all, just another subordinate official whose duty it was to carry out
the directions of the Commissioners with no obligation whatever
to the American people.[5] Therefore White advised against resignation. Henry White was a dispassionate and temperate elder statesman. The younger Bullitt was emotional and passionate. Having no
faith in the Treaty of Versailles, he violently reversed his feelings
toward Wilson. Once he had thanked God that the United States
had as its leader "a man so clean-hearted and so wise" as the President;[6] now in 1919 he regretted bitterly that Wilson did "not fight
our fight to the finish" and had "so little faith" in the millions who
had faith in him. In another few years Bullitt was to refer to the
President as the man who "ratted at Versailles."[7] For him there
could be no middle ground, no alternative; he must resign.

II

More formidable opposition than William C. Bullitt faced
President Wilson in the United States. The leader of the Republican
opposition to the Treaty in the Senate was Henry Cabot Lodge, of
Massachusetts. Enemies both personal and political, Wilson and
Lodge detested each other. Lodge's precise views on the idea of
a League have never been made wholly clear. At first he had
favored a League of Nations, but then turning against the plan, he
became one of the most influential of the anti-League spokesmen.
The senator was chairman of the powerful Senate Committee on
Foreign Relations. To gain information on the Treaty, perhaps
chiefly to embarrass the President, Lodge's committee conducted
six weeks of hearings; some sixty witnesses were called to the
stand.

Bullitt was fishing for trout in the Maine woods when he received a subpoena to appear on September 12 before the Senate Committee on Foreign Relations. He would be Lodge's last witness. Bullitt went before the senators with the decision to tell what he knew about the proceedings at Paris. He hoped thereby to help defeat both League and Treaty.

Woodrow Wilson and Secretary of State Robert Lansing had already appeared before Lodge's committee. They had not been entirely satisfactory witnesses. The committee wished to obtain all drafts presented to or considered by the peace commissioners relating to the League of Nations, and particularly the draft prepared by the American commissioners. When Lansing appeared on August 6, Lodge questioned him regarding the President's statement of the previous March that four plans had been presented at the Peace Conference for a league—the Italian plan, an American plan, a French plan, and a British plan—and that the American plan was not the one used for the purpose of building the league. Noting that there had been several requests and a good deal of desire to see the American plan, Lodge asked if the Secretary knew whether it existed. "I do not, sir," Lansing replied. Lodge continued: "There is no copy in the department?" "There are no copies, to my knowledge, in the department." Lodge asked another question: "Do you know who drafted the plan?" "I do not. I should say, the President." "Then that draft," Lodge said, "is practically unobtainable." "That I do not know, sir," Lansing answered.[8]

When asked about the original League plans, President Wilson explained briefly that he did not possess the formal drafts to which Lodge referred.[9]

Bullitt appeared at the hearings the following month. He was greeted with a similar line of questioning. Senator Knox began: "Were you cognizant . . . of the negotiations in relation to the league of nations?" "I was to a considerable extent," Bullitt replied. "How many plans were there for a league of nations that came under your observation, and whose plans were they? . . . You see what I am trying to get at?" The senator explained, "I am trying to get at the history of the various proposals, by whom they were discussed and to whom they were referred, and how they were considered by others. Do you see what I want?" "Yes, sir," Bullitt replied. Knox asked if he had a copy of the President's original proposition for a league of nations with him. "I have, sir. I have this in two forms. I happen to have a rather curious document here, which I hope may be returned to me, inasmuch as it is a unique copy. It is the President's original proposal, written on his own typewriter, I believe, which was presented to me on January 10 by Col. [*sic*] House, with an inscription on the top of it." In reply to Knox's request, Bullitt read, "For W. C. Bullitt, in appreciation of your help in an hour of need. E. M. House, January 10, 1919.[10] Bullitt then proceeded to supply Lodge's committee with the typewritten draft of the original League plan of the President; the printed draft of the original League plan of the President with comments and suggestions by the legal experts David Hunter Miller and Gordon Auchincloss; the draft of the President's second League proposal showing changes made in the original plan; the plan of Lord Robert Cecil; and the draft believed to have been prepared by Miller together with the British law experts. What Wilson and the Secretary of State refused, Bullitt furnished.

The President and Lansing had also been questioned regarding the availability of peace conference minutes. In reply to Lodge's request, the President declined to furnish reports of the minutes: "the reason for regarding as confidential intimate exchanges of opinion with regard to many delicate matters will, of course, occur to you," Wilson wrote Lodge, "and I beg to say that I am following the example of the representatives of the other Governments in making this explanation."[11] Lansing made a similar reply when faced with the committee's request: "if you open the door once I know it will make trouble."[12] Yet Bullitt, a subordinate official, become the most cooperative witness Senator Lodge could have found. Not only did he supply the committee with information on the League, he willingly read minutes of the private meetings to which Wilson referred. And when Lodge asked whether, besides extracts from the minutes of the Council of Ten already submitted by Bullitt, there were additional records of those meetings, Bullitt did what he could to help the senator locate minutes, copies of which he himself did not possess. Lodge asked if Bullitt knew what disposition had been made of the records.

"Mr. Chairman," Bullitt replied, "there were a number of copies for each delegation, and I presume that there must be a number of copies in this country at the present time."

Lodge: "Did Mr. Lansing have copies while he served on the Council of Ten?"

Bullitt: "Yes sir; well, I am quite sure that he did. I am sure that I have seen copies on the desk of the Secretary."

Lodge: "We have found some difficulty in getting them; that is the reason I asked."

Knox: "I am informed—perhaps Mr. Bullitt can tell us—that there is a complete set of minutes in the hands of some individual in this country. Do you know about that—perhaps Auchincloss and Miller?"

Bullitt: "I could not be certain in regard to the matter, but I should certainly be under the impression that Mr. Auchincloss and Mr. Miller have copies of the minutes; . . . Perhaps Mr. Auchincloss has left his with Col. House. . . . But Mr. Auchincloss and Mr. Miller perhaps have those minutes in their files."

Senator Brandegee: "Do you know whether or not they are in the State Department—any of these minutes or records in our State Department?"

Bullitt: "I should presume that in the normal course of events they would be certainly among Mr. Lansing's papers, which were very carefully kept."[13]

Lodge had evidently found what he was after. He now switched the line of questioning and inquired if any member of the American delegation, any member of the Council of Ten, expressed to Bullitt opinions about the general character of the treaty.

Bullitt replied: "Well, Mr. Lansing, Col. House, Gen. Bliss, and Mr. White had all expressed to me very vigorously their opinions on the subject."

Lodge: "Were they enthusiastically in favor of it?"

Bullitt: "I regret to say, not. As I say, the only documents of the sort that I have are the memoranda of the discussions that I had after I resigned, when we thrashed over the whole ground."

Lodge: "Those memoranda of consultations that you had after you resigned you prefer not to publish? I am not asking you to do so."

Bullitt: "I think it would be out of the way."

Lodge: "I quite understand your position. I only wanted to know—I thought it might be proper for you to say whether or not their opinions . . . were favorable. . . ." Bullitt was willing to reply: "It is no secret that Mr. Lansing, Gen. Bliss, and Mr. Henry White objected very vigorously to the numerous provisions of the treaty."

Lodge showed surprise: "It is known that they objected to Shantung. That, I think, is public information. I do not know that it is public information that they objected to anything else."

Bullitt: "I do not think that Secretary Lansing is at all enthusiastic about the league of nations as it stands at present. I have a note of conversation with him on the subject, which, if I may, I will just read . . .

> Mr. Lansing then said that he personally would have strengthened greatly the judicial clauses of the league of nations covenant, making arbitration compulsory. He also said that he was absolutely opposed to the United States taking a mandate in either Armenia or Constantinople; . . . Mr. Lansing then said

that he, too, considered many parts of the treaty thoroughly bad, particularly those dealing with Shantung and the league of nations. He said: "I consider that the league of nations at present is entirely useless. The great powers have simply gone ahead and arranged the world to suit themselves. England and France in particular have gotten out of the treaty everything that they wanted, and the league of nations can do nothing to alter any of the unjust clauses of the treaty except by unanimous consent of the members of the league, and the great powers will never give their consent to changes in the interests of weaker peoples."[14]

We then talked about the possibility of ratification by the Senate. Mr. Lansing said:

> I believe that if the Senate could only understand what this treaty means, and if the American people could really understand, it would unquestionably be defeated, but I wonder if they will ever understand what it lets them in for.

Then Mr. Lansing expressed the opinion that Mr. Knox "would probably really understand the treaty—" The senators laughed. Bullitt went on: "He expressed the opinion that Mr. Knox would probably really understand the treaty, and that Mr. Lodge would; but that Mr. Lodge's position would become purely political, and therefore ineffective." From the senators, appreciative laughter; from Lodge, "I do not mind." Bullitt continued: "He thought, however, that Mr. Knox might instruct America in the real meaning of it." The senators guffawed. "He has made some very valuable efforts in the direction," Lodge remarked. Somewhat belatedly Bullitt asked if he might "be excused from reading any more of these conversations." Senator Brandegee nodded assent: "We get the drift." The committee members laughed again.[15]

The white-haired senator from Massachusetts, cigar cocked over his clipped beard, smiled a cordial thanks: "We are very much obliged to you indeed, Mr. Bullitt." Lodge thought he had Wilson where he wanted him.

As much as he felt the need to divulge Lansing's opinion of the Treaty of Versailles, Bullitt wanted even more to tell the committee about his secret mission to Moscow. For Lodge, Russia was a side issue. Bullitt's mission did interest him, however, as an example of unorthodox action at the Peace Conference: "My dear Harry," Lodge was to write to Henry White, "there were many things done by the people in control of which I fear our commissioners knew nothing."[16] Lodge therefore encouraged Bullitt to tell what he knew of the Russian problem at Paris.

The committee had already heard something of Bullitt's mission. When Lansing appeared before the senators in August, he had been questioned on the subject. Bullitt's report was not in the State Department Archives, Lansing had replied to questions regarding its whereabouts; Frank Polk might have it; it might be in the Russian branch of the service. The Secretary had been vague and slightly uncomfortable. The discussion of Russia was brief.[17] Bullitt, on the other hand, supplied the full minutes of meetings which dealt with the Russian problem, described the origin of his secret mission, told of Wilson's refusal to act upon his proposals, and of Lloyd George's initial enthusiasm, followed by his "egregious" disclaimer of knowledge. Then Bullitt laid before Lodge and the committee his report on Russia, which the President had requested remain undisclosed.

III

"What are your plans, Mr. Bullitt? What are you going to do in this country now?" Senator Knox asked as Bullitt rose from his chair and made ready to leave the Senate chamber.[18] Was there a slight mocking tone to the senator's question? Knox must have suspected what Bullitt would have to face.

In official circles shocked reaction greeted Bullitt's testimony. "The tragedy of the week since I wrote you last has been the Bullitt affair . . ." commented William Phillips to Frank Polk.[19] An outraged Lloyd George called the Bullitt disclosures a "tissue of lies."[20] Colonel House, although appalled by his young friend's indiscretions, observed in his diary, "Candor compels me to record that in my opinion Bullitt told the truth."[21] Wilson was infuriated by Lansing's alleged disloyalty. And perhaps the President recalled how, in 1917, he had demanded the removal of Bullitt from his post of Washington correspondent for the *Public Ledger*: we can "never trust to his discretion again," the President had written.[22]

Bullitt suffered at the hands of newsmen. The Paris correspondents had a field day as the young emissary exposed himself to public criticism by revealing confidences and by presenting a report sympathetic to the Bolshevik regime. Yet one suspects from the snide tone of the criticism that the newsmen were rather envious of this youthful former colleague who was on terms of intimacy with leading men in Europe. Now they made the most of the opportunity to cut "Bill Bullitt" down a notch. Almost as a body they accused Bullitt of being on "Lenin's payroll." They described him reclining in his luxurious suite in Paris's Hotel Crillon in "pink pajamas" discoursing on the "joys of self-denial under Communism" and the "moral obliquity" of Wilson.[23] They recalled how he had "buttonholed the passerby, . . . led him to a bench in the Champs Élysées, and poured upon him the tale of All for Love of Lenin."[24] Journalists jeered: "All alone with Mr. Steffens, he set out to reconcile East with West, accomplished his great mission to his own great satisfaction, and returned to Paris only to be flouted and scouted and finally routed."[25]

Not only was Bullitt called a Bolshevik, he was blamed both for causing the defeat of the Versailles Treaty and for the ultimate resignation of Secretary Lansing. Senator Lodge was one of the many who regarded Bullitt's testimony as having the utmost significance. When the senator's good friend Henry White wrote from Paris trying to minimize Bullitt's performance, Lodge replied:

"I am sending you by this mail a copy of Bullitt's testimony. You had better read it before you say that it amounts to nothing. He was fortified by papers at every stage," and in Paris he "occupied a most confidential place." Whatever you may think of Bullitt, "it does not affect his testimony. . . . That his statements, backed by documents throughout . . . were true, I think there can be no doubt."[26] Lodge, as White suspected, hoped to use Bullitt's recollections as a weapon against Wilson and the Treaty. And Henry White knew that the senator was well satisfied with what he heard that day in the Senate rooms. Bullitt's statements relating to Lansing and the Treaty were what he was after. One suspects that Lodge had heard previously about the Lansing-Bullitt conversation. Bullitt no doubt revealed it to many after his resignation.[27] That the senator had previous knowledge was implied by his line of questioning. "Did any member of our delegation," he asked, "express to you any opinions about the general character of this treaty?" This was followed by, "were they enthusiastically in favor of it?" Bullitt, we recall, took it from there. What Bullitt said about Russia mattered little to Cabot Lodge, who opposed the Bolshevik experiment. Nor did he have sympathy personally for Bullitt. "I have no defense to make of Mr. Bullitt's breach of confidence. That is his affair," Lodge remarked.[28] Good friends though they were, Henry White always blamed Senator Lodge for the entire Bullitt episode. " 'Really,' " he wrote to Representative Rogers, " 'it requires some patience at times not to become indignant with him.' "[29]

Still, despite Lodge's delight with Bullitt's testimony, one suspects that it was hardly as significant as the senator believed. The Versailles Treaty was doomed not because of Bullitt's indiscretion but because of Wilson's stubbornness and Senator Lodge's determination not to allow its passage in a Wilsonian form. Bullitt simply provided the already recalcitrant Lodge with additional, perhaps unnecessary, ammunition. As for the resignation of Robert Lansing, the Secretary was destined for dismissal. It had long been political gossip that he was not in agreement with his chief. Indeed, Lansing's disapproval of Wilson's actions became known before Bullitt entered the Senate chamber. In August the Secretary had appeared before Lodge's committee and had given the Treaty halfhearted support. When questioned regarding Shantung, Lansing revealed distinct opposition. He implied that in the decision to give Chinese rights in Shantung to the Japanese, expediency had ruled over principle; that Japan probably would have signed the Treaty even without the Shantung concession; and that he himself had yielded only because he was subject to the decision of the President.[30] Bullitt's testimony cannot be blamed for causing Lansing's resignation—although it was responsible for making public and bringing to a critical point the breach between President and Secretary of State.[31]

Not the Versailles Treaty, not Secretary Lansing, but William C. Bullitt ultimately suffered most as a result of that day in the Senate. For Bullitt told as much about himself as about Lansing, the Treaty, and the situation in Russia. A cockiness, a too-light regard for confidences, this we have seen. Bullitt had had every reason to be grateful to Secretary Lansing. On the occasion of his run-in with Wilson in 1917, when he inadvertently published a news story that Wilson and Lansing had requested remain secret, the Secretary of State had come to Bullitt's defense urging that the President revoke his demand that the young man be recalled from Washington. In Paris, when Samuel Gompers, the American labor leader, complained that Bullitt had been talking with various labor representatives at the Bern conference along lines entirely opposed to those which Gompers thought desirable, Lansing had again come to Bullitt's defense.[32] It was Lansing, moreover, who had given the official approval and credentials for Bullitt's Russian mission: without these he would not have been able to proceed.[33]

Again we are faced with Bullitt's tendency to see issues in

extremes. In his opinion the Treaty was not worthy of ratification; the League not worthy of American membership. If what Lansing told him might contribute toward defeating Treaty or League, then by all means inform the Senate committee. That the information he divulged was given him in confidence, that it would at best cause the Secretary of State acute embarrassment, seemed of little consequence.

And yet, in Bullitt's encounter with Lodge there was also an idealism of which we can too easily lose sight. It has been argued that to wealthy "Bill Bullitt," his family's fortune behind him, jobs and careers meant little, that the love of a good show meant more, that a desire to hurt and "get even" with the men at Paris brought him before Lodge's committee. This was not so. If he revealed more than he should have, it was due to lack of proportion, a tendency to "go overboard."[34] Nevertheless, Bullitt's decision to appear before the Foreign Relations Committee and tell what he knew was not lightly taken.

His former wife recalls the day the subpoena came. "If I tell what I should about Russia, about the Peace Conference, my career will be ruined," Bullitt told her. There followed troubled hours in which the young man sought to reach a decision; should he sacrifice his career? Could he, with his great need to be liked, even bear the inevitable condemnation? By evening he had decided to tell the senators the whole story.[35]

Bullitt attempted after testifying to explain his behavior in a letter written to Nancy Astor, a distant relative:

> Your letter came today and we were both very glad to hear from you. As you suggest, I may be insane; but if so, it is the sort of insanity which produces illusions of perfect normality.
>
> I am not at all surprised that you were horrified by my testimony. Yet I am certain that if you had been in my place you would have done just what I did—only more. I had just spent five weeks in the Maine woods when I received the summons

to testify before the Senate and then had plenty of time to decide what I should do. I had a definite choice: Either I could take refuge behind "I have forgotten" and "I have not the documents," or I could speak the truth, and the whole truth.

I knew well that if I did give a full account of the Russian business I should be hated bitterly by three-fourths of the persons who had called themselves my friends. I knew that I should throw away any chance for a normal, advancing, political career —such as most of your friends will have. I knew that if I skimmed diplomatically over the surface of the truth in my testimony I should continue to enjoy the comparative good will of nearly everyone of importance. I knew also that, if I skimmed, my testimony would have no effect whatsoever in helping to end the murder by starvation and disease of the millions of Russians, who were being killed by the blockade—conducted by your government and assented to by mine. I thought that if I told the full truth, sparing no one—least of all, my own self—I might hasten the lifting of the blockade. You have not seen those starving millions in Petrograd and Moscow. If you had, you would not wonder that I should be willing to bust up a very pleasant way of life in order to try to get them peace and food.

"He will never hear anything really interesting again" you write: All right—suppose that is so—Life is a good deal more than conversation: And would you miss the confidences of the mighty, if in exchange you had the knowledge that you perhaps had helped to save the lives of thousands of babies and women and men? I believe the blockade will be lifted and that peace will be made with Russia a little sooner because I let go the whole truth to the Senate. Therefore, the dowagers and diplomats who are mewing for my blood do not disturb me.[36]

In reply to questions from the press Bullitt wrote further words of explanation: if he had not told the whole truth, he should have considered himself "a moral coward and a defaulter in everything that a man owes to his country." "Our country is being asked to pledge its men to enforce the provisions of a Treaty which makes certain future wars and the involvement of the US in those wars. Any man who at such a moment would flinch from throwing all the light he could upon this Treaty I consider utterly untrue to the duty which we all owe our country."[37]

Bullitt's violation of confidence seemed so flagrant that few cared to know his motivations. The previously gay and popular young man became a social pariah in political exile. Former friends looked through him coldly when passing in the street.[38] Men in government became angry when his name was mentioned in conversation. When he entered the State Department in 1917, Bullitt had been considered a brilliant, attractive—above all—honest young man. A "man of integrity" Lansing had called him.[39] "I know of no man whose personal character and habits are of a higher standard than his," John Sturgis, editor of the *Public Ledger* had commented.[40] A few hours in the Senate chair had erased the original picture.

Henry White wrote in 1919 that he liked Bullitt personally and appreciated his keenness and zeal about everything on which he concentrated his attention—particularly his aspirations toward higher levels in world conditions—but White regretted that "one of such brilliant possibilities should show himself to be so entirely unworthy of confidence."[41] In a sense, White's opinions were prophetic. Even at the height of his second career, Bullitt was never to attain the public offices he wanted most; for even those who liked Bullitt, who overlooked their qualms and took him into the government, were never to trust him in a position where he might be relatively free from control.[42] The encounter with Lodge was never to be forgotten. A picture of William C. Bullitt was impressed on the minds of men who would be important to him when, finally, he returned to politics; a picture of an emotional, erratic, not entirely trustworthy man—a person who "talked too much."

Bullitt could not know this in 1919. Hurt but not crushed, he made his rather rapid and undignified exit from government. Things would eventually be forgotten, he felt certain; someday he would be back in politics, so he told friends—perhaps in fifteen years. Meanwhile he would go away to the country and rest. Then he would amuse himself traveling, observing, writing. Americans in Europe during the frenetic twenties might have found William C. Bullitt on some foreign beach; in Cannes, Capri, or on the shores of the Bosporus, where he planned to "lie on the sand and watch the world go to hell."[43]

IV

The Way Back

I

Lying on the sand could not keep Bullitt content; he fast
became restless in the exile which began with Senator Lodge's "we
are very much obliged to you indeed, Mr. Bullitt." When former
Secretary of State Lansing published his memoirs in 1921, Bullitt
could not resist defending himself publicly. In his reminiscences,
Lansing denied the truth of Bullitt's statement that the Secretary
had opposed ratification of the Versailles Treaty. Bullitt had taken
his words out of context, Lansing contended; yes, he had criticized
the treaty, but he had at all times believed that it should be ratified
since restoration of peace had been paramount.[1] Taking heated
issue with Lansing's explanation, Bullitt published an open letter
to the former Secretary in *The New Republic*. Writing that he
could not allow certain statements in the memoirs to "pass without
comment," Bullitt insisted that in Paris Lansing had not favored
ratification no matter what he now claimed. Bullitt suggested that
the discrepancy between his conversation with Lansing in May,
1919, and the telegram which Lansing had sent Wilson in September, 1919, denying that he had opposed the treaty, was explained in a statement on page 276 of Lansing's book. Here Lansing
had written, when he became convinced after conversations with
the President in July and August, 1919, that Wilson would not
consent to any effective reservations to the treaty, the "politic
course" appeared to be to seek ratification of the treaty as it then

stood. Had you "believed in May what in September you said you had believed in May," Bullitt charged, you "would not have had to be convinced in July and August." Lansing's self-defense was "clearly an evasion" with no foundation in fact. The real difference between them, Bullitt concluded, was that Lansing had decided only in 1921 to let the people know what happened in Paris; but in 1921 the information was of no value. He himself, on the other hand, had given his fellow citizens the facts when the issue was still doubtful and the treaty almost certain to be passed.[2]

His incensed criticism of Lansing was to be Bullitt's last public comment as he reluctantly resumed the life of a gentleman of leisure. He had "all the money in the world," but his enormous energy would not let him rest.[3] After a brief retirement to the country, Bullitt and his wife, Ernesta, came to New York, to Gramercy Park. For a year Bullitt worked as managing editor of Famous Players-Lasky Corporation. One of his tasks was to select scenarios, another to reorganize the company's New York office. This new work diverted him only briefly.

Bullitt and his wife separated and were divorced in 1923. Very soon thereafter Bullitt married Louise Bryant, the beautiful and unconventional widow of the American Communist John Reed. Severing further his ties to the staid Philadelphia of his youth, Bullitt rented a magnificent villa on the Bosporus. Here, in the former home of a grand vizier, he wrote a novel, *It's Not Done*. Ridiculing the snobbery of Rittenhouse Square (which had not forgiven him for his behavior in 1919), Bullitt railed against the country he had left behind. America, the land where success was "largely futility on the upgrade," where one might witness the "antics of such matchless clowns as Bryan, Billy Sunday, Gompers . . ."; where there were "Rotarians, Ku Kluxers, readers of a Book of Etiquette . . . Volstead acts, censors, revisers of the Bible who improve on the morals of Christ by eliminating all references to wine. . . ." America, a "capering Virgin heifer with a blue face, a yellow back, and a buttoned-down tail. . . ."[4] America, a country "running away as fast as it can from every standard it ever had, from every ideal of Washington or Hamilton or even Jefferson."[5] Nor could Bullitt forget his hatred of Wilson; it persisted even after the President's pathetic end. Wilson was a "middle-class Southerner with a colossal vocabulary and an even more colossal inferiority complex," a man who could not endure near him anyone who insisted on "either mental or moral equality," who surrounded "himself with Tumultys and Creels," who therefore knew "nothing."[6]

Bullitt could not live in the United States. With Louise Bryant and their infant daughter, he moved about Europe during the twenties. Money remained no concern. As Lincoln Steffens commented, "Bullitt has been having some more aunts and uncles dying. He is rich, richer than ever. . . ."[7] Men of fame were his friends: from Sinclair Lewis and Ramsay MacDonald to Sigmund Freud.

Toward the close of the twenties, as his marriage to Louise Bryant also came to an unhappy end, Bullitt began an ambitious undertaking with the great Doctor Freud. The psychiatrist and the former State Department aide began to collaborate on a study of Woodrow Wilson and the World War. Since 1919 Bullitt had been doing sporadic research. Perhaps a desire to prove that he was right rather than scholarly instinct had impelled him to undertake a private investigation of the origins and conduct of the war.[8] Supplementing his research by interviews with most of the important men of the period, he had on his visits to the European capitals questioned those who had been at the Peace Conference as well as those statesmen who had stayed home. He conducted investigations in the German and Austrian secret archives, which contained the minutes of the German cabinet meetings during the First World War. In Austria he examined the private papers of the men concerned with launching the attack on Serbia in 1914. In

1930, as he resumed investigation with the intention of applying his findings to his study with Freud, Bullitt even had hopes of seeing the Lenin files insofar as they related to the United States.[9] In October of that year Bullitt wrote enthusiastically, "tomorrow F[reud] and I go to work."[10] By 1931 a first draft of the book was completed. Bullitt's part had been to contribute the political and historical background, Freud was to do the psychological analysis of Wilson as he revealed himself in public and private. Bullitt, however, managed to introduce his own theory: the President's breakdown resulted largely from the strain of convincing himself that the Versailles Treaty accorded with his avowed principles.[11] Working with Freud was exciting and stimulating. But in 1932, when the joint study was completed, Bullitt found himself again without a permanent interest.

II

That same year, the era in America of what one historian has termed the "Republican Restoration," drew to a close in what another writer has called "The Passing of the Old Order." The economic depression made certain that any Democrat who received the nomination in 1932 would be the next President. At the end of January, 1932, Franklin D. Roosevelt, Governor of New York, formally began his play for the Democratic nomination. By February FDR was "out in front—far ahead of any opponent."[12] Roosevelt called for the "building of plans" that rested upon "the forgotten, the unorganized . . . for plans like those of 1917 that build from the bottom up and not from the top down, that put their faith once more in the forgotten man at the bottom of the economic pyramid."[13]

Bullitt, back in the United States, listened to Governor Roosevelt's words and enthused: "all the Patrick Henry blood in me applauded."[14] The American people, he felt, were ready for "a new political or social religion."[15] So too was William C. Bullitt. The admiration that had once gone to Woodrow Wilson now found a new focus. Bullitt predicted that FDR would "make a big dent in the world."[16] No longer did Bullitt need to seek a new calling. "I am beginning to think about politics again," he wrote to his old friend Colonel Edward M. House. Would the Colonel let Roosevelt know that Bullitt might not be "altogether useless" in the coming campaign? My acquaintance with him in Washington was so slight, Bullitt explained, and I should, of course, "rather come to him through you than through anyone else in the world."[17]

One suspects that this connection with House had been preserved over the years with some calculation. Bullitt had hoped in 1919 that he might eventually resume a political career; to remain friendly with the man who could reintroduce him to the Democratic Party was therefore wise. As for House, perhaps Wilson's coldness after the Peace Conference made him more kindly disposed toward Bullitt—another outcast. Perhaps House felt it impossible not to respect the younger man for having spoken the truth in 1919. Whatever the reason, letters in the House collection at Yale testify to the persistently warm feeling the Colonel maintained over the years for his "exiled" friend. Now in 1932, as in the old days, House was impressed with Bullitt's political knowledge. "Your letter from Europe on conditions there," the Colonel had written Bullitt in December, 1931, is the "most illuminating" I have had in a long time. House further informed Bullitt that he wanted to show his letter to FDR to let him know how valuable Bullitt would be if Roosevelt did become President.[18] "I should like to see you play a great part in foreign affairs during the next administration," House replied to Bullitt's request, "and there is no reason why you should not do so provided our crowd is successful."[19]

From exchanges of this sort, there came to Bullitt the idea for a fact-finding trip to western Europe and Russia in the spring of

1932 to better prepare himself for meeting Roosevelt. Twenty years later, Bullitt would claim that FDR had been the man behind his trip, that the Governor had written House indicating his interest in latest information from abroad. The Colonel, feeling that "the Democrats no longer knew anything about world affairs," had, in turn, sent Bullitt to Europe.[20] Probably Bullitt has exaggerated the significance of his European tour. There is no indication that the Colonel "sent" Bullitt abroad. He seems merely to have shown interest in seeing whatever information Bullitt might bring back should he decide to go. When Bullitt reached Moscow, however, he must have intimated that he was in Russia at Roosevelt's bidding. The American journalist Eugene Lyons surmised after several long conversations with Bullitt that he was on an "unofficial errand, presumably for the future President of the United States."[21]

The visit itself was less than successful. To House, earlier in the spring, Bullitt had written of a dinner engagement with Commissar for Foreign Affairs, Maxim Litvinov, planned for June 1. But when Bullitt arrived in Moscow the Commissar was away. Litvinov's assistants in the foreign office received Bullitt most casually. *Intourist*, the Soviet travel bureau, placed him in the New Moscow, the worst of the tourist hotels on the "other side" of the river. No one was quite certain why Bullitt had come.

After his return to the United States, Bullitt waited for Colonel House to fulfill his assurances by putting him in touch with Roosevelt. As the weeks went by, Bullitt, having become impatient, concluded it might be unwise to rely solely on the elderly Colonel. Whatever the basis for Bullitt's feeling, his assumption was probably correct. Colonel House lacked his former political power. Although Roosevelt, his adviser Louis Howe, and Democratic chairman James Farley, interested in capturing the old Wilson following, were carefully keeping House informed and politely seeking his counsel, the Colonel sensed that he was being kept in a secondary position.[22] Never during the 1930's was House given the opportunity to do for Roosevelt what he had done for Woodrow Wilson.

Whether or not Bullitt suspected House's reduced influence, he decided late in July to approach a mutual friend, Louis B. Wehle —one-time Harvard companion of Roosevelt's college years and a prominent New York lawyer—with the request that he open the way to the Governor. Wehle, impressed by the fact that Bullitt had spent most of the past twelve years in Europe picking up information from a wide circle of highly placed friends and relatives, regarded him as the best-informed American on foreign affairs. Certainly he was a man Roosevelt should see. Yet agreeable as he was to smoothing Bullitt's way, Wehle maintained that House's support might be more decisive than his own. It would carry implications that the Wilsonian sector of the party had forgiven Bullitt for 1919. Therefore Wehle advised that Bullitt give the Colonel a bit more time. For another three weeks Bullitt waited uneasily while House's warm assurances again led to nothing.[23] Finally on August 13, Wehle wrote to Roosevelt informing him that William C. Bullitt had returned from Europe, where he had spoken with leading statesmen. Adding that he would be useful on foreign affairs during the campaign, Wehle urged the Governor to see Bullitt. Campaign trips and crowded days intervened. Then on September 30 Wehle received a wire setting October 5 at Albany for a meeting.

Roosevelt may have greeted Bullitt with some reservation. He had known him only slightly during the old Wilson days. To Herbert Bayard Swope, the journalist, Roosevelt had once written, " 'I really want to . . . see for myself whether you are still the same good old Swope or have taken on the manners and customs of a Billy Bullitt.' "[24] Yet when Wehle spoke with Roosevelt a few days after the interview, he felt that the Governor had been pleased and impressed with Bullitt and his report on Russian and European conditions. To the enthusiastic Wehle, his two friends seemed an ideal team. He considered Roosevelt and Bullitt both brilliant, both boldly intuitional; he hoped therefore that Roosevelt would avail himself of Bullitt's imagination and capacity for sustained work.[25] Evidently Wehle anticipated that the Governor would take Bullitt on as a member of that intimate group becoming known as the "brain trust"; it already consisted of Raymond Moley, A. A. Berle, Samuel Rosenman, and Basil O'Connor. For it was during these months after the Democratic convention that a parade of visitors was being brought to Albany and presented to Roosevelt in that trial-and-error process by which the famous group came into existence. Roosevelt would make the final selection, Moley, an original brain truster has recalled, as, man by man, candidates would be eliminated—one because he was "too pedantic" and kept saying the same thing over and over again; another because he annoyed Roosevelt with his "stuffy manner."[26] Bullitt went to Albany—neither stuffy nor pedantic—well-informed and possessing sparkle and charm equal to that of a Rex Tugwell or an A. A. Berle. Still, he was not chosen. Perhaps Roosevelt was suspicious of Bullitt's reliability, remembering 1919; perhaps he was wary of Bullitt's overenthusiasm and excess of emotion. The Governor was not prepared in 1932 to bring Bullitt into the "White House family." But after the triumph of November 8, he was to make use of Bullitt's talents in much the way Wehle had hoped.

III

Foreign affairs had not been a leading issue in the campaign, yet international problems were much on the minds of both President Hoover and President-elect Roosevelt after election day. Stabilization of currency, war debts, disarmament proposals, the entire question of American participation in world economic affairs were problems which immediately presented themselves.

Indeed, at no time was the muddle of war debts quite so acute as in November-December, 1932. A debt installment amounting to about $150,000,000 was coming due from the war associates of 1917-18 on December 15, 1932, the first payments since the moratorium of mid-1931. Hoover, together with Secretary of State Henry Stimson, believing that solution of the debt problem would aid in reviving prosperity in the United States, was particularly anxious to forestall the default which he feared likely.

The events of the four months between Roosevelt's election in November and his assumption of office in March have become well known to students of history. Hoover's eagerness to win Roosevelt's approval of his government's debt policy and to coordinate a program with the President-elect, and the latter's unwillingness to be associated with economic policies of the outgoing administration, have been described by the Republican President in his memoirs and by Stimson in his. Roosevelt has received censure—perhaps overharsh—for seeming casualness to foreign affairs: "debts are not my baby" he is said to have remarked. Yet Roosevelt was more deeply concerned with international problems than has appeared. A recent volume in the series of British documents on the interwar period gives clear account of the President-elect's preinauguration talks with the British and French ambassadors to the United States in an effort to lay groundwork for future debt negotiations. FDR at inauguration already had an awareness of matters abroad that has very generally been overlooked.[27]

Perhaps Roosevelt's knowledge of foreign affairs has been underrated largely because the methods by which the President informed himself were private. Grace Tully, Roosevelt's secretary, recalls an illustrative episode. On November 12, 1932, Hoover sent the President-elect a telegram asking for a conference on war debts. Roosevelt accepted. In the original text of his reply—dictated to Miss Tully—Roosevelt included two paragraphs requesting Hoover to have the appropriate department in Washington prepare materials for his use giving the history of the debt question and its current aspects. These paragraphs were deleted in the final version of the letter. The information Roosevelt wanted he had decided to acquire by another means.[28]

Roosevelt sat with Louis B. Wehle in Albany and reviewed the problem of war debts. On November 16, Wehle, still anxious to help his friend "Bill Bullitt," suggested a service the latter might render. Roosevelt wanted information on the debt situation; why didn't he have Bullitt go to Europe to seek it. Bullitt could travel on his own resources, make a special tour of England and the Continent, and bring back information as to what the European cabinets were likely to propose regarding debt installments due on December 15. The idea appealed to Roosevelt. After considering the political proprieties vis-à-vis Hoover and the Department of State, he concluded that there could be no harm in Bullitt going over "'purely on his own for a look-see.'"[29] And thus, before inauguration, Roosevelt initiated his policy of using personal emissaries who would go abroad seeking information for the President's use. That Roosevelt should not mention Bullitt's intentions to his adviser, Raymond Moley, who was studying the debt situation, was also to become characteristic.[30]

To Roosevelt, sending an emissary after private information seemed more convenient than requesting an official report. Perhaps the President-elect was also attracted by the element of secrecy involved. Certainly for the chosen emissary, "Bill Bullitt," this "Colonel House" sort of mission behind the scenes had immense appeal. Most anxious to impress Roosevelt with his value in the field of international affairs, he quickly made ready to depart. Wehle began receiving the first cables from Bullitt on November 28 in their specially arranged private code. Copies of the decoded messages Wehle relayed to Roosevelt in Albany. Bullitt, the President learned, had spoken with Prime Minister Ramsay MacDonald upon his arrival in England and had questioned him regarding the debt situation. MacDonald, who had liked and respected Bullitt in 1919, spoke frankly. He claimed to have wanted to take up the entire matter of the debts with Hoover in the spring; but Hoover, he contended, had personally requested that he not raise the debt question until after the election. MacDonald recalled assurances from both Hoover and Stimson that Hoover was certain to be reelected—after which time he would take up the matter of a new debt settlement. With "great heat" the Prime Minister declared that he had informed his cabinet of Hoover's promise of cooperation on the debt immediately after election; Hoover's reply to his request for a suspension of the December payment had therefore made him look like a fool. MacDonald gave Bullitt a message for the President-elect: " 'Tell Roosevelt that I want nothing but the most intimate friendship and that if he treats me as Hoover has I will resign and state in a public letter that my policy of co-operation with America is an absolute failure.' " The Prime Minister asked Bullitt if he thought the Governor would be ready to meet him halfway in establishing such a relationship. Although Bullitt was scrupulous about making clear that he had no authority to speak for Roosevelt on any subject, he informed MacDonald that he knew the Governor had the most friendly feelings toward England; in his opinion it would therefore be easy to build up a frank relationship.[31]

When questioned regarding the payment for December 15, MacDonald said he was having grave difficulty with the cabinet; Neville Chamberlain, he intimated, was opposed to paying and the treasury officials agreed with Chamberlain. He refused to say, when pressed, whether the payment would be made; he suggested that it was really doubtful. Bullitt and MacDonald parted on terms of extreme cordiality. Feeling that it was essential to have some means of communicating privately and unofficially with Roosevelt in case of emergency before March, MacDonald arranged a little code with Bullitt and an absolutely private channel of communication.[32]

In reporting the interview to Roosevelt (via his code with Wehle) Bullitt indicated that in his view British default was unlikely, despite Chamberlain's opposition. Yet the feeling in favor of repudiation in England he found to be much stronger than he had suspected. He reported unanimous agreement that unless some arrangement should be reached for a lump settlement before June, the June payment would be defaulted.[33]

Bullitt discovered that Premier Herriot of France was equally anxious to please a friend of the President-elect. Flinging his arm around Bullitt's shoulder, Herriot said he did not know how to present the December 15 payment to the Chamber in such a way that there would be a chance of a favorable vote. After making clear that he spoke for himself, not for Roosevelt, Bullitt suggested that Herriot urge payment on the ground that since England and Italy intended to pay, default by France would be a fatal blow to her position in American public opinion. This subterfuge apparently impressed the Premier. At the conclusion of a long talk, Herriot asked for Bullitt's American address so that they might keep in touch. At the door, he drew himself up, caught Bullitt's hand, and in a booming voice, full of emotion, said: " 'Je vous remercie pour votre amitie en mon nom et au nom de la France.' " "It was rather surprising," Bullitt afterward remarked.[34]

Bullitt returned to the United States on December 23, 1932. Four days later he and Wehle dined with Roosevelt in Albany, at which time Bullitt supplemented his cables with a full account of conditions in the debtor countries and of the views expressed to him by political leaders with whom he had conferred.[35] In London he had had conversations not only with MacDonald but with Chamberlain, Lothian, Lansbury, Cripps, and others; in Paris, with Herriot, Berenger, Leger; in Berlin, with Buelow and von Neurath. Whether for or against the December 15 payments, the European leaders had believed "profoundly" that debt adjustment was imperative for maintaining stability. The defeated administration's policy, if continued by Roosevelt, Bullitt had been warned, might cause progressive falls of European governments—and resulting conditions in some countries bordering on revolution. Bullitt had discussed purely political questions as well as economic. Von Neurath, Germany's foreign minister, had spoken with Bullitt about the chief terms of a possible Franco-German agreement. While in Britain, MacDonald had informed Bullitt that he wholly distrusted the German government, regarding it as " 'exactly the same gang that made the war.' "[36] As an old friend, Bullitt had asked the Prime Minister what was the "real attitude" of the British toward the reconciliation of France and Germany; did MacDonald want them to remain "merely friendly enemies"? " 'That's exactly it,' " MacDonald replied. He "screwed up his left eye," nodded, and added, " 'we do not want them to come to war but we do not want them to be friends.' "[37]

For Roosevelt, this first-hand information was of immense interest. Bullitt's description of the European political scene deepened the President-elect's understanding of European problems, giving him the background for handling the situations in foreign affairs that he would soon encounter. Bullitt's personal conversations, carefully relayed, helped Roosevelt estimate the statesmen with whom he might have to deal—particularly MacDonald and Herriot, both of whom arrived in Washington that spring.[38]

The President-elect soon had another, more official, briefing on the foreign situation. Through Felix Frankfurter, Roosevelt had made known to Secretary Stimson his desire to meet with him to discuss the war-debt situation. When Stimson broached the subject to Hoover, the President had protested: Roosevelt was a "dangerous and contrary man. . . ."[39] Still, the Secretary believed that the President-elect should have information on foreign affairs if he desired it; to refuse information, he insisted, was a serious responsibility.[40]

Reluctantly, pessimistically, Hoover finally agreed to the meeting, and Stimson on January 9, 1933, took the New York train up the Hudson to Hyde Park. Judging from the summary Stimson later made in his diary, the Secretary did most of the talking, with the President-elect asking the questions. War debts had been the ostensible purpose of the meeting. But perhaps Roosevelt felt that he had learned a sufficient amount via Bullitt. At any rate, he led Stimson over a wide range of subjects—Latin America, the Philippines, disarmament, the coming World Economic Conference, the Far East, and recognition of Soviet Russia. Stimson also wanted the conversation to proceed beyond war debts; perhaps because the Far East was his particular province, that area dominated the conversation.

Stimson had informed Roosevelt fully on Far Eastern affairs. Four days after the Secretary of State bid the President-elect goodby at Hyde Park, Bullitt was again requested to obtain further information on European conditions. A new code was arranged of which Roosevelt had a copy so that he might receive cables directly. The President-elect had toyed with the idea of this time accompanying Bullitt. He even had the latter work out an itinerary for their projected tour of some of the capitals. Then, increasingly grave domestic conditions forced Roosevelt to abandon the idea (which probably he had never seriously considered).

Bullitt now made a serious error. He confidentially disclosed his intended trip to a fourth party, one of the few Americans, Wehle was to observe ruefully, who could have been relied on to keep a secret.[41] Yet there was a later leak to the press resulting in distorted reports that Bullitt would be negotiating in Europe as a representative of the President-elect. Bullitt saw leading political figures secretly and successfully in England, Germany, and France, making reports on political and economic conditions to Roosevelt, but suddenly British newspapers made lurid "disclosures" that Bullit was in reality a mysterious advance emissary from

Franklin D. Roosevelt. Both Bullitt and the President-elect denied that Bullitt was abroad in any official capacity, but further intended meetings with European leaders were made useless. His services as secret fact-finder were terminated. From Berlin, Bullitt cabled on January 29 that he was canceling scheduled appointments and would sail for home: "recent publicity has made conversation with others dangerous."[42] He arrived at Wehle's New York office a few weeks later, hat down over his eyes and face mostly concealed under a turned-up fur collar. In his anxiety to avoid reporters he lived at Wehle's apartment for several days as Mr. Williams.

Reporters, unwilling to drop the story, made efforts to question the President-elect. Roosevelt immediately disclaimed Bullitt. In Warm Springs on January 25, he canceled his usual afternoon press conference on the plea that he had no news. Later, "it was learned authoritatively" that FDR had no one representing him in Europe. In London, government officials repudiated assertations that Bullitt was representing Roosevelt in conversations with MacDonald on war debts. According to official statement, the Prime Minister had neither seen nor received a communication from any emissary of President-elect Roosevelt.[43] In Paris, a foreign office spokesman suggested that Bullitt had arrived as an emissary of Colonel House rather than as an envoy of FDR. Colonel House in New York denied that Bullitt was acting as his agent in Europe: " 'there is nothing to represent me for,' " the Colonel observed wistfully.[44]

Since Bullitt was not representing Roosevelt in any official fashion, the Warm Springs and London denials were technically correct—if more diplomatic than honest. Bullitt, however, went further in his protestations. To reporters, he denounced rumors that he was making unofficial inquiries on the war debt question on Roosevelt's behalf as " 'ridiculous and sheer nonsense.' " He was merely on one of his usual trips to Europe gathering material for a projected book on statesmanship.[45]

Then accusations began to be leveled that Bullitt, if he were not emissary of the President-elect, was violating the Logan Act by attempting to speak on behalf of the United States.[46] The issue grew more confused. Furor over Bullitt's secret activities moved from the newspapers to the Senate floor, with Senator Robinson of Indiana charging that Bullitt had falsely described himself as representing Roosevelt and had preached cancellation of war debts. Picturing Bullitt as flitting from one capital to another under an assumed name and making the United States a laughing stock, Robinson called for his immediate arrest.[47] The issue was temporarily dropped when one senator recommended that Robinson, rather than have Bullitt prosecuted for talking too much, send him a cablegram suggesting he keep quiet. Senator Glenn, in reply to Robinson's angry "who is William C. Bullitt?" suggested that he might be a "Colonel House in disguise."[48]

If certain of the senators regarded the issue with amusement, Bullitt himself was considerably disturbed. Even as the publicity leveled off, he feared his chances of returning to government service had been irreparably injured. Were his missions for Roosevelt, undertaken largely in the hope of proving himself a valuable asset to the new administration, going to boomerang and become the factor forcing him to continue in political exile? Again Bullitt turned to the sagacious Colonel House, inquiring whether his chances for the post he wanted—the Paris embassy—had been destroyed. The Colonel assured Bullitt that the publicity, far from hurting his position, might be helpful because it revealed Bullitt's wide acquaintance in Europe and the many statesmen who were his friends; House was certain Roosevelt would want Bullitt in Paris.[49]

House's reassurances tell us something more about the Colonel's position in the Democratic Party in 1933. For Roosevelt, two months earlier in Albany, had informed Louis Wehle that the Paris embassy was not available for Bullitt: the President-elect had made prior commitments.[50] On the other hand, Roosevelt may have been playing one man against the other while he himself was reaching a decision, for Bullitt has claimed that Roosevelt did offer the Paris post to him. Bullitt recalls being present before inauguration at Roosevelt's 65th Street house when William McAdoo phoned threatening to prevent William Woodin from receiving the Treasury position if FDR did not appoint Daniel Roper, McAdoo's floor leader in the Democratic convention of 1924, as Secretary of Commerce. According to Bullitt, Roosevelt slammed the phone in irritation, asking what was he going to do now. Jesse Straus, President of Macy's, long an outstanding supporter (Straus at his own expense had organized the Roosevelt Business and Professional Men's League and had contributed $10,000 to the campaign), was expecting the Commerce post. Bullitt claims that he thereupon offered to give up Paris in favor of Straus in the interest of helping Roosevelt out of an awkward spot.[51]

Straus did go to Paris; and when the Democrats took over on March 4, 1933, Bullitt was still without an official place in the New Deal. Everyone recognized his talents and erudition; but they also remembered his unorthodox action in 1919. Whether he might be suitable in the government in an official capacity, therefore, remained an embarrassing question. Roosevelt, however, did not use the recent unfavorable publicity as a reason for dropping Bullitt, nor did he in any way discourage Bullitt's hopes of entering the administration. If not actually prepared to offer him an official position, Roosevelt evidently enjoyed having ebullient, well-informed "Bill Bullitt" around. When the French Ambassador, Paul Claudel, came to New York on February 22 for conversations with Roosevelt and his advisers on economic matters, he found Bullitt in the Roosevelt home together with Moley and the President-elect.[52] Bullitt continued to sit in on the February economic conferences Roosevelt had asked Moley to arrange, anticipating discussions with foreign representatives which would take place after March 4.[53] Along with Herbert Feis and James Warburg, Bullitt worked on preparations for the conferences.

Ultimately, neither Wehle nor House, but Raymond Moley claimed the credit for getting the "bad boy" of the Wilson administration back into the government. Shortly after Roosevelt's administration had gotten under way, Bullitt established himself near Moley's rooms in the Carlton Hotel. He visited often with the brain truster, who found Bullitt interesting and well informed. Again and again, Moley recalls, Bullitt spoke of his desire to fit in somewhere. Feeling that the New Deal needed friends in the State Department, Moley claims to have reminded the President almost daily that there was an obligation of sorts to Bullitt.[54] Roosevelt, however, remained dubious as to whether Bullitt should be given an appointment. It was kindly William Phillips who presented the real opposition. Phillips countered the suggestion that Bullitt be given a job with an emotion astonishing to Moley. "The tragedy of the week . . . has been the Bullitt affair," Phillips had written Frank Polk in 1919 after Bullitt's report to the Senate.[55] After that, William Phillips had hoped he would never have to see Bullitt again. Now in 1933 the memory of his former subordinate's appearance before Senator Lodge was still vivid. Phillips bitterly reminded Moley that Bullitt had been "disloyal" to the Wilson administration. Moley countered that the years had shown Bullitt to have been right; did not loyalty to one's country supersede loyalty to a President? Finally Phillips succumbed; it was arranged that Bullitt should be special assistant to the Secretary of State—rather than Assistant Secretary, also an open position, for the latter appointment required senatorial confirmation and might have involved a revival of old issues. Roosevelt gave approval.

After fourteen years of "exile" and months of seeking to bring himself to Roosevelt's attention, William C. Bullitt was back in government. Curiously, he was at the start of his second career what he had been in 1918, an assistant in the Department of State.

V

Bullitt and Recognition
of Russia

I

Undersecretary William Phillips has suggested that Bullitt was brought into the Department of State in order to facilitate Russian recognition.[1] Possibly so. If Raymond Moley did not have this idea when he urged Bullitt's appointment, Roosevelt, in agreeing to take Bullitt into the government, very likely did recall his enthusiasm for relations with the Soviet Union.[2] And, by the spring of 1933, the President had decided on recognition.[3] Even before inauguration he indicated to Democratic Party chairman James Farley that he would seek relations with the Soviet Union. In January he broached the subject to Stimson in their Hyde Park conference.[4]

Why Roosevelt wanted to recognize Russia is not completely clear. The majority of Americans who favored the move in 1933 did so on the ground that resulting American-Russian trade would boost the economy.[5] Although Roosevelt, of course, favored steps likely to increase trade, a study of the documents in no way suggests that this factor impelled the President.[6]

In assessing Roosevelt's motives, we should start with the most obvious. Just as he favored repeal of prohibition as a break with the Republican twenties and a step in the direction of decisive, positive action, Roosevelt wanted also to end unnatural relations

89

between the United States and Soviet Russia, a regime firmly estab-, lished for nearly fifteen years.[7] Another, more significant factor was the world situation. Although certain historians have expressed doubt as to the Roosevelt administration's appreciation in 1933 of international dangers, and skepticism regarding the President's willingness to take steps against such threats,[8] there is reason to believe that Russian recognition was motivated largely by international considerations. People do not yet realize, Henry Morgenthau, Jr., has contended, how early Roosevelt saw the dangers presented to the world by the "smash and grab attitudes" of Germany and Japan. Continued isolation of Russia, Roosevelt feared, might destroy hopes of preventing war through the collective moral sense of the nations.[9] Secretary of State Cordell Hull recalls that he and Roosevelt were in complete agreement in 1933 that the world was moving into a dangerous period in both Europe and in Asia, that Russia could therefore be "a great help in stabilizing this situation" as time went on and peace became "more and more threatened."[10] By recognizing and thus strengthening Russia, Roosevelt felt he would be able in a single move to bring pressure on the outer flanks of both Japan and Germany.[11]

Possible Japanese aggression gave the President particular concern. Roosevelt's apprehensions over Japan have been questioned by at least one historian, who contends that had the immediate aim of the Roosevelt administration been to check Japanese expansion, a visible tightening of joint American-Soviet diplomacy toward Tokyo would have been logical. Since such a tightening did not occur, she concludes that the Asian situation was not a serious factor in American recognition.[12] We may question this assumption. Roosevelt, even before inauguration, made apparent his uneasiness regarding Japan. At a dinner at the home of James Farley on January 11, 1933, FDR elaborated on the danger from Japan. " 'After extending herself in China,' " Roosevelt said, " 'Japan will be casting her eyes about for new fields of conquest. It is likely she will move southward and try to extend her possessions along a chain of islands even as far as Australia.' " Japan, he predicted, " 'would give a lot of concern to the world generally within the next ten years.' "[13] Again, at a Cabinet meeting in March, 1933, the President turned to the possibility of war with Japan. There was much discussion, Farley recalls, of Japan's attitude in the Orient, Japan's clashes with China, and other possible avenues of Japanese activity.[14]

To be sure, Roosevelt had no intention of taking positive action against Japan. First of all, the public would never have supported such a move. Whatever his feelings, Roosevelt's actions were decisively hampered by American isolationism. Then too, the government (particularly the Department of State) wished to avoid action which might antagonize the antiwar party in Japan.[15] Desiring to avoid a direct affront, Roosevelt found another way open. In a conversation with British Ambassador Sir Ronald Lindsay before inauguration, the President-elect gave a clue with regard to the future. There was nothing to be done at present to stop the Japanese; this the President made clear. His policy, however, would be to avoid action tending to relieve the strain on Japan.[16] In recognition of Russia, the President saw a twofold means of increasing that strain. Russia would be strengthened by American recognition, thus providing a counterweight to Japan's increased power. Japan, uncertain as to possible American action, might become wary of precipitous moves against Asiatic Russia.[17]

Ambassador Grew in Japan sensed what the President was doing. "The President has played his cards well," Grew commented in his diary after recognition was achieved. "He said not a word about Manchuria but started building up the fleet and recognized Soviet Russia."[18]

Not only did Roosevelt want recognition, he desired personally to direct the negotiations. " 'If I could only, myself, talk to one man representing the Russians,' " he told Henry Morgenthau, Jr., in midsummer, " 'I could straighten out the whole question.' " According to Morgenthau, the President sensed opposition to recognition in the Department of State and wished to avoid departmental obstructions.[19]

Whether opposition existed is questionable. Some members of the East European division were not overenthusiastic about recognizing Russia, but Secretary of State Hull definitely favored the move.[20] Very likely Roosevelt wished to stay clear not so much of possible opposition as of very probable caution. From Hull down, the Department of State believed that in the matter of Russian recognition the United States should move slowly, with circumspection. In a conversation with Roosevelt in September, 1933, Hull made clear his attitude. He "earnestly argued" that three questions—no Soviet interference in American internal affairs: freedom of religion for Americans in Russia; and debt settlement—should be thoroughly taken up and satisfactory written understandings reached by informal conferences between the two governments before the United States invited a Russian representative to Washington. Meantime not a word should be uttered publicly about recognition.[21]

A politician as practiced as Roosevelt must have sensed potential pitfalls in Hull's plan—which was, of course, the usual diplomatic method. Lengthy, detailed negotiation conducted by conference would produce difficult impasses and the need for awkward compromise. The matter might drag interminably. The conferences might ultimately fail. This was not what Roosevelt had in mind. He wanted recognition, and he wanted a brilliant political success; an American diplomatic triumph accomplished with the least fuss and the most smoothness. Therefore, although he listened politely to Hull's suggestions, the President "decided otherwise."[22]

Did Roosevelt, in discarding Hull's idea, also choose to use Bullitt to bypass the Secretary of State? Henry Morgenthau, Jr., recalls that by the spring of 1933 Roosevelt had decided to recognize

Russia. Yet as late as August, 1933, in a conference with Hull, FDR discussed recognition "in a general way" and, according to the Secretary of State, "did not reach any conclusions."[23] Not only was Roosevelt keeping his decision from his Secretary of State, he had several months earlier—indeed soon after inauguration—requested that Morgenthau, then his Farm Credit Administrator, "help conduct conversations looking toward the recognition of Russia."[24]

Working discreetly through two intermediaries, Morgenthau made contact with Amtorg, the Soviet trading company. Despite the unwillingness of individual Russians to assume authority, Morgenthau made some progress toward reconciliation. By August 16 he was able to report to the President that the Soviet Union wanted to purchase 75 million dollars worth of raw materials.[25]

The President grew impatient. He wanted action which would lead more quickly to recognition. In September he asked Morgenthau what he thought of "bringing this whole Russian question into our front parlor instead of back in the kitchen?" He had a "plan in mind," Roosevelt informed Morgenthau.[26] The scheme involved an approach to the Soviet government through Boris E. Skvirsky, director of the Soviet Information Bureau in Washington—unofficial embassy of the USSR. The day after this conversation Morgenthau discussed the Russian matter with Bullitt, who had been investigating problems of recognition in a general way in the Department of State.[27] Bullitt may not have previously known that Morgenthau was involved in recognition work. Now he began walking Morgenthau to work in the morning in order, the latter recalls, to pump him on the latest developments in regard to Russia. At first this annoyed the President, who remarked that Bullitt was going over Hull's head—"the way Moley used to."[28] At some point, however, Roosevelt must have decided that Bullitt, not Hull, and not Morgenthau, was the person to handle recognition. For he planned first to have Bullitt make the contact with

Skvirsky, and later to have Bullitt handle the entire negotiation—under his personal direction. In many ways Bullitt, who had been studying aspects of recognition in his capacity as assistant to the Secretary, *was* the ideal man to carry out the President's intentions. He delighted in buccaneering diplomacy and was anxious to please FDR. Particularly important, he was known to be eager for relations with Russia; thus a move toward reconciliation coming from Bullitt would be received by the Soviet leaders as a friendly gesture. This was what Roosevelt wanted.

One suspects that the President now saw a shrewd, and quite simple way to free himself from Hull's cautious objections. On November 5 the Secretary was scheduled to depart for Montevideo for the conference of American states. Pan-Americanism was close to Hull's heart and he had long prepared for the meeting. Why not invite a Soviet representative to come to Washington when Hull was obliged to be absent?[29] Roosevelt proceeded with his plan. He had Bullitt contact the Russians. With Morgenthau's aid, Bullitt got together with Skvirsky and through him relayed to the Russian government the President's desire to open negotiations.[30] Then Bullitt drafted a note of invitation, which he took to Skvirsky after Roosevelt had approved it. He asked the Russian to transmit the note to Moscow, unsigned and in his most secret code. If it were acceptable to the Soviet government, it would be signed and retransmitted officially; if not, then Skvirsky must pledge himself not to make any public revelation of the exchange. Moscow, of course, welcomed the invitation. While Hull quietly disapproved, preferring to have the message go through State Department channels, the President personally sent the letter to President M. Kalinin.[31]

Hull had wanted to see all outstanding issues settled on the lower diplomatic levels before an important Soviet diplomat should be invited to Washington. Bullitt, however, was convinced that the success of the negotiations depended upon the Kremlin's choice of a Soviet statesman of top importance—Maxim Litvinov, Soviet Commissar for Foreign Affairs. By careful phrasing of the note to Kalinin, he made certain that this impression would be conveyed.[32] Word came from Moscow that Litvinov would arrive on November 7, 1933.

Whatever the disagreement between Hull, on the one hand, and Roosevelt and Bullitt, on the other, as to the conduct of negotiations, the State Department and the White House were in accord on the promises the Russians would have to give. The Department had been giving the question extensive study, presumably since July, 1933, when the President had requested an analysis of the issues involved in a rapprochement. Robert F. Kelley, chief of the Division of Eastern European Affairs, prepared a memorandum for the President's use in which he advised that the experiences of other nations had shown the necessity of settling outstanding issues before recognition. First among the problems was the question of Moscow-directed Communist activity in the United States. A settlement of the Russian debt should also precede diplomatic relations; for once relations were established there would be little chance that the Soviets would agree to pay the money owed. To demonstrate the truth of his prediction, Kelley cited the drawn-out, fruitless French and English attempts to reach a settlement with Russia after recognition had been granted. Finally, Kelley urged that matters involving the question of protection of life and property of American citizens in Russia be settled in order to create a satisfactory basis for American-Russian relations.[33] In September Hull sent Roosevelt a memorandum in which he outlined the points at issue; it followed Kelley's analysis. Then on October 4 Hull requested that his two assistants, Bullitt and Walton Moore, each draw up a paper for the President on the more important conditions and understandings to be considered in the forthcoming talks. Again there was virtual agreement with Kelley's original suggestions. Judge Moore warned against immediate and unconditional recognition, while Bullitt agreed with Kelley that "before recognition and before loans" they would find the Soviet Government "relatively amenable." After recognition or loans, they would "find the Soviet Government adamant."[34]

The few weeks before Litvinov's arrival on November 7 were busy ones in the State Department. Kelley and his assistant conducted a close study of every treaty Soviet Russia had entered into with other governments, concentrating particularly on the treaty of 1925 between Russia and Germany, the most favorable of the treaties the Soviet Union had signed. Draft after draft was made of the agreements to be presented Litvinov for his signature. But while the Department of State prepared the texts and made thorough plans for the Foreign Commissar's arrival, the White House planned to conduct the negotiations.

II

Commissar Litvinov, sailing toward the United States, suggested to newsmen aboard ship that he would like to see establishment of diplomatic relations first, with the subjects at issue referred later to a mixed commission of experts. At Berlin he had remarked casually that a half hour would be sufficient to resolve all difficulties between his government and the United States. No doubt the Commissar thought he was being shrewd. Since the talks, as he well knew, were likely to consume many hours, it would appear to the public that the Soviet Union had graciously made the initial concession. This was exactly the impression Roosevelt also hoped to have created—for his own public opinion purposes. Newsmen were cooperative. Walter Duranty wrote: "Roosevelt and Bullitt . . . have, unless this correspondent is mistaken, maneuvered Comrade Litvinov into a position of discussion prior to recognition" of a number of points "he would have vastly preferred to discuss afterward."[35]

Meanwhile in the White House on the evening of November 6 a last-minute briefing was held. Bullitt was present—along with Morgenthau, Phillips, and Moore. So, too, was Secretary Hull. He had requested Roosevelt to allow him to delay his departure one week so that he might take part in at least the beginning of negotiations.[36] The Commissar arrived on schedule, and the next day, November 8, exploratory conversations were begun at the State Department. The first days went badly. Secretary Hull, flanked by Bullitt, Phillips, Moore, Kelley, and Morgenthau, informed Litvinov of the guarantees the United States expected regarding propaganda, religious rights, and legal protection of American citizens. Litvinov, however, gave the Department to understand that he expected recognition first, discussion after. Since he soon left off his argument, one is inclined to believe that the Commissar's protest was merely tactical.

Even after he agreed to settle issues before recognition was granted, Litvinov remained stubborn. When shown the agreement on mutual abstention from interference in internal affairs, he read it and said, "We can't agree to this." Then Hull explained that Russia had already done so; for the text had been prepared using entirely the wording of treaties Russia had already signed. When handed the agreement on freedom of religion for Americans in Russia, Litvinov again objected. It was "impossible." But it developed that the Commissar, although he spoke and read English, had somehow assumed that the draft referred to religious freedom for Russians as well as Americans. Still, Litvinov insisted that Russian laws were sufficient to protect the religious freedom of Americans.

In his memoirs Hull tends to emphasize the role of the Department of State in the recognition negotiations. Thus he suggests that by November 10, the third day of talks, he and Litvinov had reached specific agreements on religious protection in Russia and discontinuance of Communist propaganda in the United States by all Soviet agencies.[37] Bullitt and William Phillips, however, give a different impression—stressing the part played by the President and his assistant, "Bill Bullitt." Phillips recalls the first two days of negotiation as "completely unsatisfactory." So unsatisfactory were they that the negotiators met with the President on November 9, in a conference which Hull does not mention, informing him of the deadlocked negotiations. Suspecting that the Commissar wanted to deal directly with the President, rather than with the Department, they requested that Roosevelt try to break the stalemate.[38]

The President now came to the foreground. He affably assured the Commissar that the United States wanted nothing more than a just settlement. For about an hour he reviewed the problems under consideration, then suggested that he and Litvinov meet again in the evening, this time in private, so they could insult each other freely. The President and the Commissar laughed heartily. That evening, November 10, the two spoke together for three hours. The religious question was resolved to the President's satisfaction.

Roosevelt was enthusiastic over his first conference with the Commissar. He felt justified in his opinion that if he could only talk privately with one Russian, matters could be settled. To Jim Farley, with whom he dined shortly afterward, he declared, " 'everything is coming along splendidly and I am confident everything will work out all right.' "[39] Then Roosevelt told Farley a story, interesting in what it revealed of the tenor of Roosevelt's and Litvinov's talk. " 'Jim,' " the President said, " 'I threw one straight from the shoulder at him. . . . I told Litvinov that I knew he had his opinion of me, and that, in turn, I had my own ideas of him. Then I followed that up by saying I was willing to wager that five minutes before his time would come to die, and he was conscious of it, that he would be thinking of his parents and wanting to make his peace with God. Jim, he looked at me closely, but didn't say a word.' " Roosevelt threw back his head and laughed.[40]

In his memoirs Hull gives the further impression that before his departure for Montevideo he and Litvinov reached agreement on the propaganda pledges. Perhaps so. But Bullitt claims that he, as Roosevelt's personal representative, and not the Department of State, achieved the settlement. Despite his interest in seeing relations established with Russia, Bullitt was convinced that the first condition of recognition must be a Soviet pledge to refrain from all activities in the United States aimed against American institutions. The first point in Bullitt's memorandum concerning problems involved in recognition had been prohibition of Communist propaganda in the United States by the Soviet government and the Comintern.[41]

Anxious to see the pledges against propaganda signed, Bullitt recalls asking Roosevelt if he might try himself to "handle" the protesting Commissar. Since the President was agreeable, Bullitt met with Litvinov in Skvirsky's house on Massachusetts Avenue, where the Commissar was staying. When Litvinov again demonstrated unwillingness to sign the prepared agreement, Bullitt handed him the documents together with the ship sailing schedules. The alternatives were clear. Litvinov paced the floor in irritation, studying the detailed pledges. His government, he read, must promise to refrain from participation in or encouragement of any propaganda or subversive activity which would affect the United States. It must pledge to prohibit any such activity by the agents of its government or by individuals or organizations directly or indirectly under its control. It must further promise not to permit the residence on Soviet territory of any organization claiming to be the government of the United States or any military group planning armed invasion of the United States. Point Four was the most significant: the Soviet government must promise "not to permit the formation or residence on its territory of any organization or group—and to prevent this activity on its territory of any organi-

zation or group, or of representatives or officials of any organization or group—which has as an aim the overthrow or the
preparation for the overthrow of, or the bringing about by force
of a change in, the political or social order of the whole or any part
of the United States. . . ."[42]

The Commissar continued his pacing. He turned suddenly. "You
are too hard on me, Bullitt," he shouted. Finally Litvinov spit out
the words, "accept it!"[43] "Accept it!" the Commissar said. But how
far did his acceptance go? Was Litvinov, on behalf of his government, promising Bullitt that the American Communist Party and
the Third International, for which the Russians had hitherto disclaimed responsibility, would now be curbed in their activities?
Litvinov gave hints of the future before leaving Washington.
After his address to the National Press Club the night of November 17, newsmen asked the Commissar what effect Point Four
would have on the American Communist Party. "The Communist
Party of America is not concerned with the Communist Party of
Russia and the Communist Party of Russia is not concerned with
the Communist Party of America," Litvinov replied. Later, the
Commissar pointed out to inquiring newsmen that the Third International was not mentioned in the document he had signed. You
must not read into it more than was mentioned, Livinov admon-
ished.[44]

There are indications that Roosevelt was aware in November,
1933, of Litvinov's reservations. When the Soviets blandly ignored
their pledges and in 1935 allowed the Comintern to hold a meeting
in Moscow with American delegates present, an illuminating conversation regarding the recognition pledges took place between
Litvinov and the outraged Bullitt. In response to Bullitt's accusations of bad faith, the Commissar asserted that his conscience was
entirely clear. Did not Bullitt recall his warning to the President
that Russia could assume no responsibility for the Third International? Litvinov then repeated the President's supposed reply:

Roosevelt would hold the Soviet Union to its pledge only in case of important injury to the United States. Bullitt's memory was different. He recalled Litvinov saying he could make no promises about the Third International but he also recalled Roosevelt's reply that he would hold Russia to strict accountability with regard to that organization. Litvinov subsequently signed the pledge. When the Commissar insisted that he had made his statement to Roosevelt only *after* signing the propaganda pledge, Bullitt countered that the Commissar's moral position was thus weakened still further.[45]

We are not concerned at this point with the weakness of Litvinov's moral position; it is significant, however, that the Commissar had made clear his refusal to be responsible for the Third International when he signed the pledge. In the interest of restoring good relations between Russia and the United States, Roosevelt preferred to hope for the best and not press the issue.

We have seen that the propaganda pledges were given during an unorthodox debate between Bullitt and Litvinov, while pledges regarding religious freedom were granted in another informal discussion, this time between the Commissar and the President. In neither case did Hull, as the chief representative of the Department of State, play a decisive part. Hull's role was to be slighter still in the third facet of the pre-recognition talks: the negotiations concerned with payment of the Russian debt. This matter had barely been touched on when the Secretary of State departed for Montevideo and Bullitt took unofficial charge of the negotiations.

The total debt figure included several different classifications, the most important being the money owed the American government by the former provisional government of Russia. Besides United States government loans, there were two other debt categories: the claims of American holders of prerevolutionary bond issues (repudiated by the Communists) and the claims of American citizens whose properties and other interests in Russia had been confiscated by the Soviet government at the time of the revolution.

The Division of East European Affairs had in July prepared a lengthy memorandum detailing the claims. While Kelley recommended that the Soviet government not be asked to pay obligations accruing from sale of supplies to the Kolchak government, he urged that Russia acknowledge its liability on a share of the debt incurred by the provisional government. Kelley emphasized the need for a definitive settlement before recognition: as a great creditor nation, the United States had a "profound interest" in maintaining the principle that a new government is responsible for the financial obligations contracted by the state under preceding governments.[46] The State Department emphasized in particular that if the questions of repudiated debts and confiscated property were not completely settled before recognition, there was little likelihood that subsequent negotiations would result in a settlement.[47]

Roosevelt and Bullitt decided, however, to risk another arrangement. Complicated discussions had revealed the difficulty in settling an exact amount of payment. At some point, perhaps in conference together, Roosevelt and Bullitt therefore agreed that despite the Department's warnings, a statement of intent in principle would be sufficient. With this purpose in mind, the President and Bullitt saw Litvinov on the morning of November 15. They endeavored at this time to fix two figures—the higher representing the amount America wanted, the lower representing the limit below which it would not go. The assumption was that a compromise figure would result. At the conclusion of the meeting no agreement had been reached. Despite his eagerness for relations with Russia, Bullitt was Litvinov's match in driving a bargain. Alone with Litvinov, he continued to argue for another two hours. He urged the Commissar not to fix the lower figure at $50,000,000, as his government would surely insist that that sum be accepted as the maximum. "What sum would you consider might be acceptable to Congress?" Litvinov asked; then added, "You will, of course, say $150,000,000." "No, I will say nothing," Bullitt replied, "I cannot predict what Congress will do, but the President can predict very exactly what Congress will do, and you should address that question to him."

Litvinov maintained that he was sure that when the President had looked at the facts relating to America's loan to the Kerensky government he would see that the loan had for the most part been spent by Russian Ambassador Bakhmeteff to buy supplies for Kolchak's army. Litvinov was confident the President would agree that the Soviet government could not be obliged to assume liability for money used by its enemies.[48] But Bullitt pointed out that this could not be so since two-thirds of the Kerensky loan was telegraphed at once to Kerensky's government and was used in fighting the Germans. When Litvinov contended that the private claim had been so padded that $50,000,000 would be a fair settlement of all claims and debts, Bullitt dismissed the argument as "absurd."

"I finally managed to shake him a bit," Bullitt observed in a hasty memorandum to the President, "by telling him that the Johnson Bill, forbidding loans to countries in default on their indebtedness to the Government of the United States, was certain to be passed in January and that if the Soviet Government should make any absurd offer of settlement such an offer would surely be turned down by Congress and the Soviet Government would be unable to obtain one penny of credit from either the Government or any private corporation or individual in the United States. . . ." Bullitt suggested that the President "endeavor forcibly" to get Litvinov to set at least $100,000,000 as the lower limit. "I shall stop at your office at ten minutes before two, in case you should wish to draw up a final plan of campaign," Bullitt concluded. At the bottom of his memorandum Bullitt scrawled a hasty P.S.: "I think we were a bit too gentle with him this morning."[49]

There is nothing to indicate, however, that a get-tough policy prevailed at the two o'clock meeting. Roosevelt's geniality reigned instead. A settlement of sorts was reached between Roosevelt and

Litvinov. It took the unique form of a "gentleman's agreement" in which the gist of the afternoon's discussion was recorded in a four-paragraph memorandum. The two signatories agreed that over and above all claims of the Soviet government and its nationals against the government of the United States and its nationals, the Soviet government would pay to the United States a sum to be not less than 75 million in the form of a percentage above the ordinary rate of interest on a loan to be granted it by the government of the United States. The President then said that he believed confidently that he could persuade Congress to accept a sum of 150 million but feared that Congress would not accept any smaller sum. Litvinov countered that he could not on his own authority accept any such minimum as his government had already stated that it considered this sum excessive—but he added that he had "entire confidence" in the fair-mindedness of the President and felt sure that when the President had looked into the facts he would not feel that a sum greater than 75 million was justified. So far as he personally was concerned and without making any commitment, he would be inclined to advise his government to accept 100 million. The "gentleman's agreement" concluded with a statement of Litvinov's willingness to remain in Washington after resumption of relations to discuss with Morgenthau and Bullitt the exact sum between the limits of 75 million and 150 million to be paid by the Soviet government.[50] The President and the Commissar then affixed their initials to this casual document. A few days later in Cabinet meeting the President optimistically predicted that because of the agreement the United States could now collect 150 million in debts.[51]

Although the series of recognition documents—eleven in all—were released to the press on November 17—the day after recognition had been formally granted—one document remained unpublished. This was the "gentleman's agreement." In 1945 the still-secret agreement caused consternation when its existence was discovered by a researcher working in an archive index file. During the resultant interdepartmental discussion over whether to make the "gentleman's agreement" public, State Department experts described the document as ambiguous and misleading. Unless all the papers explaining America's position on the word "loan" were published, the Department maintained, the government would be put in a false light, for the word "loan" used in the "gentleman's agreement" seriously weakened Bullitt's subsequent argument during Moscow negotiations with Litvinov that no loan had been intended.[52]

One wonders why, if the "gentleman's agreement" appeared ambiguous in 1945, it could seem adequate to Roosevelt and Bullitt in 1933. One reason is offered by Henry Morgenthau, who, we recall, sat in on some of the recognition negotiations in his capacity as acting Secretary of the Treasury. "I don't think," Morgenthau has written, "that Bullitt and some of the others were much interested in the financial aspects of recognition."[53] Assistant Secretary of State Walton Moore in a radio address following the announcement of relations with Russia quite frankly described the debt settlement as "altogether ancillary."[54] Another reason is suggested by the title Roosevelt gave to the brief document. The President and Bullitt both expected Litvinov, as a gentleman, to live up to the arrangement.[55] When questioned recently regarding the ambiguous phrasing of the agreement, Bullitt insisted that at the time it did not seem vague at all; he and the President knew precisely what it meant. They assumed Litvinov did as well.[56]

Assuming then that Roosevelt was personally satisfied with the "gentleman's agreement," another question is raised. Why was the document kept secret while the other recognition agreements were immediately made public? On this point one can only fall back on conjecture. No doubt the President, realizing that he had, after all, not gotten a debt settlement, sensed that the initialed memorandum might not appear adequate to the public. Perhaps there seemed to him little point in releasing an agreement which merely detailed the situation to date. A brief statement which played down the debt by referring to an "exchange of views" and assured the public that both governments wished to have the question out of the way as soon as possible was politically more expedient.[57]

Bearing in mind Roosevelt's purpose—the reestablishment of American-Russian relations with the least bitterness and the greatest facility—the negotiations and the resultant documents were a brilliant success. Bullitt, an enthusiastic friend of the Russians, had exerted the pressure. Roosevelt, the amiable President, had smoothed things over—he had not irritated Litvinov too far on the propaganda question; he had not insisted on immediate settlement of the debt. Between them, Roosevelt and Bullitt achieved agreements with Russia which were the most sweeping the Soviets had ever signed.[58] Litvinov on behalf of his country had promised no interference in America's internal affairs; freedom of religion and legal protection for Americans residing in Russia; protection from charges of economic espionage for Americans sending out information on Russian economic developments; and had waived Russian claims arising out of activities of American military forces in Siberia (but not north Russia) after 1918.[59] All this Roosevelt achieved while skillfully avoiding a prolonged and unpleasant negotiation.[60]

If one starts from the assumption that recognition was necessary in order to protect American interests in Russia and to give the United States a much-needed observation post in the Soviet Union, then one may doubt whether Hull's more orthodox plan for negotiations could have achieved much more. Roosevelt and Bullitt may have been guilty of overlooking Litvinov's reservations on the Comintern, but the propaganda pledge as signed was ironclad. It required only Russia's good faith to carry it through; this Hull could have obtained no better than FDR. Probably a more carefully conducted debt negotiation would have resulted in more

specific agreement and less confusion when Bullitt took up negotiations in Moscow. But again, would Russia have paid her debt
any more than she was to honor the detailed propaganda pledge?

Still, Roosevelt's handling of recognition, following so soon
after the painful embarrassment of the London Economic Conference, must have hurt the Secretary of State.[61] One is struck by
Hull's failure in his memoirs to allude to the role of either Bullitt
or Morgenthau in initiating negotiations. Rather he refers with
some irritation to Morgenthau often acting "as if he were clothed
with authority to project himself into the field of foreign affairs."[62]
Hull's sensitivity regarding his position was well known to friends.
In a conversation with Louis B. Wehle, eleven years after recognition, Hull looked back through his long tenure as Secretary of
State and recalled that he knew when he accepted office that there
would be " 'humiliations that no man in private life could accept
and keep his self-respect. . . . I have suffered all these things,' " Hull
remarked, " 'but have just kept right on.' "[63]

III

To the day of Litvinov's departure from the United States,
Bullitt remained in charge of Russian matters. He drafted the fare-
well letter from Roosevelt to Litvinov and, in the President's
absence (he had left for Warm Springs), presented the note on
Roosevelt's behalf. When the recognition correspondence was released to the press on November 17, Bullitt's appointment as ambassador to the Soviet Union was also made known.

As early as December, 1932, Roosevelt had agreed with Louis
Wehle that Bullitt would make an ideal first ambassador should
Russia be recognized. And before Hull left for Montevideo, it had
been arranged that Bullitt would be ambassador if recognition
materialized.[64] Perhaps to assuage faint doubts, Roosevelt detained
William Phillips after signing the recognition agreements on No-

vember 16, to ask him his opinion of Bullitt. Once he had hoped never to have to see Bullitt again; now Phillips generously praised his ability.[65]

In many ways, Bullitt seemed the ideal choice. He combined the usual ambassadorial qualifications—loyal party support and generous contributions—with friendship for Soviet Russia. Since his mission of 1919 he had kept up his acquaintance with Russian leaders and appeared to be well regarded in Soviet circles. Important, too, Bullitt possessed the imagination and enthusiasm necessary for a post where life did not follow the normal diplomatic routine.

For Bullitt the appointment was a special triumph. Although he had hoped originally to be sent to Paris, where he might remain in close touch with officials who were old friends and where the social life was that to which he was accustomed, the Russian post had captured his imagination. Not only would he be in the tradition-making role of first ambassador, he would be picking up a thread of history dropped in 1919, and righting a historical wrong. Here would be an opportunity to implement, on his own, the sort of "genuinely friendly" relations with a "sister nation" that he had originally hoped for.

Certainly no one suspected, least of all Bullitt, that the Russians were uneasy over the choice of their old friend as ambassador. Outwardly the Kremlin evidenced much satisfaction with Bullitt's appointment. Karl Radek, the Soviet publicist, paid tribute to Bullitt as one of those Americans who had long worked for a resumption of relations with Russia.[66] The Soviet-inspired *Daily Worker* presented him as "an old personal friend of Litvinov."[67] Indeed, the only objections to Bullitt's appointment came from Daughters of the American Revolution chapters outraged over the fact that as "good an American" as the President could appoint as ambassador a man who had married Louise Bryant, widow of the Communist John Reed.

Still, American writers in close contact with Russian leaders, men like Eugene Lyons and Louis Fischer, have contended that

Moscow distrusted the "liberal" like Bullitt, having learned from experience that a militantly pro-Soviet diplomat was a dangerous gamble. [68] A career diplomat or a businessman who would approach problems on a practical basis with no illusions or emotional involvement was at least proof against disillusionment.[69]

In fact, Bullitt was not ideal for the Russian post; this events were to prove. The nature of his personality (combined with his emotional attachment to Soviet Russia) was to make him particularly susceptible to disappointment, for Bullitt needed to be liked. The hurt of his long, political exclusion made it especially important that he be on the inside now. Few documents are more revealing of a man's temperament than are Bullitt's letters to the President. While Roosevelt maintained his breezy, cordial tone, Bullitt's communications were often intense. From aboard the ship on which he sailed to Russia in December, 1933, in order to locate embassy quarters, Bullitt wrote: "I think you know what a joy it is to me to be able to work with you and under your orders. I know you refuse to admit it—especially to yourself—but the fact is you are a very great human being and a great President. It has just occurred to me that I have never thanked you properly for this assignment to Russia. The reason is, I think, that I feel myself so completely at your disposal and am so entirely ready to do anything anywhere that you may wish that I have the feeling of carrying out a job for you rather than any feeling of personal success." And later in 1934, "I am deeply sorry that I shall not see you. I should like to hear the sound of your voice and be with you for a few days. I don't like being so far away from you."[70] We would be losing sight of Bullitt's personality were we to dismiss these and similar letters as mawkish flattery. Rather they were a sincere reflection of what Bullitt, at the start of his second career, hoped his relationship to the President might be. Unfortunately Bullitt went to Moscow hoping to develop similar intimacy with officials of the Soviet government.

From the beginning, the Russians divined the nature of Bullitt's personality and played upon his weakness. In Moscow, Bullitt was given an extraordinary welcome. For the first time in Soviet history, representatives from Litvinov's office were sent to meet a foreign ambassador at the frontier. The Hotel National in Moscow, to which Bullitt was escorted, had an American flag suspended over the entrance. "Imagine my feelings," Bullitt later commented, when we "entered the identical rooms in which . . . I had heard the first outcries of the great war."[71] The apartment reserved for the ambassador and his young daughter was the same one he and his mother had occupied in July, 1914. Litvinov invited Bullitt to his home for a private luncheon at which Bullitt's nine-year-old daughter Anne and Litvinov's two children were present. At the Bolshoi theater, where Bullitt attended the ballet, the presence of the ambassador was announced. The audience stood and cheered.

Dinner at Voroshilov's apartment in the Kremlin on December 20 was the chief event of Bullitt's visit. In addition to Voroshilov, Kalinin, Molotov, Litvinov, and other officials, Stalin himself was present. Stalin offered the first toast: " 'to President Roosevelt, who in spite of the mute growls of the Fishes, dared to recognize the Soviet Union.' " This reference to Hamilton Fish, a foe of recognition, created considerable laughter.

At one point during the evening Stalin said to Bullitt: " 'I want you to understand that if you want to see me at any time, day or night, you have only to let me know and I will see you at once.' " Then, accompanying the ambassador to the door, Stalin asked, " 'is there anything at all in the Soviet Union that you want?' " Bullitt, who had been experiencing difficulty locating appealing embassy quarters, told him he would be glad to know if the lovely property on the bluff overlooking the Moscow River might be given to the American government as a site for an embassy. " 'You shall have it,' " Stalin said.[72]

The cordiality of Bullitt's reception was astonishing. Why was Bullitt's susceptibility to flattery being played upon? Why was

Stalin "honoring" him with a personal conversation? During the evening at Voroshilov's apartment, Stalin supplied most of the answer. For in discussion with Bullitt, the dictator made it clear that he regarded an attack that spring by Japan as certain. On introducing Egorov, the chief of staff, Stalin said, " 'this is the man who will lead our army victoriously against Japan when Japan attacks.' " Stalin was gauging the potential of American-Soviet relations. The second line of the Soviet railroad to Vladivostok was not completed, he remarked. To complete it 250,000 tons of steel rails were needed at once. " 'Your railways,' " Stalin observed to Bullitt, " 'are reequipping themselves and will have many old rails to dispose of immediately. Cannot you arrange for us to purchase the old rails? . . . Without those rails,' " he declared, " 'we shall beat the Japanese, but if we have the rails it will be easier.' "[73] Bullitt said he would be glad to do what he could.

Stalin asked for steel rails. Litvinov was more blunt. In Washington in November he had asked Roosevelt if the United States might conclude a bilateral nonaggression pact with the Soviet Union. The President had refused.[74] The Commissar had also discussed the international situation with William Phillips. He wondered if the United States might be willing to conclude a nonaggression pact with Russia coincident with certain other pacts covering the Far East including the United States, Russia, Japan, and China. Phillips had been cautious in his reply: the Kellogg pact, he suggested, had already given the United States similar engagements with those countries. Litvinov pointed out that the Kellogg pact was no longer in existence thanks to Japan, that anyway individual pacts between nations gave a greater sense of security than a worldwide arrangement including all nations. Phillips had assured Litvinov that his idea was interesting; the United States would give it careful study. Yet the Undersecretary had not indicated enthusiasm. The State Department was taking great care at the moment not to jeopardize its relations with the Japanese.

Russia's fear of Japan in 1933 and early 1934, then, made her particularly interested in seeking American support. After Washington's cold reaction to Litvinov's suggestion, it seems unlikely that the Soviet leaders actually hoped for a pact with the United States. Yet on December 21, Litvinov suggested to Bullitt that in addition to supplying steel rails, the most effective means of forestalling an attack by Japan would be initiation by the United States of proposals for nonaggression pacts to cover the Far East. When Bullitt explained the domestic difficulties in the way of such a proposal and repeated that the United States had no intention of getting into war with Japan, Litvinov remarked: " 'Anything that could be done to make the Japanese believe that the United States was ready to cooperate with Russia, even though there might be no basis for the belief, would be valuable.' "[75]

The Soviets were determined to squeeze every diplomatic advantage from American recognition. The act of recognition in itself promised to have a restraining effect on the Far Eastern situation. Ambassador Grew in Japan reported that in the event of a Japanese-Soviet conflict, American action would be to the Japanese an unknown factor.[76] An unusual display of public attention for the newly arrived American ambassador was well calculated. The Japanese might take it to mean a special relationship between the two countries.

What of the more private, unpublicized effort to please Bullitt? How did that fit into Soviet strategy? From the moment he crossed the Russian border, the ambassador met with an eager cooperation which would have startled (and perhaps aroused the suspicions of) diplomats more accustomed to life in the Soviet Union. The Chief of the Central Administration of Economic and Social Statistics, Mr. Osinski, promised he would place at the disposal of Bullitt's embassy all the statistics available in his department. Grinko, Commissar for Finance, guaranteed that he would make a private, special arrangement for members of the American diplomatic staff in

Moscow to obtain rubles at a fair rate of exchange. Then Stalin appeared at a private dinner for Bullitt and not only promised him a hitherto unobtainable piece of property, but urged that he call on him any time of the day or night.

In the absence of Soviet documents one can only surmise the answer to puzzling questions. It seems that the Russians hoped that Bullitt, reportedly a personal friend of Roosevelt's, would return to the United States and urge a pact of nonaggression with the Soviet Union. For this reason, Stalin, Litvinov, Molotov, Voroshilov, indeed all the officials with whom Bullitt spoke, stressed the immediate danger of the Japanese situation and the urgent need for American help. In all likelihood this was but one more example of Russian inability to comprehend the workings of government in the United States. Bullitt had explained that the American people would never allow a nonaggression pact; that Roosevelt could not possibly propose such an idea. Still, the Soviet rulers, suspecting that a friend of theirs (and of Roosevelt) might persuade the President to do so, discounted the need for public approval.

Certainly Bullitt was aware of the motives behind the grand reception, for he reported to the State Department that the Russians, valuing even the moral influence of the United States, were anxious to have this factor on their side.[77]

One suspects, however, that the ambassador was to some extent overwhelmed by the cordiality of his reception and, despite his knowledge of Soviet hopes, accepted many of the overtures as expressions of personal regard. With a surprising naiveté Bullitt reported that Litvinov had offered as a "special politeness, contrary to diplomatic precedent," to give him an advance copy of the replies Kalinin would make when on the next day Bullitt presented his credentials. This, of course, is standard diplomatic procedure. With pleasure he repeated Kalinin's assurance that Lenin had talked about him on several occasions, that he therefore felt as if he were welcoming someone he had known for a long time. Stalin's astounding offer to see Bullitt at once, any time of the day or night, seemed to the ambassador only a "somewhat extraordinary gesture," and he was pleased to point out that the dictator had hitherto refused to see any ambassador at any time.[78] That Bullitt accepted Stalin's assurances at face value seems indicated by his report to the State Department that in order to "avoid the jealousy" of colleagues he had arranged with Litvinov to make known to the press merely that he had been at Voroshilov's and that "Stalin had dropped in." Perhaps the Commissar grinned as broadly over the idea of Stalin "dropping in" as over the assurance that Bullitt might call on Stalin any time of the day or night, but Bullitt solemnly observed to Hull, "it is valuable to have the inside track, but it seems to me not desirable to emphasize the fact to the world."[79]

If the Russians hoped that Bullitt on his return to the United States might call for cooperation with the Soviet Union, they must have delighted at the ambassador's address to the Philadelphia Chamber of Commerce on January 19, 1934. "Until we resumed diplomatic relations with the Soviet Union," Bullitt declared, "it was impossible for the two nations to work together intimately for the preservation of peace. We can now work together," he added, "and shall work together for the preservation of peace, and the cooperation of our nations will be a potent force in preserving peace."[80]

A "potent force in preserving peace." What did Bullitt mean when he used this phrase? Bullitt's plea for American-Russian cooperation in the interests of world peace meant nothing more at the time than cooperation in a friendly, tactical sense. The United States, he was convinced, must not bind itself to long-term entangling alliances.[81] When Bullitt returned to the Soviet Union to begin his formal duties as ambassador, his interpretation of "potent force" would seem insufficient and vague to Foreign Commissar Litvinov, who preferred to conclude an immediate treaty of non-aggression.

Even in 1933, then, the misunderstandings which we shall see in later chapters were foreshadowed. A fundamental divergence in foreign policy, as well as the ambiguous debt arrangement and Litvinov's reservations regarding Comintern propaganda, would all be sources of friction. Most significant, Bullitt expected to have the inside track in Moscow; but the Russians would give the impression of conveying such an honor only so long as there seemed tangible advantages afforded in return.

VI

The Ambassador and the Commisasr

"I do congratulate and admire you, the second most persistent son-of-a-gun in my history. The third is probably Litvinov."

Early one morning in June, 1932, a car slowed to a stop on Red Square outside the Kremlin wall. William C. Bullitt stepped to the street, a large floral wreath in hand. Solemnly he walked through the iron gate surrounding the burial place of the heroes of the revolution. Pausing at the grave of the young American Communist John Reed, he placed his flowers on the stone and stood, head bowed, for many minutes. "Tears were rolling down his cheeks and his features were drawn with sorrow" when he returned to the car.[1]

Eugene Lyons, the American journalist, talked with Bullitt a good deal during the latter's springtime visit to the Soviet Union. Bullitt's conception of the new Russia, Lyons recalls, was "deeply colored by the romanticism of the earliest period. . . . He was still seeing Russia through the fresh ardors of the John Reeds. . . ."

The embassy at which Ambassador Bullitt arrived on March 7, 1934, was, in the recollection of its third secretary, George Ken-

* Lincoln Steffens to Bullitt on learning of Bullitt's appointment as ambassador. November 25, 1933. *The Letters of Lincoln Steffens*, II, 967.

nan, a "madhouse."[2] Since no office building existed, the staff worked on the top two floors of the Savoy Hotel but ate at Ambassador Bullitt's home. Of his own temporary residence the ambassador commented: "When we arrived the only furniture in the place consisted of six wall clocks! . . . we camped rather than lived here for some months."[3] But all the members of the staff seemed to be of excellent pioneer stock and in the absence of wardrobes or chests of drawers made no objection to "hanging their clothes on the floor."[4]

Even when the office building to be rented, Mokhovaya, was completed, the Soviet authorities refused to allow the Americans in. Among embassy personnel the conviction grew that the Russians feared the new structure would sink through to the subway being constructed below. To add to the chaos, the marines who guarded the embassy were frequently drunk and fighting. Often during the first few months, its members feared that the disorganized American embassy would have to close up and go home.[5]

Still, the high-spirited staff of budding Russian experts—Charles Bohlen, George Kennan, Loy Henderson, and Charles Thayer—could find the discomforts amusing, while the new ambassador, delighted with the warmth of his reception, overlooked daily irritation.[6] During his first months in Russia, Bullitt's enthusiasm was to be tested in every way; yet the ambassador remained optimistic about the possibilities of friendship with the Soviet Union.

I

Shortly after his arrival Bullitt sent the Department of State a lengthy dispatch describing three "extraordinary misunderstandings" which had arisen between him and the Soviet authorities. The Soviet government was not prepared to provide paper rubles for embassy use although Grinko, Commissar of Finance, had previously promised to do so; the property Stalin had said was to be Bullitt's for an American embassy no longer seemed available; and, most serious, Commissar Litvinov was interpreting his "gentleman's agreement" with Roosevelt in a disturbing way.[7]

When Bullitt called at the foreign office on the day of his arrival to see about obtaining the rubles much needed by his embassy staff, he casually repeated Grinko's assurance that of course the embassy would have no difficulty in buying rubles at reasonable prices. To Bullitt's surprise he was told that the Commissiariat of Finance felt it could not fix a rate for the American embassy because it would involve doing the same for others. Since the Commissar for Foreign Affairs upheld the altered position of the Commissar of Finance, the matter became an issue between Bullitt and Litvinov. "It semes to me," Bullitt finally remarked, "that we have embarrassed you greatly by our attempt to play fair and to live in accord with your laws." "That is quite true," Commissar Litvinov rejoined amiably, "and if the worst comes to the worst, you know that we shall have no possible objection to your obtaining paper rubles in any way you think fit." That Litvinov was advising him to patronize the "Black Bourse" (as did the other embassies in Moscow) seemed to the ambassador incredible.[8]

More "extraordinary" was the "misunderstanding" regarding the property on Lenin Hills above the Moscow River promised Bullitt in December for the new American embassy. On this site, which he considered the most desirable in Moscow, the ambassador envisioned constructing an embassy which would duplicate Monticello with its red brick and marble pillars. When Bullitt first indicated interest in the property in December, 1933, the Moscow Soviet expressed misgivings on the grounds that a new canal was going to run close to or through the property; the Soviet hesitated giving the Americans land which might cause future complications. Consequently, when Stalin asked Bullitt some days later in December if there was anything in the Soviet Union he wanted, Bullitt told him he wished the Lenin Hills property for an embassy. Although the ambassador explained the canal complication, Stalin had replied: " 'You shall have it.' " The next day Litvinov telephoned with the news that Stalin had instructed the Moscow Soviet to give Bullitt the land. In March, when he returned to take up his duties, Bullitt was dismayed to learn that the Soviet would not part with the river site.[9]

The third "misunderstanding" was the most far-reaching. In his first Moscow debt discussions with Bullitt, Commissar Litvinov took the "surprising position" that he had agreed to payment of the Soviet debt only in return for a straight loan to be spent anywhere and not a commercial credit to be utilized in the United States.

These three "extraordinary misunderstandings"—two of them relatively minor—are significant in pointing up Bullitt's mood as he undertook his Russian assignment. While vexed by the problems which developed so soon after his arrival, Bullitt was too sanguine regarding American-Russian relations to be seriously discouraged. Failing to appreciate the extent to which a desire to flatter the new ambassador had contributed to the December promises, he concluded that his difficulties were produced not so much by Russian bad faith as by Russian inefficiency. "The members of the Soviet Government," Bullitt observed, "seem disposed to make promises without taking into consideration all the factors involved." He had also learned that in dealing with the Russians "oral promises of members of the Soviet Government are not to be taken seriously."[10] If the United States maintained its position "energetically and forcibly," however, a solution favorable to American interests would be reached.[11] But the debt controversy, the ambassador was soon to decide, could not be thus easily resolved.

The extent to which Litvinov's understanding of the Washington arrangement differed from Bullitt's became irritatingly apparent at the outset. To launch the Moscow discussions, the Department of State had prepared a draft proposal setting the amount of indebtedness at 150 million, bearing interest at the rate of 5 per cent. Retirement of the debt was to be achieved by payment of an additional interest of 10 per cent on all credits or loans to be extended the Soviet government by the United States government or its nationals. This additional interest would be applied first toward the interest accruing on the 150 million and thereafter to reduction of the principal. These were obviously the Department's maximum demands. When Bullitt presented them to the Commissar, the two men resumed the disputation which had begun in Washington the previous November. Litvinov objected to almost every sentence. He protested the sum of 150 million, vehemently opposed paying interest, maintained that he had agreed to pay extra interest only on straight loans—not on credits—and objected to fixing 10 per cent as the amount of additional interest.

Bullitt met Litvinov's arguments by pointing out that since their November arrangement the dollar had been cut to 60 per cent of its former value—therefore the sum of 150 million actually represented only 90 million. As for a direct loan to be spent anywhere, Bullitt emphasized as vigorously as possible that the President had never had any idea of a direct loan to the Soviet government; he had contemplated nothing more than a loan in the form of credits. The United States could not possibly grant a loan to any nation at the present time. Still, Litvinov insisted, although he had known it would be difficult for the United States to grant a loan, he had thought the President would find a way of doing so.[12]

In the months following, the form of payment—whether an outright loan or a credit—became the focus of dispute: amount of payment and interest rates, Litvinov soon acknowledged, were "details."[13] The Commissar refused consent to any agreement which would give the Export-Import Bank the right to approve or disapprove Soviet transactions in the United States; such an arrangement, he maintained, would give the Bank control of Soviet trade with the United States. Bullitt, however, denied that Soviet trade would be controlled by the Bank, which would be authorized only to approve or disapprove transactions freely contracted by the Soviets. A straight cash loan to be expended as the Soviets might think proper, or a straight uncontrolled credit enabling it to make purchases in the United States at will, might, the State Department maintained, result in discrimination and confusion. Under such an arrangement, the Soviet government would be free to purchase war material, or to place manufacturers of the same product in bitter competition with each other. Therefore, an extension of credit with no bank control was deemed "unthinkable."[14]

When, on April 2, Litvinov announced he would not insist on a loan but would arrange for payment of the Soviet debt by way of a long-term credit operation, Bullitt was again encouraged. The Commissar envisioned a twenty-year credit for purchases in the United States to be extended his government by the Export-Import Bank for double the amount of the sum to be paid in settlement of the Soviet debt. Bullitt considered Litvinov's suggested interest rates too low to be accepted, but he received Litvinov's plan optimistically. Did it not mark a retreat from his position that there must be a loan or no settlement?[15]

Secretary Hull reacted differently: "I regard the proposal as wholly unacceptable," indeed "fantastic," he cabled Bullitt. The type of credit Litvinov suggested Hull considered the equivalent of a loan. Were the credit extended, he explained to Bullitt, the indebtedness of the Soviet government at the end of the twenty-year period would be twice what it was at the beginning.[16]

Meanwhile Congress passed the Johnson Bill (April 4, 1934) forbidding loans to governments in default to the United States.

Since the Soviets were presumably in the process of negotiating a settlement, the Export-Import Bank passed a resolution which was read to Congress that day: "No actual credit transactions with the Soviet Government shall be undertaken unless and until that government shall submit . . . an acceptable agreement respecting the payment of the Russian indebtedness. . . ." Litvinov received the news bitterly: the resolution was a threat designed to pressure his government into agreement.

To Bullitt the best strategy seemed now to await a further proposal from Litvinov. This he suggested to the Department, adding that he himself would act as though the question of claims and credits did not exist. The Commissar did oblige with an alternative proposal on May 9, before his departure for the Geneva Disarmament Conference. The Export-Import Bank, Litvinov suggested, should undertake to discount for a period of two or three years bills of exchange issued by agencies of the Soviet government in payment of goods purchased in the United States to double the amount of the debt, at the total rate of 7 per cent, the bills of exchange to mature in twenty years. He was willing, he indicated, to discuss amount of payment, interest rates, and time for maturity, provided there was agreement on the form of credit. A few days later, when Bullitt outlined to Litvinov the State Department's modification—which provided for revolving credits with the Export-Import Bank approving each transaction in advance and carrying only part of the credit risk—the Commissar seemed to the ambassador to "acquiesce in principle"[17] despite previous objections to any form of bank control.

Since the Commissar departed forthwith for Geneva, Bullitt conducted further discussion with subordinate members of the foreign office. Here the ambassador was informed by Litvinov's assistant, Rubinin, that the Soviet government had not changed its position. Consent would never be granted to an arrangement giving the Export-Import Bank the right to approve or disapprove

Soviet business transactions. Such an arrangement, Rubinin reiterated, would afford the Bank control of Soviet trade with the United States. When Bullitt exclaimed irately that Litvinov only two weeks before had no "decided objection" to the plan, Rubinin remarked that the Commissar had just been in a hurry to get away from Moscow; therefore he thought it not "worthwhile" to begin one of his customary disputes with the American ambassador.[18] Negotiations were back to where they had begun three months earlier.

After Litvinov's return, Bullitt urged that between them they attempt to overcome the "misunderstanding" arisen with regard to the "gentleman's agreement." " 'There is no misunderstanding,' " Litvinov replied. The United States government was simply trying to back out of its agreement. Bullitt rejoined with the accusation that it was Litvinov who was trying to retreat from the agreement. Their "customary dispute" ensued. The Commissar ended the argument with the declaration that he and his government were ready to let the matter of the United States debt drop " 'immediately and permanently. . . . No nation today pays its debts. Great Britain has defaulted. Germany is defaulting. And no one will be able to make propaganda against the Soviet Union if we do not pay one dollar on a debt we did not contract.' "[19]

Was this what Litvinov had been planning all along? Did the Russians, as the *New York Times* was to charge, sit back and kill time, gravely going through the forms of negotiations while "laughing in their sleeves at American simplicity?"[20] Did Litvinov, as Bullitt believed, deliberately retreat from his Washington promises as soon as recognition was assured? The answer can be partly determined by looking back at what Litvinov promised in his "gentleman's agreement." The memorandum reads:

> Over and above all claims of the Soviet Government and its nationals against the Government of the United States and its nationals, the Soviet Government will pay to the Government

of the United States on account of the Kerensky debt or otherwise a sum to be no less than $75,000,000 in the form of a percentage above the ordinary rate of interest on a *loan* [italics mine] to be granted to it by the Government of the United States or its nationals, all other claims of the Government of the United States or its nationals and of the Government of the Union of Soviet Socialist Republics or its nationals to be regarded as eliminated.

One will notice use of the word "loan"—an American synonym for credit, to be sure—but an unfortunate bit of carelessness on the part of Roosevelt and Bullitt. The absence of any reference to control of credits by the Export-Import Bank is of further interest. In his arguments with Litvinov, Bullitt asserted that supervision of future credits by the bank was an assumption on his and the President's part. Yet there is no document to prove that such control was explicitly discussed in the Washington talks. On the other hand, there exists positive indication that it was not. An interdepartmental memorandum written in July, 1934, by Assistant Secretary Walton Moore to Assistant Secretary Francis Sayre reviewing the debt situation noted that "Mr. Litvinov left here with everything undetermined except recognition."[21] Moore then proceeded to point out that when Litvinov and Bullitt got together in Moscow the Commissar insisted on a straight cash loan or an uncontrolled credit. But the dangers inherent in giving the Russians such purchasing freedom "led the President to say that a loan in either form . . . without the Government having any control, is unthinkable."[22] A breakdown of the Moscow negotiations, Moore wrote, then developed. Implied in Moore's chronology is the suggestion that control of credits, though all along an American assumption, was not made explicit until after the onset of talks in Moscow.

Litvinov protested further that he had never agreed to pay interest on the debt itself but only an extra interest which would go toward retiring the principal. Technically the Commissar was correct. Only after negotiations had started did Hull make clear that once existence of a debt was recognized, interest automatically accrued.[23]

The "gentleman's agreement" implied, moreover, that Roosevelt would accept the sum of 100 million as a compromise between 150 million and 75 million. Devaluation of the dollar, occurring soon after recognition, caused the American negotiators to exert pressure for a higher sum.

Therefore Litvinov was not, in a strict sense, backing out of his agreements with FDR: on details such as total amount of payment and interest rates nothing definite had been decided. As for the main dispute, whether the Commissar had been promised a loan or a controlled credit, assumptions aside, the one written document substantiated the Russian claim.[24] Both Roosevelt and Bullitt revealed a scant knowledge of diplomatic procedure, let alone of dealing with the Soviet leaders, when they assumed that Litvinov knew precisely what they meant, and, what is more, would graciously abide by their unwritten intentions.

Secretary Hull himself emphasized the anomalous nature of the Washington debt arrangement when, in July, 1934, he asked Bullitt to send him a statement explaining the debt understanding in Washington. In view of the stalemate between Bullitt and Litvinov, Hull was about to begin efforts (which were to prove futile) to reach an agreement with Soviet Ambassador Troyanovsky. Since Bullitt was present at all the debt talks in November, Hull hoped he might produce a summary to be shown Troyanovsky, "negativing suggestion that a straight cash loan or a straight uncontrolled credit was ever contemplated."[25] The Secretary suggested that Bullitt in his reply use a nonconfidential code and not refer to Hull's request for information. Hull would then show Bullitt's message to Troyanovsky. That Hull was forced to resort to Bullitt's memory in the absence of documents substantiating the

American position is significant commentary both on the inde-cisiveness of the Washington negotiations and on the "gentle-man's agreement" which resulted.[26] In his reply—which, as Hull suggested, made no reference to the request—Bullitt insisted that in their pre-recognition talks Litvinov never indicated that he ex-pected either a loan or an uncontrolled credit. Yet Bullitt could only fall back on recalling the tenor of conversations which he claimed were such as to make it difficult for him to imagine anyone mis-understanding Roosevelt's intention.[27]

Although the Soviet Commissar cannot be accused of directly breaking his pledged word, it should not be assumed that the dif-ficulty in reaching a debt settlement was simply the result of a misunderstanding stemming from a carelessly worded memoran-dum. While he may have been technically right, it is clear enough that the Commissar did not expect to pay the debt, that he was somewhat relieved by American determination not to agree to his terms, and that he preferred no settlement at all even to an out-right loan. Litvinov had agreed to payment at a time when re-spectable European nations were defaulting—when nonpayment was becoming almost internationally accepted. In view of the circumstances, it is likely that Litvinov never expected Roosevelt or Bullitt to be naive enough to believe all the recognition agree-ments would materialize. Consequently, the Commissar could not understand Bullitt's growing anger; the American ambassador seemed ridiculous.[28]

In the autumn of 1934 a discussion more heated than usual oc-curred between the two men. The ambassador declared that a loan was "impossible, and always would be impossible." The Commissar "grew purple" and retorted that his government had no desire even for a loan, that it desired now to let the matter drop; that if the question of payment of debts were settled in any way *what-soever* [italics mine] he would have grave difficulties in his rela-tions with England and France.[29] Bullitt departed from the Commissar's office in rage, reporting that he felt he had been "talking with the traditional bazaar bargainer of the Near East."[30]

Bullitt was unsympathetic to Litvinov's own protestations,[31] but if the Commissar's arguments were presented to him by someone else, he reacted differently. Skvirsky, counselor of the Soviet embassy in Washington, called on the American ambassador to explain that the Soviet government could not make any settlement which would cause a revival of the claims of England and France. Bullitt saw "no reason to disbelieve Skvirsky's assertation" that the chief obstacle in the minds of the Soviet leaders was the difficulty of devising a method of distinction between the claims of the United States and those of other governments at a time when the Soviet government was making every effort to establish intimate relations with England and France. To Hull, Bullitt suggested that the United States "exercise whatever ingenuity we may possess in attempting to devise a basis of settlement which while acceptable to us could not be acceptable to France, Great Britain and other claimants."[32]

Secretary Hull was unappreciative of Bullitt's advice: "We are not responsible for the Soviet's relations with England and France," he replied.[33] Nor did Hull share Ambassador Bullitt's optimism that a settlement would eventually be reached. "Personally," Hull wrote, "I have little idea that the Soviet officials will come to any reasonable agreement. Litvinoff won his victory when he obtained recognition and regards everything else as of minor importance."[34] Hull, who had had little part in the debt discussions prior to recognition, was doubtless implying, "I told you so."[35]

II

How could the ambassador after so many irritations persist in his initial feeling that the Kremlin desired "genuinely friendly relations"?

One answer is that Bullitt's irritations were frequently channeled into personal antagonism toward Litvinov, rather than into hostility toward the Soviet government. The two men—one an "old Bolshevik" born of a middle-class Jewish family in Byalostok, Poland; the other a wealthy "Yaleman" from Rittenhouse Square—were bound to clash. Bullitt, sparkling and ebullient, almost boyish, delighting in elaborate parties and dinners, seemed to Litvinov "not serious." The Commissar, a devoted family man, stolid and businesslike but quick-tempered, impressed the ambassador as pugnacious, intransigent, not to be trusted.[36] The only qualities both men shared were a strong will and the skill for effective argument.[37] One suspects that rather than being disturbed by their mutual antagonism, the ambassador enjoyed those bouts in which Litvinov "turned purple." Certainly they provided amusing copy for his jocular correspondence with FDR. "I get a lot of chuckles out of the scrapes you and Litvinov have," the President replied on one occasion.[38]

His scrapes with Litvinov did not discourage Bullitt; they made him more determined to combat what he took to be the Commissar's influence. After a conversation with Voroshilov, Bullitt reported, "I found as I had suspected that Litvinov had not given Stalin and Voroshilov an altogether accurate version of our discussions with regard to claims and indebtedness." Since Voroshilov expressed an intense desire that relations between Russia and the United States be friendly and intimate, Bullitt felt sure the Marshal would "use his influence with Stalin which is very great to soften Litvinov's obduracy."[39] A few months later Bullitt was further cheered by a conversation with Karl Radek, in which the Soviet publicist expressed an opinion that Litvinov's objection to America's suggested basis of negotiations was due to a "desire to obtain a personal triumph as a bargainer." Radek, moreover, echoed Voroshilov's suspicion that Litvinov had not informed Stalin accurately of the differences between America and Russia on debt settlement. He would drop in to Stalin's secretariat, Radek promised, and find out exactly what Litvinov had reported; then, when he visited Stalin, who was vacationing in the Caucasus, he would take up the matter in detail.

Trusting in Radek's "considerable influence" with Stalin, Bullitt advised in September, 1934, against any drastic United States action such as dissolving the Export-Import Bank, created to facilitate American-Russian trade.[40] The idea of thwarting Litvinov by dealing directly with Stalin had captured Bullitt's imagination. He hoped word might come from Radek that Stalin would like to talk the matter over personally; in that event Bullitt thought he might "make an airplane tour of the Caucasus and drop in casually on the boss."[41] Radek soon informed Bullitt, however, that he had read the entire dossier on debts and credits in Stalin's office. Insofar as he could judge, Litvinov had reported the facts without noteworthy distortions.[42]

Bullitt continued, nevertheless, to differentiate between Litvinov and the rest of the Soviet government. For along with the belief that Litvinov was causing most of the trouble, another factor seems to have influenced Bullitt's feelings: the adroit manner in which Russians other than Litvinov played upon his ego. The techniques employed during Bullitt's December visit—praise of the United States and its President, and intimations that Bullitt was much liked—proved still effective. In June Bullitt reported "private information" that Stalin and the military authorities felt strongly that cooperation with the United States must be strengthened, not destroyed; therefore, he did not consider Litvinov's "intransigence" irreversible.[43] In July the ambassador called the State Department's attention to "unusual demonstrations of friendliness" on the part of the Soviet government; these, he believed, had been "ordered by the Kremlin" out of apprehension that Litvinov's obstinacy regarding debts and claims might result in prolonged disinclination of the United States government to cooperate in any field with the Soviet government.[44]

Almost always Bullitt informed the President of the kind sentiments. "I got word from the Kremlin the other day," Bullitt confided in a personal letter to FDR, "that all the leaders of the government including Stalin would be glad to see a great deal more of me than they have been. . . ." There were, Bullitt reported, "dozens of indications" that Stalin, Voroshilov, and Molotov were most anxious to develop "really friendly" relations: Stalin was said to be encouraging social intercourse with the American ambassador and "chiding his intimates" for not seeing more of him.[45] "In the end," Bullitt predicted, "I think we shall be able to beat down Litvinov's resistance."[46]

It was chiefly through the military men that Bullitt hoped to counteract what he took to be the Commissar's influence. Diplomats like Litvinov and Sokolnikov[47] were contending that Japan would not be ready for war before the summer of 1935—a time when they expected the Red Army to be strong enough to prevent a Japanese attack.[48] They assumed further that France and Czechoslovakia would enter an alliance with the Soviet Union protecting Russia's western frontier from German or Polish action should Japan make war.[49] For these reasons the maintenance of intimate relations with the United States appeared less important than when Litvinov had negotiated recognition. Yet Bullitt suspected that the Red Army leaders were still uneasy. "The Soviet diplomatists are convinced," he reported in July, 1934, "that there is no possibility whatever of an early Japanese attack but the military men are so sure that an eventual attack is inevitable that they view Litvinov's stubbornness with disquiet."[50]

As Bullitt explained to Roosevelt, he was therefore seeking to "build a backfire in the Kremlin" by way of men like Voroshilov and Karakhan[51]—an outstanding opponent of Litvinov.[52] As a means to develop close relations with the Marshal, Bullitt hit upon a unique idea: why not teach the Red Army cavalry to play polo? The ambassador imported the equipment and with the exuberant aid of his young interpreter, Charles Thayer, personally taught the Russian proletariat the game. During the summer of 1934, the cavalrymen, with "his Excellency" Ambassador Bullitt galloping along as referee, played every other day.[53] Litvinov, Voroshilov, General Feldman and other Soviet dignitaries accompanied Bullitt to the first polo match ever held in the Soviet Union. Afterward, Voroshilov and Feldman returned to the American embassy, where they enjoyed a party lasting until the early hours of the morning. The results of his idea delighted the ambassador: "The Polo has brought not only myself," he told the President, "but our military men into the closest relations with the Red Army leaders and has been most useful."[54] Besides polo, Bullitt started baseball, importing uniforms and equipment at his own expense.[55]

Bullitt's most spectacular effort to establish rapport with the Russians was a springtime ball conceived to surpass anything Moscow had yet experienced. " 'The sky's the limit,' " he told Charles Thayer, the young embassy official charged with its organization, " 'just so long as it's good and different.' "[56] Different it was. A thousand tulips were imported from Helsingfors, birch trees were forced into premature leafage in the attic of the embassy, grass was made to grow on wet felt, and one end of the dining room was arranged as a collective farm with peasant accordian players, dancers, and baby animals.[57] Except for Stalin, "practically everyone who mattered in Moscow turned up:"[58] the diplomatic corps, most of the Politburo—including Voroshilov, Kaganovich, and Bukharin—and the leading generals of the Red Army. At ten the following morning the party wound up with Chief of Staff General Tukhachevsky doing a Georgian dance with Lolya Lepishinkaya, the ballet star. His ball was called the best Moscow had seen since the revolution, Bullitt proudly reported to Roosevelt.[59]

III

In seeking to thwart Litvinov by building a "backfire" with men of the Red Army, Bullitt believed that the Commissar was the proponent of a policy specific enough to be counteracted. He assumed that the Commissar possessed the political power to carry through his policy. He was convinced that its alternative would lead to improvement of American-Soviet relations. How accurately did Bullitt interpret the Soviet situation?

One cannot offer a definitive answer. Litvinov departed from public life without leaving written memoirs, so far as we know. Dossiers on him remain closed; his correspondence, private and official, is not accessible.[60] Equally unavailable are the Politburo archives and the records of the Commissariat for Foreign Affairs. In view of these unfortunate gaps, one can suggest only the most plausible interpretations.

When Maxim Litvinov became People's Commissar for Foreign Affairs upon the retirement of Georgi Chicherin in 1930, Ambassador Dirksen, Germany's representative in Moscow, felt uneasy. His task had become more difficult, Dirksen later wrote, because Litvinov was not a really convinced adherent of the Rapallo policy —friendship with Germany—but gave it only lip service.[61] Yet not until after the National Socialist victory in 1933—as Dirksen himself acknowledged—did Litvinov publicly deviate from the Rapallo line. In the period after Hitler came to power, Litvinov, while never denying his belief that the capitalist system was doomed to ultimate destruction, warned repeatedly that the Nazi menace was an immediate danger requiring the cooperative resistance of the peaceful powers. Whereas it had been common Soviet practice to group the capitalist nations together as "the enemy," Litvinov now differentiated between Fascist belligerent nations and those interested in the preservation of peace. In a speech to the Central Executive Committee, December 29, 1933, Litvinov made this distinction clear. Admitting that he would not evaluate the motives of the "peaceful" capitalist nations, he went on to say: " 'The maintenance of peace cannot depend upon our efforts alone. It depends upon the cooperation and assistance of other countries as well. By striving, therefore, toward the establishment and maintenance of friendly relations with all countries we devote particular attention to the strengthening of relations and maximum rapprochement with those countries which, like ourselves, furnish proof of their sincere desire to preserve peace and show that they are prepared to oppose any violators of peace.' "[62]

Litvinov thus declared to his compatriots the essence of what came to be called the "Litvinov policy"—inspired, to be sure, by fear of Germany rather than by a desire to align with the democracies. As the League of Nations looked on in embarrassment while Abyssinia succumbed to Mussolini, Litvinov gave to his policy its most eloquent expression. "We are gathered here," he declared, "to close a page in the history of the League of Nations, the history of international life, which it will be impossible to read without a feeling of bitterness." The League had failed to come to the aid of one of its members. Litvinov sought to arouse his audience from apathy: "I say we do not want a League that is safe for aggressors. We do not want that kind of League, even if it is universal, because it would become the very opposite of an instrument of peace. . . . As for myself, I would rather have a League of Nations that tries to render at least some assistance, even if it proves ineffective, to a victim of aggression than a League of Nations that closes its eyes to aggression and lets it pass unperturbed. . . . In an ideal League of Nations, military sanctions, too, should be obligatory for all. But if we are unable to rise to such heights of international solidarity, we should make it our concern to have all continents and, for a start, at least all Europe covered with a system of regional pacts, on the strength of which groups of States would undertake to protect sectors from aggression."[63]

In the absence of more definitive documents, we can do no more than suggest Litvinov's sincerity. Indeed most foreign observers in Moscow—Germans, English, and French—recognized a "Litvinov policy" and believed that Litvinov was "an ardent supporter of the course he had advocated since 1933."[64] A student of the League of Nations has commented: "No future historian will lightly disagree with any views expressed by Litvinov on international questions. . . . Nothing in the annals of the League can compare with them in frankness, in debating power, in the acute diagnosis of each situation. No contemporary statesman could point to such a record of criticisms justified and prophecies fulfilled."[65]

Although there seems adequate justification to speak of a distinct Litvinov policy—representing the views of its exponent—was Bullitt further correct in assuming that the Commissar during the 1930's possessed significant power and influence within the Soviet hierarchy?

Despite the fact that Litvinov was an "old Bolshevik," he never ranked high within the Communist Party. Though a member of the Party's Central Committee for a number of years, he was never a member of the policy-forming Politburo, and even before the revolution seems to have been valued chiefly as a competent technician.[66] Ambassador Dirksen felt that Litvinov suffered from "a certain inferiority complex" due to his position in the Soviet hierarchy. Although, Dirksen says, Litvinov had achieved his ambition in 1930 of emerging from the shadow of his rival, Chicherin, the new Commissar "was still far from happy." Although neither Litvinov nor Chicherin were members of the Politburo, Litvinov "remained of much lower standing in the party hierarchy than his predecessor."[67] And, according to one expert on Soviet affairs, Merle Fainsod, the Politburo exercised a particularly taut control over Litvinov's commissariat. When Stalin chose to intervene, his views were decisive. The foreign office moved along on its own momentum only so long as existing Politburo directives covered the contingencies with which it was confronted. If a policy arose which could not be covered by past directives, Litvinov was obliged to refer the matter to the Politburo.[68]

The post of foreign commissar consequently did not, in itself, carry a great deal of weight in the Soviet system. Therefore, to assume that Litvinov could pursue a policy at variance with Stalin's desires is impossible. How, then, could we have spoken of a "Litvinov policy" implying a line of action of which Litvinov was not only the agent and advocate but probably the formulator? Should we not refer to any Soviet policy during the thirties as "Stalin's policy"?

The explanation that seems most plausible is that which pictures Stalin as "having several strings to his bow."[69] If one assumes that the dictator was capable of considering simultaneously two separate, even conflicting lines of policy, not making any decision in advance, but waiting to see how events developed, then it is possible to understand how Litvinov could have been given more or less a free hand in his efforts to build European resistance to Nazi Germany.

What, however, were the other strings to Soviet policy? We know that Bullitt resented Litvinov largely because the Commissar in his determination to organize European resistance to Germany was showing slight interest in American friendship. Judging by his efforts to overcome what he took to be Litvinov's influence, Ambassador Bullitt evidently believed that the "other string" included heightened attention to Washington's desires. To many, however, it seemed apparent that the alternative to Litvinov's collective security was the Rapallo connection—closer ties with Germany.[70] Gustav Hilger, counselor of the German embassy in Moscow, recalls in his memoirs "a deep and lasting nostalgia for the old days of German-Soviet collaboration" among many Soviet leaders who were reluctant to endorse Commissar Litvinov's views.[71] Germany's ambassador to Moscow in 1934, Rudolph Nadolny, consequently pleaded again and again with his government that Litvinov's thesis regarding the German danger had not yet been fully adopted by the Politburo. Stalin, Molotov, and many others, Nadolny reported, seemed only too willing to remain on friendly terms with National Socialist Germany.[72] Even Karl Radek, in whom Bullitt placed a certain confidence, stated in private conversation in 1934 that nothing could forever block Russia's friendship with Germany.[73] And nowhere, Hilger recalls, was the nostalgia for the "good old days" greater than among the same Red Army officers whom Bullitt was seeking to woo.[74] In October, 1933, five months after the Red and German armies had ceased collaboration, Tukhachevsky in a long conversation with the German charge d'affaires, von Twardowski, deplored recent political developments and stressed that sympathy and good will toward the Reichswehr had not diminished among his fellow officers. As late as October, 1935, Tukhachevsky was expressing his regret over the break in German-Soviet collaboration, declaring that the German Army's valuable aid in building up Russia's forces would always be remembered. Similarly, regrets were offered by Soviet Chief or Staff Egorov and other prominent Red Army commanders. Even Voroshilov, whom Bullitt supposed to be his friend, would have liked to see the Rapallo line continued. Thus the Marshal, with nostalgic words for the former smooth collaboration between the two armies, urged Ambassador Nadolny in 1934 to influence his government to adopt a less anti-Soviet policy.[75]

It has been suggested that Stalin himself preferred the Rapallo connection, but that in light of Hitler's hostility was willing to countenance Litvinov's efforts—at least on a trial basis.[76] Others have contended that Stalin kept both the Litvinov and Rapallo policies going simultaneously. According to this latter view, Stalin was all along hoping for a deal with Hitler. Entry to the League, collective security, the pact with France, the intervention in Spain, were all undertaken with a view to making Hitler find it advantageous to be on good terms with Soviet Russia.[77]

Where then did resumption of relations with the United States fit into Stalin's policy? Was Bullitt correct in his opinion that Stalin sought American friendship? It is likely that Stalin regarded relations with America chiefly in light of his relations with Japan and Germany. Bullitt was given a magnificent welcome in December, 1933, when there existed hope—however vague—that the United States might cooperate with Russia against Japan. Then Bullitt made it abundantly clear that his country's cooperation would be limited to moral suasion. For a time even this was a valued factor. As the danger of Japanese attack lessened in 1934,[78] the importance of American good will correspondingly declined. On this point Litvinov and Stalin were in close accord. In his interpretation of Litvinov's policy in the mid-thirties, Henry Roberts has written: "American-Soviet relations are not discussed here primarily because they were not of great importance to Litvinov's major diplomatic efforts."[79]

One more question should be considered. Did the Kremlin err in lightly regarding Bullitt's overtures at "genuinely friendly relations"? Could America have contributed to the success of Litvinov's efforts and made unnecessary the Rapallo connection?

The prospect was unlikely. When Bullitt spoke of American-Russian policy lines running parallel—as he did in June, 1934—he envisioned nothing more than moral cooperation.[80] Nor was Secretary of State Cordell Hull interested in collective security: "We are not responsible for the Soviet's relations with England and France," he had declared in September, 1934.[81] The State Department, although not appeasement-minded in its basic view, Secretary of the Treasury Morgenthau observed in his diary, was "timorous, conventional and correct" in its approach to European Fascism. Hull, while disliking Fascism, did not always see it as a threat to peace to be met by vigorous, combined action.[82] World peace could be preserved, Hull thought, by lowering trade barriers; Bullitt, on his part, looked toward moral suasion; and Roosevelt, whatever his feelings, knew that international action by the United States beyond recognition of the Soviet Union was politically unfeasible. We recall that he had refused Litvinov's request in November, 1933, for a bilateral nonaggression pact between the Soviet Union and the United States.[83] When Russia asked in March, 1934, if Roosevelt might propose a pact of nonaggression between the United States, the Soviet Union, China, and Japan, this suggestion was also discouraged.[84] In October, 1934, Roosevelt privately expressed interest in a multilateral pact of nonaggression to be signed by the Pacific powers, including Russia and China.[85] Later that month he mentioned to William Phillips, "as a mere thought, not in any sense as something that we were necessarily to follow," the idea of a multilateral nonaggression pact which defined aggression as the illegal crossing of a border and provided for an embargo against the aggressor.[86] Phillips forwarded the suggestion to J. P. Moffat, who replied unenthusiastically. Instead of assisting us to remain out of further European war, Moffat observed, the pact would "bid fair to involve us in a future conflict, as there is little doubt that 'declining to trade in any manner, shape or form with an aggressor' as a means of sanction comes pretty close to a *casus belli*, and would in any event be inconsistent with the duties of neutrality." To Moffat's memorandum Phillips attached a note: "The President says we can let this matter rest."[87]

Bullitt was astute enough to know that the Kremlin did not necessarily believe in Litvinov's policy. Yet his knowledge of the Soviet system was not deep enough to permit him to recognize that while Litvinov represented and advocated a particular line, he could not pursue it without Stalin's approval. Bullitt was well enough informed to know also that the Soviet government would have liked to make a defensive alliance with Germany.[88] Despite this knowledge, despite his experience in international affairs, Bullitt seems not to have appreciated in early 1934 how unimportant

American isolationism had rendered his country in Soviet plans. Even if the Japanese situation grew more acute, American "friendship" in the mid-thirties could remain only a secondary factor. Largely because he exaggerated the importance of America in Politburo policy, Bullitt failed fully to realize that for Stalin, for Voroshilov, for all the Russians with whom he was friendly, the only plausible alternative to Litvinov was Rapallo. In afteryears Bullitt would claim to have understood Stalin's great interest in rapprochement with Hitler.[89] Yet his dispatches make it clear that in 1934 Bullitt appreciated neither the extent of Stalin's interest in Germany nor that of his disinterest in the United States. His education was to come late.

And thus Bullitt completed his first half year in Moscow in a mood of optimism and good will. He had not made progress in his negotiations, but he had found in Litvinov a scapegoat. He had been soothed by Soviet flattery: the unprecedented December interview with Stalin, the cheers at the theater, the enthusiastic reaction to his baseball, polo, and parties. His emotional friendship for the Soviet Union, which dated back to 1917, his idea that memories of John Reed and of his own mission in 1919 placed him in a special position in Russia, all caused Bullitt to expect that ultimately his difficulties with the Commissar would be resolved.

VII

The Education

American Ambassador to Germany, William E. Dodd, noted in his diary the evening of November 25, 1935, that the ambassador to Moscow had visited that morning. Bullitt's remarks, Dodd wrote, "were directly contradictory to the attitudes he held when he passed this way last year. Then he was to all intents and purposes enthusiastic." Dodd was amazed at Bullitt's observations, coming as they did from a diplomat "who had done much to get Russia recognized in 1933." "The President must know the man's mentality," Dodd concluded, "but if so, how could he have appointed him Ambassador to Soviet Russia?"[1]

I

By mid-1935 Bullitt had abandoned friendship for Russia, so conspicuous a part of his political outlook when he began his Moscow embassy. In attempting to determine the reasons for Bullitt's radical change of opinion regarding the Soviet Union, the most obvious factor should be evaluated first: how did the experience of living as ambassador in Russia affect him?

Conditions were extraordinarily unpleasant—so much so that a few months after his arrival Bullitt requested that Moscow be classified as a hardship post. Expert medical or dental care was unobtainable—as was clothing and such civilized appurtenances as fly-screening. Recreation, regarded as normal in Western Europe or America, did not exist in Russia. Congestion of human traffic was such that a walk in the Moscow streets was "as refreshing as a ride in the New York subway during rush hours." Russian food, even though obtained at great expense in the best hotels, produced digestive upsets "dignified by purple blotches." A leave of absence within the Soviet Union Bullitt did not consider a rest: travel was so expensive and "verminiferous" and hotel conditions so bad that health was apt to be affected unfavorably by a vacation in Russia.[2] These inconveniences were annoying, but Bullitt accepted them with equanimity. He decided that the intellectual stimulation of his post compensated in large degree for lack of physical comfort.

Other aspects of Russian life he could not shrug off philosophically. Threats to the ambassador's Russian servants, spying by servants on embassy personnel, the arrest of Bullitt and his daughter for crossing the Nevsky Prospekt where crossing was forbidden, the abject terror in which the *Intourist* guide who attempted to intercede for the ambassador was placed by the police, all were profoundly repugnant to the American in Moscow.[3]

Eugene Lyons, after speaking with Bullitt in 1932, had commented that although he was thoroughly informed about the physical changes that had taken place in the thirteen years since his mission of 1919, Bullitt was wholly innocent of the far greater changes in the mood of the revolution—"the hardening of its emotional arteries, its callousness and unromantic 'realism.'" Bullitt's enthusiasm for Russia, Lyons predicted at the time, would not survive a long residence—it was based on romantic assumptions which no longer held good.[4]

Lyons' words were prophetic. Bullitt developed, late in 1934, the uncomfortable realization that what he had heard in 1918, what he had seemed to be witnessing in 1919 were merely transitory moods in the revolution. Russia had evolved in a different direction. As a young man in 1918, Bullitt had exulted: "I know a lot of men who have been in Russia since the Revolution began and they have all suffered conversion. They are done with Emperors, political emperors, financial emperors, and moral emperors. They have exiled the Czar. Taken over the banks and buried Mrs. Grundy. As a nation they have become brotherly, open hearted, free from convention and unafraid of life."5 In 1919 Bullitt had spoken with certainty of the Russian situation after a one-week visit. It was a measure of Bullitt's maturity when in 1934 he could write: "No generalization on the Soviet Union can have more than momentary validity. The Russian Revolution is still moving with such rapidity that any picture is certain to be false after the lapse of a few months." With that qualification he offered his government tentative observations gathered after living in Russia for nearly a year.

Russia of 1934, he wrote, still had no greater freedom than under the Czars; it was a nation ruled by fanatics ready to sacrifice themselves and everyone else for their religion of Communism. Freedom was conspicuous only by its absence, and Soviet citizens lived in a state of terror. For the miserable millions of Russians who were neither Communists nor sympathizers, life meant present suffering and eternal hope. Bullitt was aware of positive aspects of Russian life. The speed of change since 1914 struck him as incredible: there were many spots of cleanliness and progress where once only squalor existed, there was education everywhere, and there were magnificent dams and factories. Soviet culture remained on a high level, and emphasis on traditional scientific research had increased. While the men and women above the age of twenty-five felt their lives to be drab and dreadful, Bullitt recognized another spirit among the young, drilled since childhood in the Communist catechism. The youth of Russia believed in its future.

In Bullitt's view the Soviet future promised little positive change. That the revolution would ever advance to the pure Socialism promised in 1917 seemed to Bullitt doubtful. Nor would there be relaxation of the regime of tyranny and terror, a move in the direction of greater freedom. Human freedom and personal liberty would continue to be regarded as "liberal bourgeois aberrations." Whatever alteration might come in the form of state organization, the dictatorship would undoubtedly remain.[6]

And still, despite his insights to the Soviet system, Bullitt continued in 1934 to cherish the hope of personally implementing genuinely friendly relations between Roosevelt's government and the Kremlin. Debt negotiations with Litvinov failed. Bullitt's plans for a Monticello-embassy were discarded. Litvinov intimated that good relations with America were no longer considered important because America refused to become involved in European problems. Even then Bullitt held to his dream. But in mid-1935 he abandoned it abruptly.

The disappointments suffered by the American embassy reached a climax in July, 1935, when the Seventh Communist International met in Moscow. Russia's entry into the League of Nations in 1934, the signing of mutual assistance pacts with France and Czechoslovakia in May, 1935, proved to be events heralding a new role for the Russian-controlled Comintern. Following the evolution of Soviet policy, the Communist International now accepted Russia's view of the tactics required to meet changing Soviet defense needs. Hitler's avowed hostility to the Soviet Union demanded a mobilization of forces against his rise. The Comintern Congress therefore called for a worldwide collaboration among the foes of Fascism, whether Communist, liberal, democratic, or Socialist. The "Popular Front" was thus launched in Moscow in August, 1935.

Throughout the world many non-Communists were pleased by the cooperative tone Russia appeared to have assumed. The immediate effect of the new policy was to increase Soviet prestige in democratic and moderate leftist circles. In France, Léon Blum was to come to power as the head of a Popular Front government. Still, a reading of the speeches of Dimitrov, newly elected Secretary General of the Comintern, should have dispelled the notion that the International had abandoned its revolutionary doctrines. Although pursuit of the millennium was to be postponed, world revolution remained the Comintern's goal.

Ambassador Bullitt was unaware, as the meeting began, of the new tactic about to be proclaimed at the Congress. What did concern him were the facts that the meeting of the Congress was permitted in Moscow, that quarters in one of the largest government buildings were assigned to it, and that the official government press and Tass agency were placed at the disposition of the Congress. That the Seventh Congress of the Comintern was taking place under the auspices of the Russian government seemed sufficiently proven. Bullitt's primary interest was therefore in attempting to spot violations of the Soviet pledge of November, 1933. The Soviet government, we recall, had promised "not to permit the formation or residence on its territory of any organization or group—and to prevent the activity on its territory of any organization or group, or of representatives or officials of any organization or group—which has as an aim the overthrow or the preparation for the overthrow of, or the bringing about by force of a change in, the political or social order of the whole or any part of the United States. . . ."[7] The text of the pledge stood as a solemn government commitment.

The Congress began and progressed as though no promises had ever been given to the United States. Representatives of the American Communist Party were present from the outset, among them William Z. Foster, chairman, and Earl Browder, general secretary. Foster and Browder were elected to the presidium of the Congress, and Browder delivered a speech in which he discussed conditions in the American party, activities among the unemployed, and Communist gains in leadership of the strike movement. Reference to the activities and achievements of Communists in the United States were also contained in the report on the activity of the Executive Committee of the International. Future activities of the American

Communist Party were forecast in a speech by Wilhelm Pieck of
the German party. Like Browder, Pieck spoke of the need for
continued work among the unemployed and the Negroes in order
to create class warfare. Americans, Foster and Green, emphasized
the problems of winning over American youth.[8] The Russian
pledge was thus violated by the participation in a Congress held in
Moscow of representatives of the Communist Party of the United
States; and by discussion at a Congress held in the Soviet Union of
the policies and activities of Communists in the United States.

Bullitt was unimpressed by Comintern calls for cooperation
against Fascism; he noticed instead the urgings for American
Communists to continue agitation for class warfare. A reading of
the Comintern speeches[9] had convinced him that the Third International continued to be devoted to world revolution. The Congress had occurred under Soviet auspices; therefore the violations
of Russia's pledge seemed to him more significant than any tactical
policy the Soviets chose now to pursue.[10]

Ambassador Bullitt took this newest breach of faith as a personal insult. Nearly all of the November pledges had already
been broken or strained. Now the promise he personally considered
the most important in the recognition series, the one which he
credited himself with obtaining, had openly been violated. The
wrong was the more shocking to Bullitt since he had not expected
the Comintern Congress, the first in seven years, to take place in
Moscow that summer. The seat of the Comintern, rumor had had
it, would be moved from the Soviet capital to London or Antwerp
in the interest of Soviet foreign relations.[11] Bullitt had reported
further talk that the Congress, originally scheduled for August,
1934, might be postponed indefinitely. In any event, he was certain
it would not occur in the near future since Russia could not allow
its relations with the governments of Western Europe to be
jeopardized by Comintern activities.[12] Bullitt believed Litvinov
personally resented the International since its activities had often

diminished the good will which he was engaged in building up'
abroad. Indeed, the postponement of the Congress from August,
1934, to sometime in 1935 seemed to Bullitt to be intimately con-
nected with Litvinov's delicate negotiations on the Eastern Pact.[13]
The Commissar, who hoped in 1934 to match the Locarno system
in the west with parallel border guarantees in the east, did not wish
to have his plans upset by wild speeches in Moscow.[14]

Early in July, 1935, Bullitt learned, however, that the Comintern
Congress would begin in Moscow on or about July 20. To various
Soviet officials he had made it clear that if the Third International
did meet, and if it concerned itself in any way with the United
States, relations would be too gravely prejudiced to predict the
consequences.[15] The following day the ambassador reported
"definite information" that the remarks he had dropped regarding
the effect on Soviet-American relations of the scheduled assembling
of the Comintern Congress had caused Litvinov, Voroshilov, and
Molotov to protest vigorously to Stalin against the meeting. In
view of this fact, Bullitt felt the decision to hold the Congress
might be reversed.[16]

When the Congress duly occurred later that month disproving
Bullitt's predictions, the ambassador realized that in this instance
he could not blame the Commissar, that indeed he and Litvinov
were for the first time on the same side. The Commissar thought
of European complications rather than his November assurances—
but for him the meeting was profoundly embarrassing.[17] In a
League speech on September 18, 1934, Litvinov had stressed the
importance of noninterference in the internal affairs of other nations. At the time of the Congress, Litvinov was chairman of the
council of the League and was not himself present in Moscow. In
Marienbad he was preparing for the difficult task of conducting the
session of the League council which would be concerned with the
Italo-Abyssinian conflict. Clearly the violations of the November
pledge were not the fault of Maxim Litvinov. The men in the

Kremlin were responsible. Bullitt's antipathy toward the Foreign Commissar spread now to the entire Soviet government. Here was a case which could be attributed only to bad faith, which could not possibly be excused as Soviet inefficiency.

When he sat down at his desk on August 21 to compose his report on the events of the past days in Moscow, Bullitt was more righteously indignant than at any time since arriving to take up his ambassadorial duties. The Congress of the Communist International which closed last night, Bullitt began, was a flagrant violation of Litvinov's pledge to the President. Bullitt went on to explain the nature of the violations. "There is, of course, no doubt concerning it, also no proof, that the entire course of the Congress was dictated in advance by Stalin." Bullitt considered the possibilities open to the United States. To break relations, he contended, would satisfy the indignation felt by all and would be juridically correct. In his opinion, however, the question was to be decided on neither emotional nor juridical grounds but on the basis of a cold appraisal of the wisest course to pursue to defend the American people from "the efforts of the Soviet Government to produce bloody revolution in the United States." Severing relations on the ground that the Soviet government had broken its pledge and could not be trusted would make resumption of relations inordinately difficult. And Bullitt foresaw the Soviet Union in the next decade becoming either the center of attack from Europe or the Far East or one of the "greatest physical forces in the world." In any event an official observation post of the United States in Moscow would be needed. American diplomatic representatives in the Soviet Union are harassed and restricted, Bullitt observed parenthetically, but there is no way in which a sense of reality with regard to the Soviet Union may be obtained and preserved "except by the painful process of living within its confines." As the Soviet Union grows in strength, he predicted, it will "grow in arrogance and aggressiveness, and the maintenance of an organization in Moscow to measure and report on the increasingly noxious activities and breach of faith of the Soviet Union seems definitely in the interest of the American people." He advised therefore against severing relations.

Neither should there be a written protest to the Soviet government; such a protest would produce only a violent and insulting reply and a fruitless exchange of notes. He suggested rather that Washington employ the occasion to make clear to the American people the aims of the Soviet government which lay behind the "mask" labeled "United front against Fascism and war"; that the *exequaturs* of all Soviet consuls in New York and San Francisco be revoked, leaving only the consular section in Washington; and that the granting of American visas to Soviet citizens be restrained to a minimum. Finally, Bullitt urged Roosevelt to make a speech stating that although at the time of recognition the Soviet government expressed the hope that relations might forever remain normal and friendly, the rulers of the Soviet Union were in reality directing preparations for the overthrow of our system of government. The President should describe how at the Comintern Congress American Communists were ordered to worm their way into labor unions, farmers' organizations, peace organizations, youth organizations, all liberal and religious organizations, and Negro groups.[18]

Neither Roosevelt nor Hull accepted Bullitt's suggestions. Instead they requested him to deliver a note to the foreign office which would afterward be released to the United States press. Despite his reservations, Bullitt handed the State Department message to Krestinski on August 25. " 'If your note is a protest with regard to the Congress of the Communist International,' " Krestinski observed, " 'I can tell you before reading it that it will be rejected.' "[19]

In reply to the American note the Soviets declared that they had not taken and would not take upon themselves obligations of any kind with regard to the Comintern. This denial of responsibility

Bullitt expected. What particularly incensed him was the "lie" being propagated to foreign press correspondents by chief censor Konstantin Umansky and also to foreign ambassadors by Krestinski that Roosevelt orally made a secret agreement with Litvinov in November, 1933, excluding the Comintern from the scope of Litvinov's pledge.[20]

In Bullitt's opinion it was incompatible with the dignity of the United States, in view of its protest and the nature of the Soviet reply, still to take no action. He therefore pressed Hull to make a statement announcing that the *exequaturs* of Soviet consuls had been canceled; that American military attachés in Moscow were being withdrawn; and that the Soviet military, naval, and air attachés in Washington were being asked to leave. "The Soviet foreign office," Bullitt wrote, "does not understand the meaning of honor or fair dealing but it does understand the meaning of acts. . . . We shall never find a better moment to act against the direction of the communist movement in the United States by the dictator in the Kremlin."[21] Again Roosevelt considered Bullitt's suggestions "premature." They would have soothed the ambassador's wrath but they would not have eased the situation. Probably Roosevelt felt that since relations with Russia were to continue, it would be unwise to drag out an unpleasant incident. He preferred therefore that the United States issue another protest; a formal statement of great dignity.[22]

II

A few months after the episode of the Comintern Congress, Bullitt and Litvinov had a discussion regarding Soviet-American affairs. Bullitt told the Commissar that the United States had desired "really friendly relations" with the Soviet Union but now felt the direction of the activities of the Communist International by Stalin was incompatible with friendship. Litvinov expressed the view that there was no such thing as friendship or "really friendly relations" between nations.[23]

The climax of Bullitt's Russian education came with his realization that Litvinov was right—at least insofar as Russia's international contacts were concerned. The sort of friendship he had come to Moscow to develop, that he had worked for since 1919, would be impossible. His mission and the Roosevelt-Bullitt Russian policy had failed. Not only Commissar Litvinov, but the Soviet government had made clear their lack of interest in "genuinely friendly relations." Bullitt concentrated after the summer of 1935 on informing Washington of his unhappy education.

In the opinion of one historian, there were three major hypotheses available to Bullitt to explain Soviet conduct during the thirties.[24] The first, promulgated by the German ambassador, Werner von Schulenburg, and shared by his British and French colleagues in Moscow, Viscount Chilston and Robert Coulondre, held Soviet behavior to be shaped by power politics. Communist theory made little difference in this analysis; the Kremlin, they felt, was moved primarily by considerations of power, not ideology. A second hypothesis was shared by most American foreign service officers in Moscow, the men who were training to become Russian experts—Loy Henderson, George F. Kennan, Charles E. Bohlen. It was based on careful knowledge of Communist theory and practice. These experts acknowledged the influence of considerations of power on the Kremlin, but they assigned equal importance to Marxist-Leninist-Stalinist ideology. A third hypothesis viewed the Soviet regime as an experiment in the right direction and pictured the Russians as eager for friendly cooperation with the West. Such ideas Bullitt held when he came to Moscow, and such his successor, Joseph E. Davies, maintained throughout his Russian embassy. Once discarding the enthusiastic naiveté with which he began his mission, Bullitt, to his credit, was able to balance in his analysis both hypotheses, power politics and ideology, regarding the mainsprings of Soviet conduct.

Any attempt to formulate American policy toward the Soviet Union, he told Washington, would have to begin with a discussion of the Communist faith as expounded by Marx, Lenin, and Stalin. Perhaps, Bullitt observed, men like Litvinov were mere profiteers of the revolution, and men like Radek found in its violence outlet for hatred of their childhood superiors. But in Stalin, in Voroshilov, and in other top leaders, he felt sure, one would find love of mankind as well as hate; such men were ready to sacrifice not only all others to the triumph of their faith but also themselves. To consider Communism as a religious movement, Bullitt thought, was to enter the labyrinth of the Soviet Union by the right path. And belief in world revolution was the core of the Communist religion. Neither Stalin nor any other party leader, he warned, had deviated in the slightest from his determination to spread Communism to the ends of the earth.

Bullitt considered it particularly important for Washington to be aware of this ultimate determination—particularly in view of the widespread opinion in the mid-thirties that Stalin had modified the fundamental attitude of Communism toward the capitalist world by establishing as a goal permanently peaceful relations with those neighbors which did not threaten Soviet independence. Bullitt believed the division of forces determined immediate Soviet attitudes toward external relations, that Soviet policy would vary in the exact proportion to the real force which the Kremlin felt it could exert in world affairs. Every increase in Russian strength, Bullitt predicted, would invariably lead to increased arrogance and aggressiveness, and eventually to stiffening of Moscow's foreign policy. Such increases in strength, Bullitt warned, were inevitable.

There were indications that Soviet foreign relations would

soon be approaching a turning of the way. The first decade and a half of defensive policy, designed to preserve the existence of the country through a crucial phase of economic and social change, was coming to an end. Bullitt saw approaching a new era in which an increasingly powerful Kremlin would be able to take the offensive in world affairs, to retract one after another of the concessions it had made to its capitalist environment, and to apply the enormous weight of its concentrated political and economic power for the achievement of its goals. These goals were essentially imperialistic. The Soviet government was really "the greatest capitalist group the world had ever seen." Its imperialism would differ from that of other capitalist nations, Bullitt thought, "only because it holds actual political sovereignty in the great territory it controls."[25] Bullitt predicted the line of Soviet advance in the East: from Mongolia and Sinkiang, Communism would eat its way steadily into the heart of China using the Chinese Red Army as its teeth. Indeed, the "heartiest hope" of the Soviet government was that the United States would become involved in war with Japan. The Soviet Union would then attempt to avoid becoming an American ally until Japan had been thoroughly defeated and would then merely use the opportunity to acquire Manchuria and Sovietize China.[26]

The Bolsheviks did not expect Communist revolutions in Europe except as a result of a general European war, Bullitt maintained. Hence their policy would be to keep Europe divided and to promote enmity between France and Germany. They were convinced that if either Poland or Rumania should become involved in war, social revolution would follow. If war could be delayed until the Red Army was prepared, the Russians would then be ready to send their army at once to assist Communist governments which might be set up in the border states, even for a day. Already, Bullitt observed, representatives of Russia's neighbors on the west were beginning to look on the future in much the same manner as the statesmen of Athens, Thebes, Sparta, and Corinth must have viewed the future of their city states during the days when Philip of Macedon was training his armies. Possibly, Bullitt concluded, the Kremlin leaders believe that should their power be undisputed throughout the world, a new and better era will dawn for humanity. They know, however, that it will be many years before this goal can conceivably be reached. In the meantime they will be engaged in a battle for power, pure and simple—a battle in which such things as principles, ideals, human lives and even the welfare of entire peoples will be no more than pawns.[27]

What then should be the policy of the United States in regard to the Soviet Union and the world Communist movement? The United States should maintain relations with the increasingly powerful Soviet Union. But the American government should remain unimpressed by expansive professions of friendliness and unperturbed in the face of slights and underhand opposition. And above all, America "should not cherish for a moment the illusion that it is possible to establish really friendly relations with the Soviet Government or with any . . . communist individual."[28]

Despite his sober analysis of Soviet policies, and his measured advice that the United States remain "unperturbed" in its dealings with Russia, Ambassador Bullitt was too emotional to be philosophic in personal contacts. "I deviled the Russians," after the Comintern Congress, he recalls with relish. "I did all I could to make things unpleasant."[29] Bullitt did not merely deliver his notes of protest to the Soviet foreign office. He launched a fierce propaganda campaign in Moscow against Moscow. According to Louis Fischer, Bullitt met the American correspondents every day and urged them by their dispatches to "fan the flames of anti-Sovietism in America."[30] He ignored precedent and summoned non-American foreign correspondents to do the same in their own countries. He also pressed foreign diplomats to have their governments protest

against the Comintern Congress. Bullitt's presence in Moscow became impossible—both for the ambassador, in view of his inability
to take disillusionment with equanimity, and for the Soviet officials,
who considered his anger obnoxious. Having failed to accomplish
the purpose of his mission, Bullitt saw little left for him to do as
ambassador to Russia. "I know how anxious you are to have some
definite work," Roosevelt wrote him in April, 1936, "and I hope
to Heaven you will have it by the middle of May. . . . I can tell
you this, however, that when the change is made you will pack up
your furniture, the dog and the servants—where you deposit them,
we will have to tell you later."[31]

III

Bullitt returned to the United States in June, 1936, ostensibly on leave of absence. The Russians were not informed he did
not plan to return. Washington friends also believed that, when
his vacation had ended, Bullitt would resume Moscow duties.
Throughout the summer he remained in the United States studying, on Roosevelt's orders, the problem of "reforming and regener-
ating" the Department of State and the foreign service.[32] Bullitt
had looked forward during the dreary months in Moscow to working also on Roosevelt's campaign (that the President would be
renominated seemed to him obvious). He was pleased, therefore,
to be included—one hot Sunday night in June—in the White House
group responsible for drafting the reelection platform. Bullitt continued through the summer to work with Tommy Corcoran, Ben
Cohen, and Stanley High on the campaign speeches.

Meanwhile, he denied rumors that he would resign his Russian
post: "These reports are 100 per cent untrue, flatly."[33] But on
August 25, 1936, Bullitt was appointed ambassador to France in
place of Jesse Straus, who had recently died.

France was home to William C. Bullitt. His new position de-

lighted him. Paris's warm reception boosted the spirits of the ambassador, whose angry departure from Moscow was marked by a
sigh of relief—emanating from the diplomatic corps as well as the
Soviet government. For several reasons Bullitt appealed to the
French. His ties with their country were old and deep: the Bullitt
ancestry could be traced to a family in Nîmes named Boulet, part
of Bullitt's childhood had been spent in Paris, and he spoke the
language of the country as though it were his own. His expansive
personality, his love of elaborate balls and entertainments were
particularly suited to the French capital. He promptly leased a
magnificent château in Chantilly, installed a superb chef, and
stocked the cellar with 18,000 bottles of the choicest wines. Harold
Ickes once commented of his friend Bill Bullitt, "In many respects
he is more French than the French themselves."[34]

Bullitt's influence in Paris was to become so great he would be
dubbed minister without portfolio in the revolving French cabinets. Cabinet ministers were constantly at his dinner table, and
almost every day the American ambassador lunched with a prominent government official. To Washington came lengthy reports
detailing table-time political gossip. With politicians as far apart
as Léon Blum and Edouard Daladier (minister of war from 1936 to
1938, and then premier) Bullitt developed personal friendship. He
sat with Blum at the bedside of Madame Blum the night she died.[35]
Daladier, lacking confidence in his subordinates, leaned heavily on
Bullitt for advice—as Bullitt's cables to the State Department revealed. Bullitt spoke of himself as Daladier's closest friend; this may
have indeed been so: when the war came, Daladier asked Bullitt to
serve as guardian for his young son in the event of his own death.

Bullitt's influence in Paris came to be unique; similarly his relationship with Roosevelt was never so close as during these prewar
years. Bullitt had free access to the White House and was one of
the few men privileged to phone the President at any time. In
Europe he came to be regarded as the President's personal spokes-

man. Roosevelt and Bullitt, in the tense months before the outbreak of the war, even utilized a personal code, for Bullitt feared leaks in the Department of State. Bullitt advised the President directly on foreign service matters and diplomatic appointments. The embassy in Paris, due to Bullitt's extraordinary political contacts, became the channel through which a great deal of information from Europe passed to Washington.

An American diplomat's chance to influence decisions was greater during the thirties·than it is today in the era of traveling secretaries of state personally conducting their own diplomacy. Then, as now, Washington's foreign policy remained unsettled. The choices open to the executive were admittedly limited both by isolationist sentiment in the nation and the Congress, and by unfortunate neutrality legislation. Still, there was much the President and State Department could do to awaken the nation to the danger to America in the progressive deterioration of world affairs. Italy had attacked Ethiopia in 1935. Hitler, having withdrawn from the League, rearmed Germany and in 1936 reoccupied the Rhineland, both in defiance of Versailles. General Franco led a revolt against the Republican government in Spain; Germany and Italy aided the insurgents, while Russia sent help to the loyalists. Hitler and Mussolini in 1936 formed the Rome-Berlin Axis; Japan and Germany, the Anti-Comintern Pact (which Mussolini joined the following year).

In 1936, however, Roosevelt had yet to be convinced that the perils to the United States inherent in Europe's disintegration could not be met but by direct American participation in world affairs. Roosevelt has been accused by revisionist historians of tricking the nation with hypocritical assurances that he would never send American boys to battle. Yet, as Langer and Gleason have so thoroughly shown, Roosevelt was sincerely anxious to maintain American neutrality—anxious to the degree that he has been criticized by close associates (and by Langer and Gleason) of moving too slowly, of being inexcusably dilatory in warning the country and in providing for national defense. All his public pronouncements in 1936 conformed to the line of nonentanglement—a policy he had followed since 1932. Not until the world situation became so crucial that America could no longer stay out did FDR even remotely consider taking his country to war.

Similarly, the State Department needed to be convinced that it must take a hand in halting the deterioration of European conditions. Close observers of American politics and intimates of high officials have summed up the situation in Washington during the thirties with the astute observation that policy was the product of cables received rather than of a clear conception of American interest in world affairs. Hull, convinced that economic problems caused war, concentrated on trade agreements, which he hoped would reconcile nations. The idea that the United States might formulate a comprehensive program of action and bring influence to bear in Europe in order to implement it was, in the opinion of one historian, quite alien to the thinking both of Hull and of his influential subordinate, Sumner Welles.[36]

Washington's policy was fluid; so too was foreign policy in France. In private conversation with Bullitt in 1937 Léon Blum admitted both France and England were vacillating between two opposing views: one, that real peace with Germany might possibly be purchased by great sacrifices to Hitler; the other, that Hitler's insatiable appetite prevented any confidence in promises made by the German government, and that it was therefore impossible to make peace with Germany. Assuming the latter, the only possible course would be to construct as strong a coalition as possible to deter Germany from attack or to defeat her if attack were inevitable. Such a coalition envisioned cooperation with Russia[37]—a meaningful development of the "Popular Front."

Bullitt would be asked his opinion by both Roosevelt and the several French leaders. His newly acquired Russian education became particularly significant when it began to influence the advice he offered Washington and Paris.

Shortly before his departure from Russia, Bullitt had informed his government that Germany could not be in a position to make war on the Soviet Union for many years. All Litvinov's "propaganda trumpetings" to the contrary, Bullitt declared, the only real threat to Russia, and Russia knew it, was Japan. The Soviet Union hoped, however, to promote hostility between France and Germany, for only as a result of European war could Communism spread in Europe. Bullitt therefore advised Hull to instruct American diplomatic representatives "to use all opportunities in personal conversations to point out the danger to Europe of the continuation of Franco-German enmity and to encourage reconciliation between France and Germany."[38]

Bullitt began early his efforts to persuade the French not to develop closer relations with the Soviet Union. He condemned the idea of cooperative action among England, France, and the Balkan states to bring Russia into a moderate policy, and he declared himself in full agreement with the Lloyd George-Lord Lothian opposition to including Russia in a European combination to check Germany.[39] As early as mid-1935 he argued at length with French leaders for defeat of the Franco-Soviet pact then being negotiated.[40] Later that year Bullitt did what he could to prevent a possible French loan to the Soviet Union by informing a strategic official in the French government that Russia would never repay.[41] Unable to prevent ratification of the Franco-Soviet treaty, Bullitt did what he could to hinder its development. When he heard reports that France was acceding to the Soviet demand for military conversations in order to put meaning into the innocuous treaty, he went to Gamelin demanding whether the reports were true. General Gamelin assured his American friend the stories were mere rumors.[42]

Besides warning against the futility of moving toward Russia,

Bullitt urged closer relations with Germany. To Blum in 1937 he suggested that the time was propitious for France and Germany to get together on the basis of removal of barriers to international trade and limitation of armaments.[43] He encouraged Prime Minister Chautemps in the latter's suspicion of Soviet promises and admired his "realistic" policy of seeking a settlement with Germany.[44] He approved Daladier's intentions, if he were to come to power, of abandoning the mutual assistance pact with Russia and attempting to reach reconciliation with Germany. When Foreign Minister Yvon Delbos mentioned the possibility of inaugurating moves for agreement with Hitler on humanization of warfare, Bullitt thought Hitler would probably cooperate.[45] On his own, Ambassador Bullitt sought to mediate in December, 1936, between German Ambassador Count von Welczeck and Bonnet, both of whom had assured him that they would welcome rapprochement.[46] And it was Bullitt who brought Hjalmar Schacht to Paris for conversations with Léon Blum.[47] Should the French decide to give Germany the Cameroons in an attempt to reach reconciliation, Bullitt assured Paris the American government would not disapprove.[48] When Bonnet expressed to Bullitt the need for prior American blessing of Franco-German reconciliation, Bullitt told the Frenchman that any effort to reach agreement would have the full benediction of his country.[49]

Bullitt's advice both to the French and to the State Department consistently aimed at a goal formulated during the 1936 Presidential campaign. In one of his speeches—at Chautauqua on August 14 —Roosevelt dwelt at length on foreign policy. This speech had been prepared by Bullitt.[50] A prophetic expression of the policy of both the President and his adviser in the mid-thirties, its keynote was desire to keep America out of war. Bullitt had written:

> We can keep out of war if those who watch and decide have a sufficiently detailed understanding of international affairs to make certain that the small decisions of each day do not lead

toward war and if, at the same time, they possess the courage to say "no" to those who selfishly or unwisely would let us go to war. . . .

Bullitt contributed to the "small decisions of each day" by urging the United States to lend encouragement to rapprochement efforts —perhaps by letting it be known in private conversation that America favored Franco-German reconciliation as Europe's only hope for peace. He even envisaged some public statement by Roosevelt to this effect.[51]

Ambassador Bullitt was moving in the direction of appeasement. Other diplomats in the tense years before Munich were sending their governments analyses which differed radically from Bullitt's. Men like Robert Coulondre, French ambassador to Moscow, and Sir Eric Phipps and William E. Dodd in Germany possessed remarkably similar views. Phipps worried not about Russia, with whom he hoped for cooperation to keep the peace, but about Hitler. He reported his fears as early as 1934. After a June day spent visiting General Goering's new bison enclosure in the Schorfheide, Phipps reported to the British foreign office his impression of a "big, fat, spoilt child" showing off his primeval woods, his bison and birds, his shooting box and lake—"all mere toys." "And then I remembered," Phipps wrote, that "there were other toys, less innocent, though winged, and these might some day be launched on their murderous mission in the same childlike spirit and with the same childlike glee."[52] The British ambassador's fear of "murderous missions" grew. Germany's continuing refusal to agree to disarmament proposals seemed to him ominous. If Germany continued to withhold agreement, Phipps foresaw the collapse of Europe, unless the League, including Russia, could unite to defend any state attacked.[53] The Franco-Soviet pact, development of which Bullitt argued against, seemed to Phipps Europe's only hope of peace.[54] Unlike Ambassador Bullitt, the British ambassador saw not the faintest possibility of coming to an agreement with Hitler—a fanatic, who he believed would be satisfied with nothing less than domination of Europe.[55] He was certain by 1937 that military force alone could impress the Germans. Otherwise German rapacity could be satisfied—and only temporarily—by nothing less than the return of all her colonies taken by the Treaty of Versailles. Indeed, any negotiations begun with Germany would end in failure, he believed, unless France and England were prepared to accord the Nazis absolute domination of the international situation.

In Germany, Ambassador Dodd was similarly convinced by 1936 of the validity of the encirclement program. If supported by all the border states east and west of Germany, and by England, France, and Russia, it held the only promise of peace for Europe.[56]

Robert Coulondre, during the years of his mission in Moscow, 1936 to 1938, and Berlin, 1938-1939, reaffirmed that Germany would have to be stopped; and only a tight military alliance between the Western powers and the Soviet Union could stop her. If such an alliance should not materialize, the alternative, he knew, would be victory for those who sought French security by collaborating with Germany. Like Phipps, he was convinced the Nazis could not be diverted or appeased, but could only be checked by greater force.[57]

Ambassador Phipps was transferred in 1937 to Paris, where he had opportunities for long conversations with his American colleague, William C. Bullitt. Bullitt's failure to grasp the essential nature of the Nazi movement is further revealed by his appalled reaction to Phipps' warning. Phipps pointedly expressed his disappointment to find people in Paris who still believed it possible for France to come to terms with Germany. His settled belief in the total impossibility of such reconciliation made little positive impression on Bullitt. Instead Bullitt reported to Washington that Phipps "exhibited a hostility to Germany and the German Government surprising to me." The American ambassador suspected the Englishman's intentions, believing Phipps feared to reveal a British policy of keeping the European continent divided. Bullitt therefore expected little or no support from Britain for the policy of restoring the world's economic life through reduction of trade barriers. Britain, he was convinced, was merely determined to rearm.[58]

Bullitt's failure to understand what seemed clear to Phipps, to Coulondre, even to W. E. Dodd, who lacked the experience and sophistication of the trained diplomat, was due not to a dearth of evidence on German intentions; a great deal of information became available before Munich. There was not only the evidence of *Mein Kampf*, the statements of leading Nazis, and the record of internal persecution, rearmament, the Rhineland, and Spain. Such prominent German officials as Weizsäcker in Berlin and Schulenburg in Moscow also supplied data to their friends. Colonel Lindbergh was treated to intimate, detailed views of the growing might of the *Luftwaffe*. Churchill was able to learn that the *Wehrmacht* had at its disposal at least thirty-six infantry and four armored divisions. As early as 1934 Churchill was warning that Germany had a military air force awaiting only the order to assemble in full, open combination; that if both Germany and Britain continued with their present programs, Germany by the end of 1936 would be nearly 50 per cent stronger.[59]

Bullitt came in contact with this information, but his views of the international situation were hampered by obsessive fear of the Soviet Union. His awakening to the nature of the Russian regime, his realization that beliefs held for over fifteen years were erroneous, had been too recent: the enormity of his discovery blinded him to the other dangers in Europe, dangers more immediate than those emanating from the Kremlin. A man like Churchill, who from the outset lacked illusions about Russia's intentions, could keep the ultimate Soviet threat in proper focus and, as early as 1934, sound a warning against Hitler. Bullitt was incapable of similar perspective.

Certain historians have blamed Bullitt's failure to gauge Hitler's intentions entirely on his preoccupation with the Russian danger.[60] Another factor should be included: Bullitt's hatred of the Versailles Treaty—"one of the stupidest documents ever penned by the hand of man."[61] Bullitt had never forgotten 1919. He attributed Europe's problems largely to Clemenceau's "criminal errors" in the treaty.[62] Hatred of Versailles reinforced Bullitt's feeling that Germany deserved appeasement. After the signature at Munich, the American ambassador rushed to Bonnet's apartment, tears in his eyes, his arms full of flowers, to convey *"le salut fraternal et joyeaux de l'Amerique."*[63]

Although in a position of influence far greater than that of his colleagues—British, French, or American—Bullitt failed to warn leaders who sought his advice on the futility of appeasement, and the impossibility of neutrality. The meaning of the Munich surrender eluded him until after the crisis had passed. Then, after conversations with French leaders, Bullitt understood. In October, 1938, he reported, " 'Daladier sees the situation entirely, clearly, realizes fully that the meeting in Munich was an immense diplomatic defeat for France and England and recognizes that unless France can recover a united national spirit to confront the future, a fatal situation will arise within a year.' "[64] Finally, for Bullitt, the point had been passed when he could debate whether Europe should be preserved in the form set up at Paris, 1919. No longer were his own diplomatic disappointments relevant. The situation had become one of self-defense. Only after Munich and the shock of Hitler's occupation of Prague and Memel, did Bullitt declare to his countrymen, "You cannot appease the unappeasable. . . . Hitler will not stop; he can only be stopped." Again, Bullitt's education came late.

Why Bullitt altered his views regarding the possibilities of appeasement needs further explanation. It would be incorrect to say that he switched abruptly from viewing the United States as aloof observer to urge that she become a concerned, interventionist

power. Bullitt has tended always to see international situations instance by instance and to respond to each individually. Already
in September, 1938, he had begun to suggest for Roosevelt the role
of a peacemaker who might bring the contending nations together.[65] As the European crisis developed, the ambassador had
himself progressed both intellectually and emotionally from a pas-
sive to an active position; but only after Munich did Bullitt call
upon the United States to eschew neutrality and take sides.

The journalist Louis Fischer, who spoke with Bullitt in Paris in
1938, sought to explain the ambassador's new outlook by comment-
ing that "Bullitt being the sensitive artist, reacts to atmosphere and
is influenced while he influences."[66] Fischer is an astute observer.
The complexities of the European scene in 1938 were evidently too
great, too confusing for Bullitt to trust completely to his own
judgment. In those tense days he responded chiefly to Daladier's
perceptions and moods. In late September he had shared the French
Premier's dread of an imminent war; in October, Bullitt's dispatches
reflected a new awareness on Daladier's part. Daladier had been
firm at Munich, Bullitt told Fischer, "at least in the morning." But
he had been unable to resist Hitler's ultimatums. Still, unlike Chamberlain, Daladier had understood the significance of France and
Britain's surrender. And this dreadful knowledge the Premier had
imparted to his friend Ambassador Bullitt.

Although he did not abandon his convictions that Stalin's ultimate aim was world revolution, Bullitt turned his thoughts in 1939
to the more immediate Nazi danger, his energies to the improvement of Anglo-French-Soviet relations. When Daladier asked Bullitt in March, 1939, if he thought Herriot ought to be empowered
to go to Moscow to negotiate a military understanding with the
Soviet Union, Bullitt replied that in the present situation "no stone
should be left unturned even though one might expect to find
vermin under it."[67]

Britain and France did endeavor in the spring and summer of

1939 to come to an agreement with the Soviet Union. Perhaps their efforts were begun too late. In August, 1939, Russia signed a pact of nonaggression with Germany.

Bullitt grew more urgent in his insistence that the United States forswear isolation.[68] France and Britain were desperately searching for arms and allies, he warned Washington. America would not be an ally but it must supply the arms. He begged Roosevelt in 1939 to denounce the Nazi aggression against Czechoslovakia and to ask Congress for repeal of the neutrality laws. Then after Mussolini's occupation of Albania he urged that Italian funds in the United States be frozen.[69] It was Bullitt who was behind Roosevelt's message of April 15, 1939, asking Hitler and Mussolini to guarantee the independence of certain European states believed to be in immediate danger.[70]

In the spring of 1940 Bullitt bombarded the President and State Department with suggestions he believed might halt Mussolini. First he urged Roosevelt to invite the Pope to take refuge in the United States in case of need. This curious idea was followed a few days later by the proposal that the Atlantic fleet be sent to the Mediterranean.[71]

When Roosevelt, contemplating his projected "destroyers for bases" deal, became worried over public reaction, it was Bullitt with whom he arranged a testing of popular sentiment. In a speech to the American Philosophical Society in Philadelphia on August 18, 1940, Bullitt warned that the nation was in danger. Hitler was not going to stop. If Britain fell, the United States would be the next Nazi target; then the Atlantic might serve as highway rather than barrier. The soothing words Atlantic Ocean were being used, Bullitt declared, by the propagandists of the dictators in hope that they might become the "lullaby of death for the United States. . . . It is as clear as anything on this earth that the United States will not *go* to war, but it is equally clear that war is *coming* toward the Americas." Some months later Bullitt went before the Congressional committee hearing opinions on the Lend-Lease bill and warned again that America's complacency could be compared only to prewar France's faith in the Maginot line.[72]

In Bullitt's view the President was moving too slowly. Together now with men like Secretary of War Stimson, Bullitt pleaded for a dramatic manifestation of Presidential leadership. Roosevelt must not wait for public initiative; it was his duty to take the lead. The President, however, was besieged with advice from two camps within his official family. On one side were ranged the advocates of caution—particularly Secretary of State Hull, who, pessimistic to a point considered defeatist by some, still believed in the spring of 1941 that an attempt to repeal the neutrality legislation would end in failure. In the opposite camp were most of the Cabinet: Stimson, Knox, Ickes, and Morgenthau, who hoped for even more than repeal of the neutrality legislation and institution of a convoy system. At lunch with Harry Hopkins, Morgenthau confided his conclusion that " 'if we are going to save England, we would have to get into this war.' " But Hopkins thought the President was " 'loathe' " to enter the fight.[73]

To the dismay of his activist advisers, Roosevelt was indeed reluctant to accept the thesis that Hitler could be defeated only by American participation in the war. He still hoped, as late as September, 1941, that the American contribution could be restricted to naval and air support and material assistance.

FDR was cautious about getting too far ahead of public opinion. Bullitt was intent on arousing that opinion from its complacency. Late in 1941 he wrote bluntly: "The only way we can defeat Hitler is by the United States putting all its resources into this fight and going to war now."[74]

I V

Despite the energy with which Bullitt exerted influence against Germany after Munich, his personality was too complex to adjust fully to his dual education. Suspicion of Russian intentions —always present—occasionally burst to the surface, pulling his attention away from Fascist threats, back again to the Kremlin. Bullitt's inability to concentrate exclusively on the Nazi menace was largely responsible for contemporary disagreement which arose over his policy, and for the simultaneous accusations of "warmonger" and "Fascist." Bullitt's attitude toward the civil war in Spain helps reveal the conflict within him.

When the United States decided to recognize the Franco government in March, 1939, Bullitt was go-between in the negotiations that took place in Paris.[75] Although the ambassador found "appalling" the reprisals being taken against Spanish Loyalists, although he was aware of German influence on the *Falangistas* and anticipated a Fascist state in Spain, he made no protest over the impending move. Bowers in Spain did all he could to persuade the administration to aid the legal government. Bullitt, who rarely missed the opportunity for a crusade, this time remained quiet. As he told Harold Ickes, he thought it a "toss-up" between the Loyalists and the insurgents: if the Loyalists remained in power, there would be a purge of the Fascist leaders and Spain would go frankly Communistic; if the Fascists won, they would have a purge of their own and would set up a dictatorship.[76] Bullitt laconically carried out orders and facilitated Spanish recognition.

Similarly Bullitt's post-Munich efforts in support of an Anglo-French-Soviet coalition against Germany did not keep his attention from focusing solely on the Kremlin when Russia attacked Finland in 1939. Together with Daladier, Bullitt acted behind the scenes to have the Finnish case brought before the League. Successful in that venture, he urged Roosevelt and Hull to lend American support to a move to expel the Soviet Union from the League. Hull objected: he did not think the United States should get involved in League activities. He and FDR were anxious, moreover, not to push the Soviet Union further into the Axis camp.[77] Bullitt, unable to keep control over his hatred of the Soviets, was willing to take the risk even though both the British and his own government were dubious regarding the wisdom of the move.[78]

Bullitt's fear of Communism again became dominant when in June, 1940, he chose to stay behind in Paris as that city was about to fall to the Germans. Both Hull and Roosevelt had advised Bullitt to leave with the retiring government in the hope that the ambassador might use his influence to convince the French to fight on. But when Prime Minister Reynaud and Minister of the Interior Georges Mandel asked Bullitt to assume responsibility for order and security in the city and to treat with the Germans for its peaceable occupation, Bullitt gladly accepted the custodianship.[79]

Hull has criticized Bullitt for not retreating with the government to which he was accredited. In the Secretary's view, Bullitt, had he gone with the ministry to Tours and Bordeaux, could probably have prevented the defeatist decision not to fight on in North Africa and the resulting suit for an armistice. In any event, Hull believed that Bullitt could have safeguarded American interests in the French fleet and the colonies.[80]

In a letter written to the *New York Times* when Hull's memoirs appeared in 1948, Bullitt stated his reason for staying behind: the best tradition of our diplomatic service was that the American ambassador "did not run away in time of danger." He recalled that Gouverneur Morris remained despite the revolution and saved thousands; that Elihu Washburne stayed in Paris throughout the siege and commune; and that Myron Herrick did not leave the French capital in 1914.[81] In cables to the Department on June 11 and 12, 1940, Bullitt had elaborated these reasons. "I cannot exaggerate," he wrote, "what it has meant to those who stayed behind to know that I am here. . . . My deepest personal reason for staying in Paris is that whatever I have as character, good or bad, is based on the fact that since the age of four I have never run away from anything however painful and dangerous. . . . If I should leave Paris now I would be no longer myself. . . . The fact that I am here is a strong element in preventing a fatal panic. . . . It will mean something always to the French and to the foreign service to remember that we do not leave though others do. *J'y suis. J'y reste.*[82]

Communications such as this one have led to criticism of Bullitt's act as maudlin exhibitionism—a search for martyrdom.[83] To the overemotion and self-dramatization that is part of Bullitt's personality was added, however, another factor—sincere fear that during the interlude between French departure and German arrival the French Communists would try to seize control of the city. On May 28, 1940, Bullitt had reported that both Reynaud and Mandel expected a Communist uprising. In view of this possibility Bullitt had requested Hull to have a cruiser dispatched to Bordeaux with 5,000 to 10,000 submachine guns and ammunition to be used against the Communists.[84] The French Communists, however, despite radio broadcasts calling on their followers to slay the bourgeoisie, ultimately supported Moscow's policy of imposing no organized obstacles to Nazi conquest. As Bullitt delivered Paris to the Germans, the Communists in the city remained peaceful.

Whether Bullitt deserves censure for having allowed his fear of Communist intentions to keep him in Paris is difficult to determine. His prestige with the French government was admittedly enormous. Prime Minister Reynaud, however, had assured Bullitt before he left that he would stand firm and continue the fight.[85] Whether Bullitt's words, indeed, whether any words, could have bolstered French defeatism at the last minute remains dubious.[86]

That Bullitt was willing to absent himself from the French government at this critical, historic juncture, largely to prevent possible Communist uprisings, affords further insight, however, to the deeply troubling effect of his Russian education. Long after the Nazi danger would disappear, the Communist menace was to remain Bullitt's personal gadfly—pursuing him, directing his actions, allowing him no ease of mind.

VIII

Conclusion: the Decline

Although Bullitt indubitably influenced Roosevelt's foreign policy, the precise extent of that influence must remain cloudy, for the President has left few indications of his private thoughts. We do know that next to Roosevelt, Bullitt figured most significantly in negotiating Russian recognition. Similarly, during the early years of our official relations with Soviet Russia, America's Russian policy was Bullitt's policy. The President, engrossed in New Deal political problems, left the implementation of American-Russian relations in his ambassador's hands: he delighted in Bullitt's letters describing baseball, polo, and elaborate balls. "Keep up the good work," he wrote his friend in Moscow. After Munich, Bullitt again influenced the President, urging preparedness and convincing him of the need for unstinting aid to Britain. Following the fall of France, Bullitt had much to do with the formulation of American policy toward the Vichy government.[1]

For a while Bullitt enjoyed White House privileges granted to very few. He could phone the President as he wished; Roosevelt's office door opened easily to him. He was one of the coterie known as the White House family. But this group was continually changing. Raymond Moley, Rexford Tugwell, Hugh Johnson, Thomas Corcoran, Ben Cohen, A. A. Berle, Donald Richberg, Archibald MacLeish, Sam Rosenman, Robert Sherwood, and, of course, Louis Howe and Harry Hopkins were, at one time, members. A few, notably Howe, Hopkins, and Rosenman, remained until the end.[2]

A coolness gradually developed between President and adviser in mid-1940. The first incident in the estrangement came in March, 1940, when Roosevelt offered the Secretaryship of the Navy to Ambassador Bullitt, who accepted with alacrity. FDR had long wished to have Secretary Charles Edison out of the post; he was somewhat deaf and the President found it difficult to work with him. He had therefore arranged, in the manner in which such things were done, to have Boss Hague of New Jersey name Edison as candidate for the governorship of that state. On May 20, 1940, Edison announced his resignation. Bullitt was to take over in June. Unfortunately, in December, 1939, when Secretary Claude Swanson died, Roosevelt had offered the same position to Frank Knox, a Republican. Knox had refused, but FDR left the question open, urging Knox to reconsider his stand. Then, in the spring of 1940, Roosevelt having offered the position to Bullitt, received word from Knox that he was ready to assume the job—providing a second Republican were brought into the Cabinet.³ The President, interested in having a coalition administration to gain more widespread support for his emergency policies, retracted the offer to Bullitt and gave the position to Knox.

Ambassador Bullitt returned to Washington after the fall of France, hoping now to become Secretary of State, but willing to accept another Cabinet post. He had no status in Washington and soon became sensitive about "hanging around" the State Department, an ambassador on leave with no particular duties or responsibilities. In February, Ickes had suggested Bullitt as Secretary of War to replace Harry Woodring, with whom the President had long been dissatisfied partly because of his isolationism and partly because of his inability to get along with his assistant, Louis Johnson.⁴ Roosevelt wanted to be rid of Woodring, but he did not wish to have Bullitt in his place. Ickes continued to intervene for his friend. In October he spoke to Roosevelt again but the response was not encouraging: the President would make no moves until after the election. " 'Bill wants to be Secretary of State,' " Roosevelt said scoffingly, " 'and I can't do that.' " He explained to Ickes that " 'Bill talked too much' " and intimated he was too quick on the trigger.[5] The best Roosevelt could offer was the London embassy. This Bullitt refused, countering with the suggestion, in November, 1940, that Frank Knox be sent to London and that he, Bullitt, then be made Secretary of the Navy. Roosevelt could do nothing but assure Bullitt that he did not want him out of the administration, that he was going to do a lot of rearranging. Bullitt would have to wait a little while. When the President moved finally to replace Woodring as Secretary of War, Bullitt agitated for that post with frequent reminders to "Missy" Lehand and Grace Tully, Roosevelt's secretaries, that the President had promised him such a plum. But as Miss Tully has indicated, his effort was "futile."[6] The position went to Henry Stimson—Knox's other Republican.

From time to time Roosevelt suggested brief tasks for Bullitt. He made him an ambassador at large in November, 1941, and in December Bullitt went to North Africa and the Middle East as Presidential observer. The more important positions were given to others.

Bullitt, who had been accustomed to signing letters to Roosevelt with "My love and deepest admiration,"[7] now changed toward FDR as he had toward Woodrow Wilson. In mid-1940 he was reporting that the President's mind refused to grasp an idea with the vigor he had hitherto shown, nor was he inclined to take suggestions or ideas and follow them through to their logical conclusions. He complained about Hopkins' influence, suggesting that FDR was a tired man who tended to dump important matters into the lap of another man, Harry Hopkins, who was not only tired, but very ill.[8] He felt that too much solicitude was being felt at the White House about the President's health—that the main point in everyone's mind was not to help England save the world but to protect the President.[9] He deplored Roosevelt's slowness in the

matter of going to war, and reported that the President was becoming "very sure of his own judgment."[10]

Then in June, 1941, Bullitt's antagonism found another target.
That month Hitler attacked the Soviet Union. Whether Hitler
would continue operations against Russia through the winter,
whether the Soviets would be able to resist, whether Stalin would
persist or instead make a new deal with Hitler, were immediate
questions which faced the Roosevelt administration. The decision
of whether to send American aid to the Soviets would be based
on their answer. Following Harry Hopkins' visit to Moscow at
the end of July, Roosevelt and Churchill decided that the chances
of Soviet resistance were sufficiently good to justify a commitment
providing for large-scale aid over a long-term period.[11]

Bullitt tried during the summer of 1941 to convince the President that in return for Lend-Lease to Russia he should ask for definite, written, public pledges from Stalin that the Soviet Union
renounce all claim to any territorial rights or privileges she did
not already possess in China and other areas of the Far East; and
that the postwar boundaries of the Soviet Union on the European
side should be those of August, 1939. Bullitt warned against Soviet
imperialism. Roosevelt, however, had a "hunch" that Stalin, if
treated with consideration, would respond in kind. He was willing
to gamble that the Russians were going to cooperate, that Stalin
would not try to annex territory. Bullitt pointed out that the President when he talked of *noblesse oblige* was not dealing with the
Duke of Norfolk.[12] But Roosevelt was going to play his hunch.
Bullitt departed from the White House offices in deep agitation.

Bullitt's original Russian policy had pleased the President, and,
although Bullitt had himself discarded it, Roosevelt continued to
maintain a generous and open-minded attitude toward the Soviet
Union. He had the feeling (akin to that of Jefferson toward the
French Revolution) that Bolshevik rule, for all its bad features,
was an experiment for the improvement of the lot of man. It is

difficult to document matters of influence, but it appears that Roosevelt was listening in 1941 no longer to Bullitt, but to the views of men like Assistant Secretary of State George Messersmith and Ambassador Joseph E. Davies, who at the time of the Nazi attack on Soviet Russia was serving as Hull's special assistant for war emergency problems and policies.

Messersmith considered Stalin's dictatorship to be different from Hitler's. There was reason to believe that Communism was gradually being transformed into a kind of Socialism which might accommodate itself to the economic systems of the democracies. He argued that the Soviets had no territorial designs in Europe and only doubtful ones in the Far East. The Kremlin wanted peace.[13] Davies believed in 1941 that the Russian people and its leaders were moved, basically, by "altruistic concepts." The Soviet government's purpose was to promote the brotherhood of man and to improve the lot of the common people; it was "devoted to peace." In Davies' view, the Russians had made "great sacrifices attempting to achieve those spiritual aspirations." Now they were fighting against Hitlerism and should therefore receive every possible help as speedily and with as much friendly cooperation as the United States could extend.[14] Davies was everywhere in Washington after the Nazi attack, urging these views on White House and State Department. In July he had repeatedly conferred with Sumner Welles and Harry Hopkins, two of Roosevelt's principal advisers. The President himself had a long conference with Davies in which he requested his views on Russia. The former ambassador to Moscow believed it outside the realm of possibility that the Soviet Union after the war, or for many years thereafter, would seek to project Communism into Europe.[15] Certain that the resistance of the Red Army would amaze the world, he urged all aid to Russia without stint or condition.[16]

That Joseph E. Davies should be on the inside while his own advice was being ignored upset Bullitt. He considered his Moscow successor an incompetent.[17] But Bullitt's feelings no longer carried weight. In September, as American relations with Russia grew closer, as an American mission headed by Averell Harriman went to Moscow to make Lend-Lease arrangements, Roosevelt finally told Bullitt that there was no place for him in the preparedness organization.[18] During this interview with the President, Bullitt said he understood the situation perfectly, that Harry Hopkins was responsible for his exclusion. Four people, he told Roosevelt, had related to him incidents in connection with Hopkins that proved to him it was "Harry's doing." The President vigorously denied this: " 'You may say to these people that the President of the United States says that this is a damned lie.' "[19] It may have comforted Bullitt to think that Hopkins, not Roosevelt, wanted him out of the administration, but there is reason to believe that in matters of this sort, the choice was Roosevelt's own. In the view of one biographer, nobody ever told Roosevelt whom he wanted to see or whom he should exclude. Hopkins, aware of the final test of loyalty to Roosevelt, was capable of shouldering the blame, of saying he was responsible for keeping people out, when such was not the case.[20]

Bullitt continued to linger in Washington but in eclipse. His efforts to see the President became less and less successful. His hints that he would like to be invited to luncheon were ignored. Rare appointments with FDR were cut to three minutes.[21] Roosevelt, feeling somewhat uncomfortable, did try to think up a job for Bullitt. In June, 1942, he suggested that Bullitt head some kind of Speaker's Bureau. He wrote Elmer Davis asking if in setting up his speaking organization, Mr. Davis might consider putting Bullitt in charge. "Bill makes a grand speech himself in the first place, and should make a speech on the war effort, etc., once a month."[22] This suggestion to a man of Ambassador Bullitt's ambitions and ability was insulting.[23] In a cold note, Bullitt informed the President that Frank Knox had just asked him to become a special assistant in the Navy Department, an offer which he accepted: "For this reason and others I cannot accept the post which you kindly suggested. . . ."[24] Bullitt indicated his happiness in having found a spot "however minor" in which he could render "real war service."[25] FDR's reply was equally formal: "I am delighted that you are continuing in the Government and I know you will do a grand job for the Navy. My best wishes and appreciation for your loyalty and devotion to your country."[26]

A minor position in the department he had hoped to head could not satisfy Bullitt. He made a last effort in 1943 to achieve some political eminence by running for mayor of Philadelphia on the Democratic ticket. The campaign was disastrous. Religious groups, digging up his 1926 novel, *It's Not Done*, accused Bullitt of being both immoral and anti-Semitic. Anti-Semites, noticing that his mother's maiden name was Horwitz, whispered that he was Jewish. Liberals, remembering his support of relations with Vichy France, accused him of being a Fascist. Others, recalling his marriage to Louise Bryant, widow of John Reed, declared that Bullitt was a Communist. After political defeat in the city of his childhood, Bullitt left the United States; he accepted a commission in 1944 as a major in de Gaulle's Free French forces. The French decorated Bullitt with the Croix de Guerre with Palm, and with the Legion of Honor.

One cannot say precisely why Bullitt lost his position of favored friend to the President. He went, as did Moley, Tugwell, and others. Many a former brain truster may never have known why Roosevelt no longer found him useful. Occasionally the President may simply have tired of a man's presence. In Bullitt's situation Roosevelt perhaps grew irritated by his friend's overebullience: Bullitt "talked too much" and too indiscreetly; he was "too quick on the trigger."[27] Though the President had liked his ambassador, it was a liking tinged with reservations.[28] Just as Bullitt became convinced that Roosevelt could not see straight on Russia, FDR had grown certain that Bullitt was too erratic to be relied on.

If Bullitt's retirement from the Roosevelt circle had been no more than a personal loss to William C. Bullitt, it would be a matter of slight significance. What does interest us is the fact that Roosevelt in discarding Bullitt was losing a valuable adviser on Russian affairs.[29] Bullitt's suggestions, it is true, were not always reasonable; and his reactions were often intemperate. Possibly, however, Roosevelt, once cognizant of Bullitt's shortcomings, might still have made use of his ambassador's diplomatic education. As early as 1936 the ambassador, in cables to the government, had warned that within ten years Soviet strength would be staggering, that the Soviet Union would profit from a European war by seeking to set up satellite Communist governments in her border states, that Russia would take advantage of an American war with Japan to penetrate China further with Communism. Again in the early 1940's Bullitt predicted a Soviet attempt to communize Europe. Over and over he warned of the Soviet Union's determination to spread its creed, insisting that not even Stalin's death would prevent Russian aggression.

Hopeful men criticized Bullitt's assertions that Stalin at the war's end would seek to Sovietize Europe as fomenting disunity among the wartime Allies. They accused Bullitt of adding his bit to the overwhelming difficulty of achieving a decent world. "Realistic men who know the Soviets," wrote Marquis Childs in the Washington *Post*, "believe they will cooperate in a reasonable adjustment of power in Europe." He discounted Bullitt's warnings as "silly."[30]

Russian publicists were similarly aroused. *Pravda* called Bullitt a "bankrupt spy" trying to make a career out of dirty, anti-Soviet work; it discounted his public utterances as "the ravings of an old gray mare."[31] The Soviet army newspaper *Red Star* denounced Bullitt as an "enemy of peace."[32]

Ultimately Roosevelt's hunch that Stalin would cooperate was proved wrong; Bullitt's warnings of Soviet imperialism were demonstrated to be accurate. Each year more of Bullitt's predictions came true. China has become a powerful Communist nation. Throughout Asia, Communism is a growing threat. Russia has on her border the string of satellite states of which Bullitt warned. The increased emphasis on scientific research which Bullitt reported in 1936 has been translated into celestial satellites ringing the earth. No nation has been more successful in its diplomatic victories than Soviet Russia. Yet today, Bullitt, who predicted the situation in which we now live, presents the paradox of a man whose unusual gifts of insight have come to be undermined by increasing overemotion. Ambassador Bullitt's analyses of situations have been remarkable, but his suggested remedies—as FDR recognized—have been alarmingly capricious. In 1954 Bullitt suggested, for example, that the American government organize a concerted air and ground attack on the Chinese Communists in order to recapture the mainland. Such action, Bullitt thought, might spare us annihilation by Soviet H-bombs.[33]

Along with suggestions for preventive war, Bullitt's attacks on political opponents became more personal than diplomatic.[34] Thus, despite his singular ability, circumspect administrators in the postwar era chose not to invite William Bullitt to assume influential positions. A man who began a diplomatic career in 1918 full of promise, and with the warm support of the top figures in the Wilson administration, and who came eventually to achieve a remarkable education in diplomacy, Bullitt has been forced to confine his talents to the pages of magazines.[35]

In 1926 someone commented that Bullitt was a "planet all in the making, still largely in the incandescent state, spitting blue flames and of a fearfully hot temperature, but with the chemical stuff that will make fine protoplasm when it cools."[36] William C. Bullitt, with all his education as a diplomat, has never cooled.

MANUSCRIPT SOURCES
NOTES
INDEX

MANUSCRIPT SOURCES

Unprinted collections of manuscript sources have greatly enriched my study. Material in the National Archives provides an excellent source for studying Bullitt's diplomatic career. The "open period" for researchers includes archival material before January 1, 1934. Papers pertaining to the Bullitt mission of 1919 are therefore freely available. "Limited access" extends from January 1, 1934, to 1943. The researcher working in this period must receive permission to examine the particular material he is interested in, and must leave his notes for review. The Department is liberal in its review policy; in general, only names of living persons are red-penciled. I was allowed to see what I wished concerning Bullitt's Russian embassy. Certain restrictions prevailed, however, in material dealing with his later mission to France.

On the whole, Bullitt's dispatches from Russia were more contemplative and interpretive than those from Paris. The greater part of the Paris dispatches tend to report, with little comment, casual conversations in the Quai d'Orsay, and dinner-time gossip. Not until after Munich did the Paris telegrams carry the tone of urgency and serious thought characterizing Bullitt's messages from Moscow.

Unfortunately, other governments do not allow similar access to their documents. The British diplomatic archives are presently open through 1902. The French foreign office archives are closed after 1896. Russian archival material for the 1930's, of course, remains unavailable. I wrote to the Moscow State Committee on Cultural Relations with Foreign Countries inquiring whether material pertaining to the Bullitt mission of 1919 existed in the Soviet

archives. In reply, I was informed that a search in the Central State
Archive had been made but that no such material could be found.

The Trotsky Archive at Harvard University contains correspondence between Lenin and Trotsky for the year 1919. However, Trotsky, occupied with military matters, did not discuss Bullitt's mission at any length in his dispatches.

The Yale University manuscripts collection ranks in importance
for this study with the National Archives. Some years ago Bullitt
brought the entire mass of his papers to Yale with the intention
of settling down to write a book. Later he changed his mind and
had certain of his papers returned to him. What has been left in the
Sterling Library is of immense value: material covering Bullitt's
early work in the State Department, his activities at the Paris Peace
Conference, and his report to the Senate in September, 1919. The
significance of the papers in the Sterling Library serves to interest
one further in the papers still within Bullitt's possession. That he
will make these available during his lifetime seems unlikely.

An invaluable source of material has been the Colonel Edward M.
House collection at Yale, which includes the complete House-
Bullitt correspondence. House's own diary is a rich source of information on Bullitt at the Peace Conference. Gordon Auchincloss's diary, also in the Yale collection, throws light on the extent
of Bullitt's influence on formulation of Russian policy in 1918.

The Wilson collection in the Library of Congress, although not
as rich a source for this study as the papers in the National Archives
or at Yale, provides interesting material both on Bullitt's work in
the State Department and on the Russian question at Paris. The
voluminous Wilson papers have been described in four articles by
Miss Katherine Brand, formerly in charge of the collection, in the
Library of Congress Quarterly Journal of Current Acquisitions,
February, 1945; August, 1948; May, 1953; and February, 1956.

The Robert Lansing papers, also in the Library of Congress,

contain a desk diary in which Lansing discusses Bullitt's mission to Russia.

A particularly fine source of material has been the Franklin D. Roosevelt collection at Hyde Park, which has been described by Herman Kahn, director, in the *American Archivist*, XVII (April, 1954), 149-62. The Roosevelt papers are arranged in files referred to as Official File (OF), President's Personal File (PPF), and President's Secretary's File (PSF). Also at Hyde Park are the bound volumes containing complete transcripts of Roosevelt's press conferences; an index for this series is available.

The Roosevelt papers are particularly significant to a study of American diplomacy because the President encouraged ambassadors—especially William C. Bullitt—to write him directly. Some of these letters were sent to the State Department to note and return; many never left the White House. While the personal papers of FDR must be used by anyone studying the diplomacy of Roosevelt's era, it should be emphasized that the papers do not contain records of conversations—neither face-to-face, nor by telephone. Roosevelt made it a point not to make records of his conversations. Only rarely is it possible to find even an indication of the nature of a conversation. The student should also note that the Roosevelt papers, having originally been organized as current files, present certain research problems. On almost any subject, it is necessary to go through large quantities of irrelevant material. However, the library staff, according to its director Herman Kahn, is making cross-sectional indexes and otherwise organizing the papers in such a way as to make research more feasible. Recently the library completed a monumental subject index to the 9,000 folders arranged only by name of correspondent.

Unfortunately the Roosevelt-Bullitt correspondence may not be freely consulted, due to Bullitt's references to persons still living. Although only a portion of the correspondence is available, much information pertaining to Bullitt is contained in the PPF, the OF, and the PSF. Material in these files provides a detailed picture of Bullitt's rise and decline in the Roosevelt circle.

The Henry Cabot Lodge papers at the Massachusetts Historical Society may be consulted with permission from Henry Cabot Lodge, Jr. Within this collection, the Lodge-Henry White correspondence proved especially informative. White was a devoted correspondent, writing letters of remarkable length to his friend, the senator. In their exchanges Lodge and White discussed in detail the Bullitt mission to Russia and Bullitt's report to the Senate.

INTERVIEWS

During my investigations I have profited from numerous interviews, notably two with Mr. Bullitt himself, September 19, 1955, and August 9, 1966. On both occasions, Mr. Bullitt freely offered his recollections and revealed much of his personality. Mrs. Ernesta Barlow, December 27, 1954, afforded me an illuminating hour of objective comments. Although Mr. Bullitt's former wife had forgotten details, she well remembered moods, reactions, and points of view. George Kennan, February 12, 1957, very kindly recalled events of Bullitt's Russian embassy. During these years, Kennan served as third secretary. The late Professor Charles Seymour, generous in various conversations over a two-year period, gave me the benefit of his recollections of William C. Bullitt as Yaleman, assistant in the Department of State, member of the Paris Peace Conference delegation, and American Ambassador to Russia and France.

NOTES

I. WILLIAM C. BULLITT AND WORLD WAR I

1. Undated conversation recounted by Bullitt. William C. Bullitt, "How We Won the War and Lost the Peace," *Life*, XXV (August 30, 1948), 94.

2. William C. Bullitt, *It's Not Done* (New York, 1926), p. 10.

3. R. W. Robbins, A. L. Barbour, and L. Schwab, eds., *History of the Class of 1913, Yale College* (New Haven, 1913), p. 55. Due to illness Bullitt was forced to withdraw from college for a year; he did not graduate until 1913.

4. Interview with Bullitt's first wife, now Mrs. S. L. Barlow, December 27, 1954.

5. *Public Ledger*, November 12, 1916.

6. Bullitt memorandum of conversation with Tiza, September 3, 1916, in the Bullitt papers at Yale University.

7. Memo of conversation with Von Jagow, September 16, 1916, Bullitt papers.

8. Ernesta Drinker Bullitt, *An Uncensored Diary from the Central Empires* (New York, 1917), p. 152.

9. Bullitt interview, September 19, 1955.

10. Bullitt to House, July 5, 1917, in the House papers at Yale University.

11. Wilson to Brougham, October 30, 1917, series VI, Wilson papers in the Library of Congress.

12. Lansing to Tumulty, November 6, 1917, series VI, Wilson papers.

13. Bullitt interview, September 19, 1955.

14. John Sturgis to Chief Signal Officer, December 14, 1917, copy of letter in Bullitt papers.

15. Chauncey B. Tinker to Chief Signal Officer, December 14, 1917, copy of letter in Bullitt papers.

16. Bullitt interview, September 19, 1955.

17. Bullitt interview, August 9, 1966.

18. House to Bullitt, July 10, 1918, House papers.

19. Copy of Phillips memorandum of December 26, 1917, in Bullitt papers.

20. Interview with Professor Charles Seymour, November 17, 1955.

21. Undated notes in the Bullitt papers. While these notes reflect Bullitt's early views of Russia, Bullitt has cautioned against identifying the sketch as autobiographical; for, as he explained, his own death is not a subject he ever pondered or feared. Bullitt interview, August 9, 1966.

22. The proposals provided for: 1) no forcible annexations; 2) political independence to peoples who had lost it during the war; 3) peoples not independent before the war to be assured the right to determine their political allegiance by a plebescite; 4) rights of minorities to be guaranteed; 5) no punitive indemnities but compensation for losses suffered by private persons to be met by a proportional fund contributed to by all belligerents; 6) colonial questions to be solved on basis of principles in 1, 2, 3, 4.

23. Bullitt to Phillips, January 3, 1918, Bullitt papers.

24. Bullitt to House, February 3, 1918, House papers.

25. Bullitt to House, February 7, 1918, House papers.

26. *Foreign Relations of the United States: Russia, 1918* (Washington, 1931), I, 407.

27. Ibid., 408.

28. Bullitt to House, February 7, 1918, House papers.

29. Charles Seymour, ed., *The Intimate Papers of Colonel House* (London, 1928), III, 401.

30. *Foreign Relations of the United States: the Lansing Papers, 1914-1920* (Washington, 1940), II, 346-48. Bullitt, we recall, regarded Lansing with condescension. George Kennan has written that for his own contemporaries Lansing's light was "somewhat obscured by the contrast between his quiet, unassuming nature and the President's overriding personality. . . . There was a tendency to underrate Lansing, and sometimes to ridicule him." It would be wrong to assume, Kennan states, that Lansing's lack of personal color rendered unimportant his contributions. Behind the façade of "stuffy correctness and legal precision," Kennan observes, "there lay powers of insight that might have been envied by the more boisterous natures with which wartime Wash-

ington then abounded." George Kennan, *Soviet-American Relations, 1917-1920: Russia Leaves the War* (Princeton, 1956), pp. 30-31.

31. Stephen Gwynn, ed., *The Letters and Friendships of Sir Cecil Spring Rice: A Record* (Boston, 1929), II, 423-24.

32. Ibid., 423.

33. House agreed to the need for answering the Russian demand for an explanation of Allied war aims. It was to be an answer as "might persuade Russia to stand by the Allies in their defense of democratic and liberal principles." Seymour, *Intimate Papers*, III, 331. Wilson's decision to make such a statement had been taken before Trotsky made his appeal; the Bolshevik declaration simply reinforced his judgment. The worsening Allied military situation had been the compelling factor. Lenin's and Trotsky's activities were another reason why the President had turned to a formulation of war aims. In December, 1917, the Bolsheviks had torn open Czarist archives, brandishing before the world the secret treaties by which the Allies had prearranged a territorial settlement of Europe and the Near East. Following this severe blow to Allied morale came Trotsky's appeal for peace. To meet the critical weakening of military and moral strength, Wilson issued his Fourteen Points in hope that his words might boost the Allied spirit as well as keep Russia from making a separate peace.

34. Point Six: "The evacuation of all Russian Territory and such a settlement of all questions affecting Russia as will secure the best and freest cooperation of the other nations of the world in obtaining for her an unhampered and unembarrassed opportunity for the independent determination of her own political development and national policy and assure her of a sincere welcome into the society of free nations under institutions of her own choosing; and, more than a welcome, assistance also of every kind that she may need and may herself desire. The treatment accorded Russia by her sister nations in the months to come will be the acid test of their good will, of their comprehension of her needs as distinguished from their own interests, and of their intelligent and unselfish sympathy."

35. The French note, delivered to Lansing by Ambassador Jusserand, stressed the desirability of some joint action "tending to protect . . . Siberia from Maximalist contagion, to secure the use of the Trans-Siberian and Russian railways for southern Russia to the advantage of the Allies and by isolating Vladivostok, if not too late, to protect the stocks of all kinds that are stored there." Otherwise, the French feared

a spread of German influence in the event of separate peace. *Foreign Relations of the United States: Russia, 1918* (Washington, 1932), II, 20-21.

36. According to George Kennan, there was no serious danger in March and April of attack on Murmansk by Finns under German command; but by the time the British and French had spent several weeks acting as though there were such a danger, they had succeeded in conjuring it into a real existence. By July, 1918, Wilson was to accede to Allied demands to establish a small American force at Murmansk, and in September, 1918, an American force landed at Archangel. Wilson never opposed the north Russian intervention with the vehemence and soul-searching that was to accompany his stand on Siberian intervention. He was willing to intervene in north Russia to satisfy Allied demands, and to guard military stores and make it safe for Russian forces to come together in organized bodies in the north. The British, however, also had the idea of a deeper intervention into the Russian interior, directed not only to securing the two ports but also to linking up with the effort to be made from the Siberian side. The north Russian intervention will not be discussed in this chapter since it did not enter into the scope of Bullitt's diplomatic activities in 1918. George Kennan has presented a thoughtful analysis of the situation in chapters two, eleven, and sixteen of his *American-Soviet Relations, 1917-1920: The Decision to Intervene* (Princeton, 1958).

37. *FR: Russia, 1918*, II, 29.

38. *Lansing Papers*, II, 351.

39. *Lansing Papers*, II, 354, 355.

40. Copy in Bullitt's papers in the Yale Library is to Polk and is dated March 2, 1918. Presumably the original memorandum which Bullitt read to House was written on March 1.

41. Entry of March 4, 1918, House Diary in the House papers at Yale.

42. Seymour, *Intimate Papers*, III, 406.

43. Wilson to House, July 8, 1918, Seymour, *Intimate Papers*, III, 398.

44. On March 4, Gordon Auchincloss noted in his diary: "Almost the entire morning was occupied with work in connection with the impending action by Japan in Siberia. The President called me up on the Secretary's private wire and asked me if I had seen the telegram which he had intended to send to Tokio. I told him I had not seen it until this morning and not until after I had sent him a memorandum

prepared by Bullitt concerning this action. He said that *in view of this memorandum and of a letter he had received from Colonel House* he wished me to read to Colonel House over the telephone his proposed telegram to Tokio and to get his reaction on this telegram and to call him back. [Italics mine.] This I did and reported to him in due course." Entry of March 4, 1918, in the Diary of Gordon Auchincloss, Yale University Library. (Misdated as March 3 by Auchincloss.)

45. Entry of March 5, Auchincloss Diary.

46. Seymour, *Intimate Papers*, III, 411. Unlike Bullitt, the Colonel did not expect the message to influence the Bolsheviks. "My thought is not so much about Russia," House observed, "as it is to seize this opportunity to clear up the Far Eastern situation but without mentioning it or Japan in any way. What you would say about Russia and against Germany could be made to apply to Japan or any other power seeking to do what we know German is attempting." Ibid.

47. The record does not indicate how much of the final draft of the Wilson-Bullitt message was Bullitt's, how much Wilson's. George Kennan has reached this same conclusion in his study of American-Russian relations. Kennan, *Russia Leaves the War*, p. 511.

48. Bullitt to House, May 20, 1918, House papers. Bullitt noted that Reed knew Lenin and Trotsky so intimately that his recommendations might be regarded as those the Bolsheviks would themselves make. Reed's memorandum concluded with the declaration that the anti-Soviet governments in Russia were "absolutely unsupported except by the propertied classes and foreign bayonets." Bullitt and Reed were acquaintances in 1918. Reed considered Bullitt sympathetic enough to be appealed to in May, 1918, with regard to his papers, which had been taken by the State Department and not returned to him. Bullitt made efforts through Polk and House to have the Reed material returned. See Bullitt to Reed, May 23, July 22, and July 25, 1918, in the John Reed papers at Harvard University.

49. House to Bullitt, May 23, 1918, House papers.

50. Bullitt to House, June 24, 1918, House papers.

51. House to Bullitt, July 18, 1918. It is of interest that Wilson was not consulting House on the Russian question during the summer of 1918.

52. *FR: Russia, 1918*, II, 246.

53. Kennan, *The Decision to Intervene*, p. 395.

54. Wilson's ostensible reasons, for intervention were subsequently

stated in an *aide-mémoire* presented on July 17, 1918, to the Allies. "Military action," the document read, "is admissible in Russia, . . . only to help the Czecho-Slovaks consolidate their forces and get into successful cooperation with their Slavic kinsmen and to steady any efforts at self-government or self-defense in which the Russians themselves may be willing to accept assistance . . . the only legitimate object for which American or Allied troops can be employed . . . is to guard military stores which may subsequently be needed by Russian forces and to render such aid as may be acceptable to the Russians in the organization of their own self-defense." *FR: Russia, 1918,* II, 287-90. Wilson's decision actually represented a rejection of the Allied appeal of July 2, for Wilson hoped to see the action limited to American and Japanese forces, excluding Britain and France. Kennan, *The Decision to Intervene,* p. 399. The British and French insisted, however, in joining the Americans and Japanese in Siberia.

55. *FR: Russia, 1918,* II, 328.

56. See Department of State memorandum of August 3, 1918, *FR: Russia, 1918,* II, 329. This document indicates that the Czechoslovaks were to be protected in a movement *westward.*

57. Bullitt to House, September 20, 1918, House papers.

58. Kennan, *Russia Leaves the War,* pp. 501-502.

59. George Kennan in his excellent interpretation of the factors behind the decision on Siberia suggests that Wilson and Lansing were in this instance the victims of misinformation to which they were particularly vulnerable, first because of their unwillingness to face the reality of Soviet power, and second, due to anxiety to find a means of escape from the "endless importunities" of the Allied governments. The thesis that the Czechs, an Allied force, were being opposed in Siberia by armed German and Austrian legions had come, Kennan suggests, as the perfect answer. Kennan, *The Decision to Intervene,* pp. 402-403. Unterberger in her study contends that Wilson's real reason for intervention was to enable the Americans to be present in Siberia in order to restrain the Japanese, whom Wilson believed would ultimately intervene with or without American sanction. "The 'open door' in China was at stake. If Japan went into Siberia, the United States must also go." Betty Unterberger, *America's Siberian Expedition, 1918-1920* (Durham, North Carolina, 1956), p. 88.

60. This statement was made in a meeting with Lansing, Newton D. Baker, Josephus Daniels, General Peyton March, and Admiral W. S. Benson. See Kennan, *The Decision to Intervene,* pp. 396-97.

61. Ibid., p. 408. I am indebted to Kennan for the above conclusions.
62. Bullitt to Wilson, September 27, 1918, series II, Wilson papers.
63. Bullitt to House, September 27, 1918, House papers.
64. Barlow interview.
65. Joseph Grew, another member of the American delegation, stressed the important role House played in selecting the American delegation; "the army of officials who will attend the final Peace Conference have not . . . yet been chosen except in the minds of the two men, the President and Colonel House, in whose hands their selection will lie." Diary entry of October 18, 1918, Joseph Grew, *Turbulent Era* (Boston, 1952), I, 331.

II. THE BULLITT MISSION OF 1919

1. Harold Nicolson, *Peacemaking, 1919* (New York, 1933), p. 31.
2. Undated notes in the Bullitt papers at Yale University.
3. Entry of December 4, 1918. Diary kept by Bullitt aboard ship. This Diary is in the Bullitt papers.
4. Entry of December 9, 1918, Bullitt Diary. For further discussion of this episode between Wilson and Bullitt, see Charles Seymour, *Letters from the Paris Peace Conference* (New Haven, 1965, edited by Harold B. Whiteman, Jr.), p. 21.
5. Undated notes in Bullitt papers.
6. Bullitt letter to his wife Ernesta, December 20, 1919, Bullitt papers.
7. *Foreign Relations of the United States: Russia, 1919* (Washington, 1937), pp. 5-6.
8. M. P. Briggs, *George D. Herron and the European Settlement* (Stanford, 1932), p. 146; George B. Noble, *Policies and Opinions at Paris, 1919* (New York, 1935), p. 280.
9. John M. Thompson, "The Russian Problem at the Paris Peace Conference, 1919," unpublished doctoral dissertation, Columbia University, 1960, p. 227. Ironically, Lord Northcliffe was strongly anti-Bolshevik, and the Northcliffe press ultimately attacked the idea of peace negotiations with Lenin.
10. Memorandum from Bullitt to House, January 19, 1919, Bullitt papers. Also see entry of February 17, 1919, Note-pad, Bullitt papers.
11. Steffens was not an official member of the mission but went along in his private capacity as a journalist.

12. House in conversation with Philip Kerr as cited in Thompson, p. 231.

13. House gave this explanation in private conversation to members of the American Commission, Dresel and Dolbeare. Undated and unsigned memorandum, Paris Peace Conference 184.022/11, National Archives.

14. *FR: Russia, 1919*, pp. 57-58.

15. Bullitt's proposals were based evidently on the concessions Litvinov, former Soviet emissary to London, had offered William H. Buckler a month earlier in Stockholm, and on the concessions mentioned in the Prinkipo reply. Buckler, a special assistant in the American embassy in Britain, was sent by House and Wilson to Stockholm on January 8, 1919, where he interviewed Litvinov. In an informal conversation Litvinov expressed his desire for peace and declared his government's willingness to grant an end to Bolshevik propaganda in foreign countries; to give amnesty to Russians who were anti-Soviet; and to settle their debt. *FR: Russia, 1919*, pp. 15-16. In their reply to the Prinkipo offer, the Bolsheviks offered an end to hostilities, payment of the debt, economic concessions, and territorial compensations. Ibid., pp. 39-42.

16. House observed, however, that the attitude of the French made such a statement desirable. William C. Bullitt, *The Bullitt Mission to Russia* (New York, 1919), p. 35.

17. Note from Kerr dated February 21, 1919, Bullitt papers.

18. Lloyd George later declared that he "never heard of Bullitt until after he came back from Russia." *House of Commons Parliamentary Debates*, Fifth Series, November 17, 1919, p. 719. Although it is possible that Lloyd George did not know of the proposals, since he was not in Paris when Bullitt was preparing them and since Kerr does not indicate having mentioned them to him, it is hardly likely that Lloyd George was unaware of the Bullitt mission until after it returned. Bullitt claimed that Lloyd George "had known I was going." *Treaty of Peace with Germany: Hearings Before the Committee on Foreign Relations. United States Senate. 66th Congress, First session* (Washington, 1919), p. 1252. He also noted that when he got to London on his way to Russia and found that the torpedo boat on which he had expected to go was escorting the President, Lloyd George's office called up the Admiralty and asked them to give him a boat. Ibid. Furthermore, Bullitt reports that when he saw Lloyd George upon his return and handed

him a copy of the Russian proposal, Lloyd George said " 'That is the same one I have already read. . . .' " Ibid., p. 1260.

19. In July, 1919, when *The Nation* published an article mentioning the "secret" Bullitt mission and the terms which Bullitt took with him to Russia, Wilson wrote to Joseph Tumulty, " 'This is an amazing article. I know of no such "allied terms" as are here quoted.' " Thompson, p. 237.

20. Henry White of the American delegation wrote to his friend Henry Cabot Lodge regarding the Bullitt mission: "I may say that his trip to Russia . . . was in no sense as an official representative of our Delegation. . . . He was merely sent by Lansing and Colonel House to ascertain conditions, as he was particularly anxious to do so, and they felt that he might obtain information tending eventually to the solution of the Russian situation. Neither General Bliss nor I were even aware that he had gone until some time after his departure." White to Lodge, September 19, 1919, in the papers of Henry Cabot Lodge in the Massachusetts Historical Society. In a later letter, White asserted that Bullitt went to Russia "not because anyone here was desirous that he should do so, but because of House's weakness in giving way to his own determination to get there; House's tendency, as I discovered during my association with him, being always to compromise rather than to take a firm stand about anything if it involves a struggle, much less a row." White to Lodge, November 13, 1919, Lodge papers. Regarding Joseph Grew's letter of authorization which Bullitt took to Russia, White wrote that Grew had since explained that the letter was the regular form letter given to emissaries of the Commission to obtain information in different parts of Europe. Grew recalled that Lansing asked him to give Bullitt the "usual letter of introduction." White further remarked that Lansing told him that Bullit had been "allowed" to go to Russia—rather than "ordered" there. "The whole trip was at Bullitt's own instigation," White concluded. White to Lodge, November 21, 1919, Lodge papers. An interesting reflection of Lansing's casual attitude toward the Bullitt mission is reflected in his diary comment, "Talked with House about sending Bullitt to Russia to cure him of Bolshevism." Entry of February 16, 1919, Lansing Desk Diary in the Lansing papers in the Library of Congress.

21. Lincoln Steffens, *Autobiography* (New York, 1931), p. 792.

22. Lynch had remained outside of Russia, and Pettit lingered in Petrograd to report on social conditions.

23. Undated memorandum by Bullitt for The President and the Commissioners Plenipotentiary to Negotiate Peace, Bullitt papers.

24. In a report of the Central Committee of the Communist Party to the Eighth Party Congress, March 18, 1919, Lenin predicted that the Bolsheviks would have to make changes in their line of conduct. Lenin warned that they would have to "repeat much of what we did at the time of the Peace of Brest-Litovsk." V. Lenin, *Polnoe Sobranie Sochineniya* (Moscow, 1963), XXXVIII, 135.

Later, on December 5, 1919, in a report to the Seventh Congress of Soviets, Lenin recalled that the Bolsheviks signed the "most severe terms of peace in a businesslike manner," believing that the "blood of our workers and soldiers" was "too dear a price to pay," and saying "we shall pay you, like the merchants you are, a heavy tribute as the price of peace." In this way, Lenin explained his dealings with Bullitt. Ibid., XXXIX, 403.

25. V. Lenin, *Sochineniya* (Moscow, 1932), XXIV, 59.

26. Ibid.

27. When the Bolsheviks were deciding whether to ratify the separate peace with Germany, Robins was promising American aid if they remained in the war. Nothing came of his promise. According to Kennan, however, Lenin was so determined to make peace that such aid would not have changed his decision. George Kennan, *Soviet-American Relations, 1917-1920: Russia Leaves the War* (Princeton, 1956), pp. 504-505.

28. Louis Fischer for many years lived in Russia on friendly terms with the Communists. He claims to have seen in the Bolshevik Rakovsky's private files letters from Chicherin indicating Lenin's attitude toward the Bullitt plan. Chicherin claimed that Lenin carefully weighed every word of the proposals. On March 13, 1919, Chicherin wrote that the decision to sign a statement for Bullitt was very important, for he feared " 'If we do not reach an understanding, the policy of blockade will be pressed with vigour.' " Louis Fischer, *Soviets in World Affairs* (Princeton, 1951), I, 171. I have written to the Moscow State Committee on Cultural Relations with Foreign Countries inquiring whether material pertaining to the Bullitt mission exists in the Russian archives. In reply, I was informed that a search in the Central State Archive had been made but that no such material could be found. The Trotsky Archive at Harvard University contains a dispatch in which Trotsky refers with brief disdain to the American "eavesdroppers" sent to find

out whether the Bolsheviks would survive. Trotsky to Lenin, March 17, 1919, Trotsky Archive, Houghton Library, Harvard University. In his report on conditions in Russia, Bullitt correctly observed that Trotsky disapproved of making compromise peace settlements with the West. Rather, he believed that the Red Army should go forward until more vigorous intervention by the Entente was provoked. Trotsky counted on such increased intervention to bring on revolutions in France and England. *Bullitt Mission,* p. 52. Both Trotsky and Lenin were each advocating in 1919 the same positions toward peace which they had held a year earlier at the time of Brest-Litovsk.

29. Arthur Ransome, *Russia in 1919* (New York, 1919), p. 224.

30. Undated memorandum by Bullitt for the President and the Peace Commissioners, Bullitt papers.

31. Telegram from Bullitt for the President, Lansing, and Colonel House only. Undated from Helsingfors. Received in Paris March 18, 1919, Bullitt papers.

32. Bullitt later explained to Kerr that Lenin wanted the proposal to be made by the Allies so as not to cause misunderstanding in Russia. If the Bolsheviks made the offer, it would have to be couched in revolutionary diatribe which might defeat their purpose. Sir Llewellyn Woodward and Rohan Butler, eds., *Documents on British Foreign Policy, 1919-1939* (London, 1949), First Series, III, 425-26.

33. Entry of March 25, 1919, House Diary, in the House papers at Yale University.

34. *Bullitt Mission,* p. 66.

35. The article in question was by H. Wickham Steed of the Northcliffe press. House's aide and son-in-law, Gordon Auchincloss, informed Steed on March 26, 1919, that an agreement with the Bolsheviks was being considered. Immediately, Steed wrote an editorial opposing any sort of recognition of Lenin's government. Thompson, p. 349. Whether Auchincloss "leaked" this information with the hope of jeopardizing the Bullitt proposals or whether he simply enjoyed having people know he had inside information is not clear.

36. Comment by Lansing on an unsigned memorandum to the Commissioners. The memorandum discussed Bullitt's report and was written on April 1, 1919, in the section of Current Diplomatic and Political Correspondence. Paris Peace Conference 184.02202/11, National Archives. Although Bullitt's report was not "released," news of the mission and of Bullitt's views on Russia did become known.

37. *Treaty of Peace with Germany: Hearings before the Committee on Foreign Relations, 68th Congress, First Session, Senate Document 106* (Washington, 1919), pp. 1254-58. Report also appears in the Bullitt papers.

38. Bullitt's one adverse comment was that the Soviet form of government was "unquestionably" one that "lends itself to gross abuse and tyranny." But Bullitt followed this criticism with the observation that it "meets the demands of the moment in Russia and it has acquired so great a hold on the imagination of the common people that the women are ready to starve and the young men to die for it." *Hearings*, p. 1254.

39. Lincoln Steffens, *Autobiography* (New York, 1931), p. 798.

40. Ibid., p. 799.

41. Ibid.

42. Thompson, p. 347.

43. Although the proposal for relief to Russia would be taken over by Herbert Hoover, it was Wilson's friend, Vance McCormick, head of the War Trade Board, and now member of the American delegation, who inspired the plan for feeding Russia. In his memoirs, Hoover gives the impression of having himself originated this idea, which was subsequently adopted by the Peace Conference. Thompson, pp. 341-42.

44. Entry of March 26, 1919, House Diary.

45. Entry of March 28, 1919, House Diary.

46. Entry of March 26, 1919, House Diary.

47. Paul Mantoux, *Les Délibérations du Conseil des Quatre* (Paris, 1955), I, 55-56.

48. House planned to enlist Hoover actively in the Russian matter and reach a solution with his aid. Entry of March 27, 1919, House Diary.

49. On April 2, 1919, Tumulty wired Wilson that "The proposed recognition of Lenin has caused consternation here." Series VIIIA, Wilson papers.

50. Bullitt, however, blamed Gordon Auchincloss and David Hunter Miller for discouraging House. On April 18, 1919, Bullitt wrote to Pettit interpreting his failure to get the Soviet proposals accepted in Paris. Bullitt reported that both the President and Lloyd George had left the Russian matter to House but that "At the last moment . . . David Hunter Miller, who, as you know, is the blackest reactionary we have here, . . . persuaded Auchincloss that such a proposal was excessively bad, and Auchincloss in turn persuaded House that something milder should be done first." Bullitt to Pettit, April 18, 1919, Bullitt papers.

Although Bullitt was probably correct in assessing Miller and Auchincloss's views and behavior, Wilson's lack of interest would have been more decisive with Colonel House.

51. Speech of June 12, 1920, V. Lenin, *Polnoe Sobranie Sochineniya* (Moscow, 1963), XLI, 140-41. In his report to the Seventh Congress of Soviets, on December 5, 1919, Lenin recalled, "when Bullitt came here, when he was received by Comrade Chicherin, talked to him and to me . . . when in the course of a few hours we concluded a preliminary peace treaty . . . he assured us (those gentlemen love to brag) that America was everything—and who reckoned with France in view of the might of America? And when we had signed that treaty, the French and British Ministers made this kind of gesture [Lenin makes an expressive movement of the foot]. Bullitt was left with a scrap of paper. And they said to him, 'who expected that you would be so naive, so stupid, as to believe in the democracy of England and France!' " Ibid, XXXIX, 402-403.

52. In fact, Lansing had notified the French on March 10, two weeks before Bullitt arrived back in Paris, that an unofficial, fact-finding mission had been sent to Russia. Thompson, p. 238. Thompson is critical of the secrecy which surrounded Bullitt's mission, blaming the mission's ultimate failure in large part on this secrecy, which alienated members of the American delegation and the press, who might have helped put the plan across. This conclusion seems to exaggerate the importance of those members of the American delegation whose sensibilities were offended. The secrecy did provide an element of sensationalism for press attacks but the Bullitt mission failed chiefly because the major figures who might have supported it, Wilson and Lloyd George, were beset with other problems. Bullitt's own defense of the secrecy appears valid, that the mission was secret because of " 'fears that the French Foreign Office and the conservative wings of the French, British, and American press would raise such an outcry as to prejudice in advance the success of the peace negotiations which the mission hoped to arrange.' " Bullitt to Thompson, February 25, 1953, Thompson, p. 243.

53. Entry of March 29, 1919, House Diary.

54. Nansen's scheme was finally approved by the Allies. But there followed the same difficulty that had pursued the Prinkipo decision and the Bullitt plan. White Russian groups protested that such a move would help maintain Lenin in power. The Allies began to hesitate over public reactions. Then Kolchak made further advances. The Soviets

replied that they would be glad to accept supplies but not to cease fighting, though they were prepared to enter into negotiations for a general Russian peace. This reply—that cessation of hostilities would have to be discussed—became a sufficient reason for abandoning the feeding plan. Once again the Allies could not see their way to a conference with the Bolsheviks. *FR:Russia, 1919*, p. 115. It is of interest that as with the Prinkipo plan there was difficulty in sending a message to the Bolsheviks. Nansen found that the Allied governments would not lend their facilities for dispatching a telegram to Moscow since they had not recognized Lenin. Finally the Nansen message was sent from Berlin. Fridtjof Nansen, *Russia and Peace* (London, 1923), p. 26.

55. I did not come across the letter when I examined the Wilson files; if it ever reached Wilson it was not preserved.

56. The revision read: "Individuals of neutral States are considering organization for feeding Russia. Will perhaps decide something definite within a week. Bullitt." This telegram is dated April 10, Bullitt papers.

57. The Bolsheviks in their reply to Prinkipo had offered the Allies economic concessions in Russia. *FR: Russia, 1919*, p. 40. Lenin offered similar concessions to Bullitt, who explained that Wilson was opposed to "entangling" concessions. Lenin laughed and said, " 'Here is the most humorous thing imaginable: three Communists in the Kremlin are trying to persuade a bourgeois diplomat from a capitalist country to accept valuable concessions.' " Undated memorandum of Bullitt's verbal report to S. Montgomery, Captain J. Ogden Mills, and Colonel Van Deman, Paris Peace Conference 184.02202/11, National Archives.

58. Entry of April 11, 1919, Harold Nicolson, *Peacemaking, 1919*, p. 310.

59. Ella Winter and Granville Hicks, eds., *The Letters of Lincoln Steffens* (New York, 1938), I, 522.

III. BULLITT AND LODGE

1. Letter from Bullitt to Colonel House, May 17, 1919, Bullitt papers at Yale University.

2. Bullitt to Wilson, May 17, 1919, Bullitt papers. There are no notations by Wilson on Bullitt's letter in the Wilson papers, series VIIIA; nor is there a reply.

3. Undated notes presumably penned in 1918, Bullitt papers.

4. Drafts of May 17, 1919, letter from Bullitt to Wilson, Bullitt papers.

5. Letter from Henry White to Henry C. Lodge, September 19, 1919, Lodge papers in the Massachusetts Historical Society.

6. Bullitt to House, September 27, 1918, House papers, at Yale University.

7. William C. Bullitt, *It's Not Done* (New York, 1926), p. 296.

8. Lansing testimony of August 6, 1919, as it appears in *Treaty of Peace with Germany: Hearings before the Committee on Foreign Relations, 68th Congress, First Session, Senate Document 106* (Washington, 1919), p. 143.

9. Wilson to Lodge, August 8, 1919. *Hearings*, p. 253.

10. Bullitt came to possess the original draft in this manner. The President sent the draft down to the Hotel Crillon late one night with the request that it be printed before the following morning. House tried to find the men who would do the job but at the time they were all out. As he happened to meet Bullitt in the hallway, he asked him if he would take on the job of getting it printed. Bullitt agreed to do so and stayed up all night. By breakfast he had the copy ready. House was pleased and in reply to Bullitt's request gave him the original draft as a souvenir. Joseph Grew, *Turbulent Era* (Boston, 1952), I, 395.

11. Wilson to Lodge, August 8, 1919. *Hearings*, p. 253. Lodge writes that the records of the peace conference and of the conferences of the five powers were asked for by the commitee and refused by the executive. Henry C. Lodge, *The Senate and the League of Nations* (New York, 1925), p. 167.

12. Lansing testimony of August 6, 1919. *Hearings*, p. 173.

13. *Hearings*, pp. 1275-76.

14. Memorandum of this conversation held on May 19, 1919, is in the Bullitt papers.

15. *Hearings*, pp. 1276-77.

16. Lodge to White in referring to Bullitt's Russian mission, October 2, 1919, Lodge papers.

17. *Hearings*, p. 170.

18. *Hearings*, p.1280.

19. William Phillips to Frank Polk, September 18, 1919, in the Polk papers at Yale University Library.

20. *House of Commons Parliamentary Debates*, Fifth Series, October 28, 1919, pp. 120, 451.

21. Entry of September 15, 1919, House Diary in House papers at Yale University.

22. Wilson to H. B. Brougham, October 30, 1917, series VI, Wilson papers in the Library of Congress. See above, p. 9.

23. Article by Edwin L. James in *New York Times*, September 23, 1919. Hugh Wilson summed up contemporary reaction to Bullitt's position in Paris when he wrote, "It was extraordinary to see this youth on terms of intimate relationship with so many of the leading figures of Europe." Hugh R. Wilson, *Diplomat Between Wars* (New York, 1941), p. 14.

24. Editorial in the *New York Times*, September 24, 1919.

25. Ibid. That Bullitt's resignation and testimony were hailed in the German and Austrian press did not enhance his reputation. The *New York Times* quoted the Vienna *Ostdeutsche Rundshau:* "Bullitt and his splendid and courageous letter will live forever in the history of mankind. Doubtless Wilson will also live, but Bullitt will unquestionably be infinitely better judged by the verdict of posterity than Wilson. Bullitt is our man, not Wilson." *New York Times*, September 23, 1919.

26. Lodge to White, October 2, 1919, Lodge papers. White had written Lodge regarding the Bullitt testimony, which he considered "reprehensible." Bullitt, he had declared, was "not even one of the regular experts of the Delegation, but merely an attractive and rather brilliant personality, who had been taken on by the State Department for a while during the war and got himself attached to this Commission." White to Lodge, September 19, 1919, Lodge papers. On November 13 after receiving Lodge's letter of October 2, White wrote again; he repeated his condemnation of Bullitt's action but added, "I did not mean, however, to give the impression in my letter of September 19th, that his [Bullitt's] testimony amounts to nothing, still less that it was for the most part otherwise than true." White to Lodge, November 13, 1919, Lodge papers.

27. Joseph Grew, recording in his diary a conversation with Bullitt in November, 1934, regarding the Lansing episode in 1919, concluded that Bullitt had divulged this talk in conversation because when he returned to the United States Bullitt heard that the Republican senators who wanted to defeat the Treaty were going to call on him to testify before the Committee on Foreign Relations. Grew, *Turbulent Era*, I, 398.

28. In this same letter to Henry White, Lodge wrote: "He [Bullitt] thought that Mr. Wilson had betrayed the views which he and others

represented. With all these views I have no sympathy whatsoever. He simply turned state's evidence." Lodge to White, October 2, 1919, Lodge papers. In another letter Lodge asked, "Is Bullitt the Bolshevist who was sent to Russia? I have heard nothing of the name except in that connection." Lodge to White, June 12, 1919, Lodge papers.

29. Allan Nevins, *Henry White* (New York, 1930), p. 464.

30. Lansing testimony, *Hearings*, p. 182. Lansing's testimony, writes John Blum, increased the separation between him and Wilson that had begun in Paris. John Blum, *Joe Tumulty and the Wilson Era* (Boston, 1951), p. 201.

31. In Paris, Clemenceau remarked of Lansing, "I received my bullet at the Conference; he his Bullitt only after he got home." White to Lodge, November 13, 1919, Lodge papers. On September 16, 1919, Lansing sent a telegram of explanation to Wilson in view of the fact that he found it impossible to deny that he had expressed to Bullitt opposition to the Treaty. "I told him [Bullitt]," Lansing wired, "that I would say nothing against his resigning since he put it on conscientious grounds, and that I recognized that certain features of the Treaty were bad, as I presumed most every one did, but that was probably unavoidable in view of conflicting claims and that nothing ought to be done to prevent the speedy restoration of peace by signing the Treaty. Bullitt then discussed the numerous European commissions provided for by the Treaty on which the United States was to be represented. I told him that I was disturbed by this fact because I was afraid the Senate and possibly the people, if they understood this, would refuse ratification, and that anything which was an obstacle to ratification was unfortunate because we ought to have peace as soon as possible." Wilson did not reply to Lansing's telegram. Tumulty, pp. 441-42. Tumulty recalls that Wilson showed the telegram to him and said: " 'Read that, and tell me what you think of a man who was my associate on the other side and who confidentially expressed himself to an outsider in such a fashion? . . . The testimony of Bullitt is a confirmation of the suspicions I have had with reference to this individual. . . . I could find his trail everywhere I went, but they were only suspicions and it would not be fair for me to act upon them. But here in his own statement is a verification at last of everything I have suspected. Think of it! This from a man whom I raised from the level of a subordinate to the great office of Secretary of State of the United States. . . . I did not think it was possible for Lansing to act in this way.' " Tumulty, p. 442.

32. White to Lodge, September 19, 1919, Lodge papers.

33. In "slamming Lansing," Colonel House told Joseph Grew, Bullitt had "injured his best friend for it was Lansing who had finally approved of his going to Russia and had given him his credentials." Grew, *Turbulent Era*, I, 395.

34. Expression used by Bullitt's first wife in discussing Bullitt's character, interview with Bullitt's first wife, now Mrs. S. L. Barlow, December 27, 1954.

35. Barlow interview. Fifteen years later Bullitt told this same story to Joseph Grew. As Grew records it in his diary, it corroborates the recollections of Mrs. Barlow. Grew, *Turbulent Era*, I, 398.

36. Letter from Bullitt to Nancy Astor, January 17, 1920, Bullitt papers.

37. Undated rough notes in Bullitt papers. Bullitt stressed different reasons for his testimony in his public statement and in his private letters to Nancy Astor. Both reasons impelled Bullitt to testify as he did; it is likely, however, that he suspected Nancy Astor would understand better than the press his feelings about peace with Russia.

38. Barlow interview.

39. Lansing to Tumulty, November 6, 1917, series VI, Wilson papers.

40. John Sturgis to Chief Signal Corps Officer, December 14, 1917, Bullitt papers.

41. White to Lodge, September 19, 1919, Lodge papers.

42. In a later chapter we will see that when Bullitt sought the position of Secretary of State, Roosevelt, although he liked Bullitt, refused to make the appointment and mentioned afterward to Harold Ickes that Bill "talked too much." Harold L. Ickes, *The Secret Diary of Harold L. Ickes* (New York, 1955), III, 344.

43. *New York Times*, September 23, 1919.

IV. THE WAY BACK

1. Robert Lansing, *The Peace Negotiations* (New York, 1921), p. 271.

2. William C. Bullitt, "An Open Letter to Mr. Lansing," *New Republic*, XXVI (April 6, 1921), 160.

3. Interview with Bullitt's first wife, now Mrs. S. L. Barlow, December 27, 1954. Mrs. Barlow explained that Bullitt's mother, who had recently died, had left her son a fortune.

4. William C. Bullitt, *It's Not Done* (New York, 1926), p. 340.

5. Ibid., p. 197.

6. Ibid., p. 264.

7. Ella Winter and Granville Hicks, eds., *The Letters of Lincoln Steffens* (New York, 1938), II, 747.

8. "The more I researched, the more I became convinced I was right in 1919," Bullitt has remarked. Bullitt interview, September 19, 1955.

9. Bullitt to House, July 29, 1930, House papers at Yale University. This hope was evidently unrealized.

10. Bullitt to House, October 26, 1930, House papers.

11. Although the Bullitt-Freud study of Wilson was completed, Bullitt claimed that it would not be published while Mrs. Wilson was still living. Bullitt interview. As of this writing (January, 1967), the book has appeared. Interesting light on Freud's attitude toward Wilson has recently been provided by William Harlan Hale, "President Wilson, Dr. Freud, and 'The Story of a Style,' " *The Reporter*, XVIII (June 26, 1958), 28-30. In this article Hale discusses the correspondence between Freud and Hale's father, William Bayard Hale, author of *The Story of a Style* (New York, 1920), a psychoanalytic study of Wilson's literary style. After the appearance of this book, Freud wrote to Hale telling him, " 'I detest the man who is the object of your study: as far as a single individual can be responsible for the misery of this part of the world, he surely is.' " Still, Freud disapproved of what Hale had done: " 'In my opinion, psychoanalysis should never be used as a weapon in literary or political polemics.' " Freud further remarked that psycho-analysis " 'should not be practiced on a living subject . . . unless he submits to it.' " According to William Harlan Hale, Freud continued to show interest in the study. Evidently Bullitt was able to convince Freud to collaborate with him on a similar work.

12. Frank Freidel, *Franklin D. Roosevelt: The Triumph* (Boston, 1956), p. 242.

13. Speech by Roosevelt made on April 7, 1932.

14. Bullitt to House, September 17, 1932, House papers.

15. Bullitt to House, September 3, 1932, House papers.

16. Ibid.

17. Bullitt to House, January 9, 1932, House papers.

18. House to Bullitt, December 28, 1931, House papers.

19. House to Bullitt, May 11, 1932, House papers.

20. Bullitt interview, September 19, 1955.

21. Eugene Lyons, *Assignment in Utopia* (New York, 1937), p. 499.

22. James A. Farley, *Behind the Ballots* (New York, 1938), p. 88. Farley refers to a memorandum in which House "plaintively" complained that Howe seemed unwilling to let other people know what was going on. House, Farley remarks, felt he should have been consulted more than he was. See Frank Freidel, *Franklin D. Roosevelt: The Triumph*, pp. 201-203 and 243 for an analysis of House's position.

23. There are no letters in the House-Roosevelt correspondence, in the House papers at Yale, in which House urged consideration of William C. Bullitt. House may, however, have spoken with Roosevelt directly.

24. Frank Freidel, *Franklin D. Roosevelt: The Ordeal* (Boston, 1954), p. 23.

25. Louis B. Wehle, *Hidden Threads of History* (New York, 1953), p. 115.

26. Freidel, *Franklin D. Roosevelt: The Triumph*, pp. 264-65; Raymond Moley, *After Seven Years* (New York, 1939), pp. 20-21. Samuel I. Rosenman, however, was the brains behind the brain trust in many ways.

27. Rexford G. Tugwell, *The Democratic Roosevelt: A Biography of Franklin D. Roosevelt* (New York, 1957), p. 292. Consequently, Tugwell observes, when Roosevelt became President on March 4, he did not fear dealings with other nations that had so worried his predecessor. Cf. Stimson-Roosevelt conversation, below, p. 84.

28. Grace Tully, *FDR My Boss* (New York, 1949), p. 61.

29. Wehle, p. 118.

30. Moley heard rumors about Bullitt's trip, but when he asked Roosevelt, he was told that there was nothing to them. Moley, p. 135.

31. Bullitt to Wehle, December 3, 1932. Franklin D. Roosevelt papers, PPF, 693.

32. Bullitt to Wehle, December 3, 1932, PPF, 693, Roosevelt papers.

33. Ibid.

34. Bullitt to Wehle, December 3, 1932, PPF, 693, Roosevelt papers. Bullitt added that Herriot, although he would urge the December 15 payment, expected defeat and the fall of his government. On December 15, 1932, Britain did pay her pledged installment in full—but indicated that this payment was not to be regarded as a resumption of the annual payments; they had made the payment because time did not allow detailed negotiations. Britain warned that without some debt

adjustment a general breakdown of existing intergovernmental agreements would occur by June 15, 1933. Italy paid after discovering that the British would pay. Poland defaulted; Greece deposited part payment in a blocked account; France defaulted.

35. Wehle, p. 119.

36. Bullitt to Wehle, December 3, 1932, PPF, 693, Roosevelt papers.

37. Ibid.

38. Wehle attaches great importance to Bullitt's European trips for Roosevelt. He writes, "they seem to have crystallized Roosevelt's advance determination to restore to the President the initiative in foreign relations, and educated him intensively for pursuing that policy. Again, they helped to establish the precedent that a President-elect, within appropriate limits, may properly confer with domestic and foreign officials about problems that he will have to meet." Wehle, p. 123. As an indication of the importance Roosevelt attached to Bullitt's information, the following incident is illustrative. Sometime between February 21 and March 4, 1933, Hull, after learning he was to be Secretary of State, saw Bullitt, who acquainted him "with the results of his trip to Europe for the President-elect." Hull termed the information "interesting and useful." Cordell Hull, *Memoirs* (New York, 1948), I, 160.

39. Entry of January 3, 1933, Stimson Diary, Yale University.

40. Ibid.

41. Wehle, p. 120.

42. Undated telegram from Berlin, Bullitt to Roosevelt, PPF, 1124, Roosevelt papers.

43. *New York Times*, January 26, 1933.

44. *New York Times*, January 27, 1933.

45. Ibid.

46. The Logan Act was passed by Congress in 1799. It made unauthorized missions by self-appointed American representatives a crime and punishable by a fine of not more than $5,000 and imprisonment of not more than three years.

47. *Congressional Record*, February 2, 1933, p. 3146. The Department of State on February 4, 1933, issued a statement to the press which indicated that in response to the demand of Senator Robinson of Indiana that the Department curb the alleged diplomatic activities of William C. Bullitt in Europe, the Department was inquiring of its embassies in London and on the continent as to whether they had any information concerning Bullitt's activities. This appeared in the *New*

York Times, February 5, 1933. American diplomatic missions in Paris, London, Vienna, and Berlin informed the State Department that they had not discovered that Bullitt was conducting diplomatic negotiations in Europe or was more than a correspondent—although he had been seen at Number 10 Downing Street and had talked with Foreign Minister Boncour. Ibid., February 7, 1933.

48. *Congressional Record*, February 2, 1933, p. 3146.

49. House to Bullitt, February 23, 1933, House papers.

50. Wehle, p. 119.

51. Bullitt interview, September 19, 1955.

52. *Documents on British Foreign Policy: 1919-1939* (London 1956), Second Series, V, 772.

53. Moley, p. 102.

54. Moley, p. 164. Bullitt contributed $1,000 to the campaign, which was the same contribution made by Henry Morgenthau, Jr., Chairman of the Farm Credit Bureau and later Secretary of the Treasury, and by William Phillips, Undersecretary of State. The ambassador to Britain, Bingham, gave $5,000; Straus, $10,000; ambassador to Belgium, D. H. Morris, $5,000; Breckinridge Long, ambassador to Italy, $5,000; ambassador to Sweden, Steinhardt, $5,000; and Mrs. Sumner Welles, $2,500. Louis Overaker, "Campaign Funds In a Depression Year," *American Political Science Review*, XXVII (October, 1933), 769-83.

55. Phillips to Polk, September 18, 1919, in the Polk papers at Yale University.

V. BULLITT AND RECOGNITION OF RUSSIA

1. Robert Paul Browder, *The Origins of Soviet-American Diplomacy* (Princeton, 1953), p. 104.

2. During their Albany meeting in October, 1932, Bullitt had recommended recognition to Roosevelt. Bullitt interview, September 19, 1955.

3. Henry J. Morgenthau, Jr., "The Morgenthau Diaries," *Colliers*, CXX (October 11, 1947), 21.

4. James A. Farley, *Jim Farley's Story* (New York, 1948), p. 43; entry of January 9, 1933, Stimson Diary, Yale University.

5. A public opinion analysis prepared in the Department of State indicated that the groups favoring recognition were primarily inter-

ested in the prospects of increased foreign trade. Donald F. Whitehead, "The Making of Foreign Policy During President Roosevelt's First Term, 1933-1937," unpublished doctoral dissertation, University of Chicago, 1952, p. 85.

6. One historian has quoted the remark of an unidentified member of the government to the effect that the administration considered trade a necessary "cloak" to make it easier to secure a favorable public opinion for recognition. Browder, p. 108.

7. Morgenthau recalls that FDR considered nonrecognition a futile gesture against an established government. Morgenthau, *Diaries*, p. 20.

8. See William A. Williams, *American-Russian Relations: 1781-1947* (New York, 1952), p. 237; and Robert H. Ferrell, "A Meeting at Hyde Park" in *American Diplomacy in the Great Depression* (New Haven, 1957), pp. 231-54.

9. Morgenthau, *Diaries*, p. 20.

10. Cordell Hull, *Memoirs* (New York, 1948), I, 297.

11. Morgenthau, *Diaries*, p. 72. Bullitt has since claimed that both he and Roosevelt were convinced in 1933 that " 'Hitler would eventually make war unless England, France, and the Soviet Union should stand together against Nazi aggression. . . . The primary objective [in recognition] was to prevent the launching of another world war by Hitler.' " Letter from Bullitt to Robert P. Browder, February 2, 1950. Browder, p. 111. One should note that Bullitt did not advocate in 1933 that America stand with Britain, France, and Russia against Hitler. When Bullitt advocated American aid (as Morgenthau contends he did) as a means by which the Soviet Union could break its dependency on Germany and become a bulwark against Japanese aggression, he did not mean military aid or military cooperation. See below, p. 114.

12. Pauline Tompkins, *American-Russian Relations in the Far East* (New York, 1949), p. 263.

13. James A. Farley, *Jim Farley's Story* (New York, 1948), p. 34. A cable from Bullitt to Roosevelt on January 24, 1933, contained information that he had received assurances from MacDonald that the British government would not allow a Japanese loan to be floated in England. Bullitt to Roosevelt, January 24, 1933, PPF, 1124, Roosevelt papers. One receives the impression that this possibility had been a matter of Presidential concern.

14. *Jim Farley's Story*, p. 39.

15. On October 28, 1933, State Department Far Eastern expert, Stanley K. Hornbeck pointed out in a memorandum to Hull that the Russians were trying to create the impression that recognition conversations would have an important bearing on Far Eastern policy. Hornbeck suggested reassuring the Japanese that the conversations would have nothing to do with Japanese affairs—especially since the Japanese minister of foreign affairs was trying to cultivate friendly relations with the United States. *Foreign Relations of the United States: The Soviet Union, 1933-39* (Washington, 1952), p. 24.

16. Sir Ronald Lindsay to Sir John Simon, January 30, 1933, reporting conversation with Roosevelt on January 29. *Documents on British Foreign Policy: 1919-1939* (London, 1956), Second Series, V, 751.

17. For this move the President had the advice of Hornbeck to back him. If American interests in the Far East are to be protected short of the use of military force, Hornbeck warned early in 1933, effective means must be found. One suggestion was to create effective counterweights against Japan: this could be done by recognizing Soviet Russia. Memorandum by Hornbeck on March 14, 1933. Cited in Whitehead, p. 76.

18. Entry of November 30, 1933, in Joseph C. Grew, *Ten Years in Japan* (New York, 1944), p. 108. Grew also believed that recognition had greater effect than any other single factor in restraining Japan from aggression directed at the Soviet Union. Ibid., p. 120. Grew's reference to building the fleet concerned the Executive Order on July 16, 1933, allocating $238,000,000 from the NIRA appropriations to the construction of new warships of the London treaty type. The Japanese naval maneuvers in the western Pacific in August, 1933, were matched within two months by American maneuvers in the eastern Pacific.

19. Morgenthau, *Diaries*, p. 21. Bullitt was also of the impression that the State Department was anti-recognition. Ibid.

20. This was the opinion of Samuel N. Harper. See Paul V. Harper, ed., *The Russia I Believe In: The Memoirs of Samuel N. Harper, 1902-1941* (Chicago, 1945), p. 200. Harper was strongly sympathetic to Russia and may have considered caution as opposition. Hull indicated his enthusiasm for recognition. Hull, *Memoirs*, I, 297.

21. Ibid.

22. Ibid., p. 298. The Secretary "doubted the wisdom of this course."

23. Ibid., p. 294.

24. Morgenthau, *Diaries*, p. 21.

25. Ibid.

26. Ibid.

27. During the spring of 1933 Bullitt had been more specifically engaged in preparations for the London Economic Conference. He attended the conference as executive head of the American delegation.

28. Morgenthau, *Diaries*, p. 21.

29. As it turned out, Hull managed to be present for the first few days of the negotiations (see below, p. 97). Roosevelt, however, in scheduling the negotiations for a time when the Secretary was to be out of the country, may have thought he could thus avoid embarrassing and antagonizing Hull since the negotiations were to be handled by Bullitt. Hull was, after all, still annoyed by the London fiasco (an annoyance which persisted fifteen years later when he wrote his memoirs). In this instance, Roosevelt had sent Moley to London after the World Economic Conference began, to inform Hull of latest developments in Washington. But Moley's dramatic airplane flight to meet the President on his yacht and the speculation attending his departure from New York had made it appear that the assistant secretary would be the bearer of vital instructions. The London press carried banner headlines heralding the arrival of Moley, "the man who controlled Presidents." It was suggested that Moley was possibly being sent to take over the American delegation—replacing Hull. The press "rawhided me in rough fashion," Hull later wrote, "indicating that I had proved incapable of handling the situation for my Government." Hull, *Memoirs*, I, 259. It was generally believed that at "Hull's insistence" FDR decided to remove Moley from the Department of State. Rexford G. Tugwell, *The Democratic Roosevelt: A Biography of Franklin D. Roosevelt* (New York, 1957), p. 317. Hull had originally disapproved of Moley's appointment as Roosevelt's "utility man" in the State Department. "I was not at all enthusiastic about this sort of appointment." Hull, *Memoirs*, I, 161. Moley, however, denied that Hull's objections prompted his "resignation." Moley, p. 276.

30. Morgenthau, *Diaries*, p. 21.

31. The note was dated October 10, 1933. In his memoirs Hull indicated his disapproval of the transaction. Hull, *Memoirs*, I, 297.

32. According to Robert F. Kelley, Chief of the Division of Eastern European Affairs, the note was worded and reworded with this object in mind. Browder, p. 116.

33. Memorandum by Kelley, July 27, 1933, *FR: Soviet Union, 1933-39*, pp. 6-10.

34. Bullitt reiterated the points in Kelley's earlier memorandum and

emphasized in addition the need for protection of the religious rights of Americans in Russia. This point Roosevelt considered particularly important because of the significance it had for certain segments of the American public. Bullitt also suggested an agreement regarding a waiver of Russian counterclaims based on our Vladivostok, Archangel, and Murmansk expeditions.

35. *New York Times*, November 15, 1933.

36. Hull, *Memoirs*, I, 300. Hull wanted to be sure that the agreements on Soviet propaganda and interference in the United States, and religious freedom for Americans in Russia were arranged before he was obliged to leave Washington.

37. Hull, *Memoirs*, I, 301.

38. Browder, pp. 132-33.

39. *Jim Farley's Story*, p. 43. Roosevelt assured Farley that he had convinced Litvinov that guarantees of religious freedom must be given Americans in Russia before anything could be done. Roosevelt therefore felt confident that the agreement would be very pleasing to the American people and that those who had opposed recognition on religious grounds would no longer do so. Ibid., p. 44.

40. *Jim Farley's Story*, p. 44.

41. Memorandum by Bullitt, October 4, 1933, *FR: Soviet Union, 1933-39*, p. 17. Earlier, in 1932, Bullitt had assured Louis Wehle that he understood the extent of Soviet subversive activity in the United States and the need to put an end to it. Wehle, recalling Bullitt's enthusiasm for Lenin in 1919, had been apprehensive that Bullitt might advise Roosevelt unwisely regarding Russia. Therefore he had made it clear to Bullitt that before recommending him to Roosevelt he would have to know how he stood on the question of Communist subversion. Wehle was satisfied by Bullitt's assurances although he knew that Bullitt retained his sympathy for the Russian experiment. Wehle, pp. 112-14.

42. This last pledge certainly referred directly to the Comintern, whose headquarters were located in Moscow. There was considerable skepticism in the State Department that these pledges would be observed. Roosevelt and Bullitt were thought to be more trusting of Russian good faith than were the members of the Department. Browder, p. 143.

43. Bullitt interview, September 19, 1955.

44. *New York Times*, November 18, 1933; *Daily Worker*, November 21, 1933. The former American Communist Benjamin Gitlow has

claimed that Litvinov and the secretariat of the American Communist
Party met in New York before the Commissar's departure. The Communists, according to Gitlow, were concerned over the effect the subversive activities pledges might have on their future. Gitlow claims
that Litvinov assured the American Communists that the commitments
he gave Roosevelt in no way affected the activities of their party or its
relations with the International. "After all, comrades, you should by
this time know how to handle the fiction of the tie-up between the
Comintern and the Soviet Government. . . . The letter is a scrap of
paper." Benjamin Gitlow, *The Whole of Their Lives* (New York,
1948), pp. 264-65. That such a meeting took place is extremely unlikely.
Gitlow's story is interesting, however, since it probably reflects the
feeling of the Communist Party toward the recognition pledges.

45. Bullitt to Hull, November 9, 1935, *FR: Soviet Union, 1933-
39*, p. 265.

46. Memorandum by Kelley, October 25, 1933, *FR: Soviet Union,
1933-39*, p. 23.

47. Ibid., p. 8.

48. Bullitt to Roosevelt, November 15, 1933, *FR: Soviet Union, 1933-
39*, pp. 25-26.

49. Ibid.

50. Memorandum by Roosevelt and Litvinov, November 15, 1933,
FR: Soviet Union, 1933-39, pp. 26-27. Although Litvinov remained in
Washington, no agreement was reached.

51. *Jim Farley's Story*, p. 44.

52. The documents detailing Bullitt's two years of negotiations with
Litvinov were subsequently printed along with the "gentleman's agreement." Although the problems caused by the "gentleman's agreement"
will be described in a later chapter, one should note that the document
proved to have settled nothing. In Moscow, Litvinov argued that he
had been promised a loan, basing his statement on the use of the word
"loan" in the agreement. Bullitt countered that the Commissar knew
well that no outright loan was considered at any time; that in American
usage "loan" and "credit" were interchangeable words, and only a
credit had been intended. It is of interest in this connection to note
Hull's interchangeable use of loan and credit. Hull to Roosevelt, September 21, 1933. *FR: Soviet Union, 1933-39*, p. 13. But in November,
1933, neither Roosevelt nor Bullitt suspected the subsequent disagreement.

53. Morgenthau, *Diaries*, p. 21.

54. Robert Walton Moore, "Recognition of the Union of Soviet Socialist Republics," radio address, November 22, 1933 (Washington, 1934), p. 4.

55. One is reminded of Roosevelt's hunch that after the war Stalin would act in accordance with *noblesse oblige* if he were treated trustingly by Roosevelt. See above, page 3.

56. Bullitt interview, August 9, 1966.

57. Litvinov's subsequent threats to Bullitt in Moscow that he would make public the "gentleman's agreement" suggests that secrecy was the idea of Roosevelt or Bullitt.

58. George Kennan recalls that Roosevelt regarded the recognition documents as "looking good on paper." Interview with George Kennan, February 12, 1957.

59. The State Department gave Litvinov documents to examine which made it clear that American forces had not been in Siberia to wrest territory from Russia but to ensure the withdrawal of the Japanese from the area. Hull, *Memoirs*, I, 299.

60. In October, 1932, Litvinov told Dr. W. W. Yen, Chinese representative at the Geneva disarmament conference, of his desire to see a resumption of relations with the United States. But Litvinov considered a pre-recognition settlement of the American private and public debt impossible. If that were the criterion for recognition, he told Yen, diplomatic relations between America and Russia might be delayed for fifty years. October 12, 1932, report from American minister to Switzerland detailing conversation with Yen. *Foreign Relations of the United States, 1934* (Washington, 1951), IV, 297.

61. J. P. Moffat cites an incident reflecting Hull's sensitivity to the way in which he was being bypassed. "I met the Secretary in the elevator this morning coming into the building. He asked me to come to his office and talk for a few moments. He thereupon pulled out from his inside pocket a clipping from the Hearst press [Kenneth Clark, "Evidence of Hull's Declining Influence" New York *American*, October 22, 1933, p. 14] yesterday indicating that once more he was being relegated to a secondary position in the Government and citing as instances thereof the fact that the President was going to negotiate on Russia himself, that the debt negotiations had been transferred to the Treasury. . . ." Moffat observed that "apparently the Secretary honeycombs the papers and is far more sensitive to personal press attack than I had

anticipated. . . ." Nancy Hooker, ed., *The Moffat Papers* (Cambridge, Massachusetts, 1956), p. 108.

62. Hull, *Memoirs*, I, 207. "We sometimes found him conducting negotiations," Hull continued, "with foreign Governments which were the function of the State Department." Hull does not refer directly to Morgenthau's part in recognition although since the Morgenthau *Diaries* appeared in 1947, Hull must have been aware of his activities when he wrote his memoirs in 1948. Hull may not have known, however, that Morgenthau always operated with FDR's knowledge and consent.

63. Wehle, p. 131. The recognition negotiations show clearly the direction in which Roosevelt was moving. The Department was never to focus on Hull. Assistant secretaries like Bullitt and Sumner Welles were appointed by FDR and saw the President at their own instance. Often they would be contemptuous of "old man Hull" (Bullitt's appellation; Bullitt interview, September 19, 1955). Hull was to be bypassed on important matters, his influence within the Department becoming amorphous as Roosevelt assumed more and more the role of Secretary of State. An interesting reflection on Hull's position was seen in Harry Hopkins' attitude when Hull's successor was being selected in 1944. James F. Byrnes was an obvious choice but Hopkins opposed Byrnes on the ground that Roosevelt was going to be his own Secretary of State particularly in dealings with Churchill and Stalin. And Byrnes (who had once told Hopkins to "keep the hell out of my business") was not one to conform placidly, Hopkins thought, to "the role of a mere mouthpiece." Robert E. Sherwood, *Roosevelt and Hopkins* (New York, 1948), p. 835.

64. Hull, *Memoirs*, I, 302.

65. William Phillips, *Ventures in Diplomacy* (Boston, 1952), p. 158.

66. *Pravda*, November 19, 1933, as cited in Browder, p. 161.

67. *Daily Worker*, November 18, 1933.

68. Eugene Lyons, *Assignment in Utopia* (New York, 1937), p. 564.

69. Louis Fischer, *Men and Politics* (New York, 1941), p. 303.

70. Bullitt to Roosevelt, December 6, 1933, Franklin D. Roosevelt papers, PSF, 15; Bullitt to Roosevelt, May 18, 1934, PSF, 15, Roosevelt papers.

71. *New York Times*, September 6, 1936.

72. Bullitt to William Phillips, Acting Secretary of State, January 4, 1934. *FR: Soviet Union, 1933-39*, pp. 59-60. Stalin gave Bullitt his as-

surances although Bullitt had already been told by Moscow authorities that he could not have the property.

73. Ibid., p. 59.

74. Bullitt to Hull, March 13, 1934, *Foreign Relations of the United States, 1934* (Washington, 1950), III, 74. Bullitt here refers to this conversation. No record of it exists at Hyde Park.

75. Bullitt to Phillips, January 4, 1934, *FR: Soviet Union, 1933-39*, p. 61.

76. Grew to Hull, March 8, 1934, *Foreign Relations of the United States, 1934*, III, 68. Ambassador Grew noted that American recognition was a restraining factor on the Japanese war group because the Japanese did not know what the United States would do in case of war. Even a neutrality benevolent to the Soviets might be serious to Japan.

77. Bullitt to Roosevelt, Phillips, and Moore, December 24, 1933, *FR: Soviet Union, 1933-39*, p. 54.

78. Ibid., pp. 56, 60.

79. Ibid., p. 60. George Kennan, then a third secretary in the embassy, recalls that Bullitt was "thrilled" by the honor paid him at Voroshilov's home. He returned to the embassy in the small hours of the morning, and sitting on the edge of Kennan's bed, told him all about the conversation with Stalin. Kennan interview.

80. William C. Bullitt, *The Establishment of Normal Relations Between the United States and the Union of Soviet Socialist Republics. An Address before the Chamber of Commerce of Philadelphia, January 19, 1934* (Washington, 1934), pp. 5-6.

81. Bullitt interview, August 9, 1966.

VI. THE AMBASSADOR AND THE COMMISSAR

1. Eugene Lyons, *Assignment in Utopia* (New York, 1937), p. 500.

2. Interview with George Kennan, February 12, 1957.

3. Bullitt to House, July 2, 1934, House papers at Yale University.

4. Bullitt to Hull, March 9, 1934, 123 William C. Bullitt/57, National Archives.

5. Kennan interview. Kennan claims that the lack of organizational experience of Bullitt and Wiley, Counselor of Embassy, contributed to the confusion.

6. See Charles W. Thayer, *Bears in the Caviar* (New York, 1950)

for amusing descriptions of the chaotic first months in the Soviet Union.

7. Bullitt to Hull, March 28, 1934. *Foreign Relations of the United States: The Soviet Union, 1933-39* (Washington, 1952), p. 74.

8. Bullitt to Hull, March 28, 1934, 124.613/527, National Archives. Kennan attests to Bullitt's shock at this advice. Kennan interview.

9. Due to inability to come to terms with the Soviet government on building arrangements, the United States in 1935 abandoned plans to build an embassy in Moscow. The United States rented Spasso House for its embassy residence, and Mokhovaya House for its chancery offices. For the fruitless negotiations regarding building see *FR: Soviet Union, 1933-39*, pp. 268-77.

10. Bullitt to Hull, March 28, 1934, ibid., p. 74.

11. Bullitt to Hull, March 15, 1934, ibid., p. 67.

12. Bullitt to Hull, March 15, 1934, ibid., pp. 66-67.

13. Bullitt to Hull, May 9, 1934, ibid., p. 91.

14. Assistant Secretary Moore to Assistant Secretary Sayre, July 19, 1934, ibid., p. 120.

15. Bullitt to Hull, April 2, 1934, ibid., p. 76.

16. Hull to Bullitt, April 5, 1934, ibid., p. 76.

17. Bullitt to Hull, May 13, 1934, ibid., p. 95.

18. Bullitt to Hull, May 21, 1934, ibid., p. 99.

19. Bullitt to Hull, June 16, 1934, ibid., p. 109.

20. *New York Times*, February 3, 1935.

21. Moore to Sayre, July 19, 1934; *FR: Soviet Union, 1933-39*, p. 119.

22. Moore to Sayre, July 19, 1934, ibid., p. 120.

23. Hull to Bullitt, April 18, 1934, ibid., p. 85.

24. As the State Department experts admitted in an interdepartmental memorandum of November 15, 1945, when the "gentleman's agreement" was accidentally discovered by a researcher working in an index file. 711.61/353½, National Archives.

25. Hull to Bullitt, July 16, 1934, *FR: Soviet Union, 1933-39*, p. 117.

26. Perhaps significant are FDR's replies in a press conference which touched on the subject of debts. Can you tell us, a reporter asked, whether Litvinov in his discussions with you relative to recognition made any promise that Russia would eventually settle the debt? FDR replied that the reporter had better try the State Department: "That is one thing you have to phrase exactly." Press Conferences, V (February 2, 1935), 87. The reporter continued: "Secretary Hull said he

could not remember whether you had said anything or not." The reporter asked if it was our understanding that Russia promised to settle debts. FDR: "I think there was a formal statement at that time." Ibid. When questioned further on Litvinov's statement that Roosevelt had promised him a loan, FDR refused direct comment: "You will have to try the State Department again." Ibid., V (February 6, 1935), 95. Records of the press conferences are at the Roosevelt Library at Hyde Park.

27. Bullitt to Hull, July 17, 1934, *FR: Soviet Union, 1933-39*, p. 119.

28. This was the impression of George Kennan, third secretary of Bullitt's embassy. Kennan interview. The Commissar attempted to make clear his position by explaining to Bullitt that although he desired the best possible relations with the United States he could not jeopardize Soviet relations with the rest of the world. The claims against the Soviet Union of England, France, Germany, etc., were much larger than the claims of America. These claims had been forgotten; but the moment Russia made a settlement with the United States all other nations would demand settlement. Therefore a settlement had to be made with the United States which would be on a basis that no other nation could accept. Since it was physically impossible for other nations to lend Russia double the amount of their huge claims, it was on this basis that settlement would have to occur. This was Litvinov's stand in July, 1934. Bullitt to Hull, July 9, 1934, *FR: Soviet Union, 1933-39*, pp. 115-16.

29. British documents reveal that during the spring and summer of 1934, British-Soviet relations were not of the best. Both nations in their diplomatic contact stressed their eagerness for improved relations. See Sir Llewellyn Woodward and Rohan Butler, eds., *Documents on British Foreign Policy, 1919-1939* (London, 1958), Second Series, VII, 586-743.

30. Bullitt to Hull, October 10, 1934, *FR: Soviet Union, 1933-39*, p. 159.

31. Bullitt to Hull, May 4, 1934, 761.62/305, National Archives. Bullitt here referred to Litvinov as "posing dexterously as the disappointed idealist whose peaceful proposals are rejected by scheming neighbors for ulterior motives."

32. Bullitt to Hull, September 13, 1934, *FR: Soviet Union, 1933-39*, p. 145.

33. Hull to Bullitt, September 17, 1934, ibid., p. 148.

34. Hull to Bullitt, September 17, 1934, ibid., p. 146.

35. Of interest is the fact that Roosevelt shared Bullitt's optimism. At a press conference on September 26, 1934, a reporter asked whether Roosevelt was a little disappointed over the results of recognition. "Oh, no," FDR replied. The reporter continued, "You did not expect any more?" FDR: "Oh, it will be worked out some way." Press Conferences IV (September 26, 1934), 88-89, Franklin D. Roosevelt papers.

36. Louis Fischer, who was close to the Russians during the thirties, comments on the mutual dislike which developed between Bullitt and Litvinov. Several times Litvinov told Fischer of his regret that Washington had not sent a career diplomat instead of an "ambitious and impatient" one who hoped to rise to fame on success or failure in Russia. Fischer notes also the Russian suspicion that Bullitt was "not serious." *Men and Politics* (New York, 1941), p. 303. Bullitt has claimed that he never trusted Litvinov, not from the first. Bullitt interview, September 19, 1955.

37. "He was indeed a redoubtable antagonist," Ambassador Dirksen commented of Litvinov, "being quick-witted and well versed in affairs." Herbert Von Dirksen, *Moscow, Tokyo, London* (Norman, Oklahoma, 1952), p. 81.

38. Roosevelt to Bullitt, May 9, 1934, PSF, 15, Roosevelt papers.

39. Bullitt to Hull, July 27, 1934, *FR: Soviet Union, 1933-39*, p. 124. See Kelley memorandum to Hull of November 17, 1934, emphasizing that according to embassy reports "the attitude of Litvinov" had played a large role in the difficulties the United States was encountering in reaching a settlement of the debt question. 861.44/Litvinov/12, National Archives.

40. Bullitt to Hull, September 9, 1934, *FR: Soviet Union, 1933-39*, p. 143. Earlier, Bullitt had written Hull that he had taken advantage of certain avenues to Voroshilov and Stalin to let the highest circles of the Soviet government know that in his opinion Litvinov was "playing a somewhat dangerous game of being so intransigent with regard to American claims." Bullitt to Hull, July 23, 1934, 761.00/245, National Archives.

41. Bullitt to Hull, September 9, 1934, *FR: Soviet Union, 1933-39*, p. 143.

42. Bullitt to Hull, September 15, 1934, ibid., p. 147.

43. Bullitt to Hull, June 30, 1934, ibid., p. 113. The same techniques of flattery were employed on Bullitt's successor, Joseph Davies, and with similar success. Richard H. Ullman, "The Davies Mission and

United States-Soviet Relations, 1937-1941," *World Politics*, IX (January, 1957), 220-39.

44. Bullitt to Hull, July 22, 1934, *FR: Soviet Union, 1933-39*, p. 121; Bullitt to Hull, July 23, 1934, 761.00/245, National Archives.

45. Bullitt to Roosevelt, July 14, 1934, PSF, 15, Roosevelt papers.

46. Bullitt to Roosevelt, August 5, 1934, PSF, 15, Roosevelt papers.

47. Sokolnikov was in charge of Far Eastern affairs in the Soviet foreign office.

48. Bullitt to Hull, April 16, 1934, *FR: 1934*, III, p. 110. Ambassador Grew in Tokyo reported a similar belief that the Japanese army would reach the zenith of its combat efficiency in 1935. Grew to Hull, December 14, 1933, *FR: 1933* (Washington, 1949) III, 483.

49. Bullitt to Roosevelt, September 8, 1934, PSF, 15, Roosevelt papers.

50. Bullitt to Hull, July 22, 1934, *FR: Soviet Union, 1933-39*, p. 122.

51. Bullitt to Roosevelt, August 5, 1934, PSF, 15, Roosevelt papers.

52. Lev M. Karakhan was assistant commissar for foreign affairs, 1931-1934. Litvinov liked him no better than he did Bullitt. Of Karakhan, Dirksen has written: "Karakhan, an astute and wily Armenian . . . could play tennis, drive his own smart cabriolet, and court the ballerinas of the Bolshoi Theater without prejudice to his party standing," Dirksen, p. 82. See Fischer, pp. 128-29 for Litvinov's antagonism to Karakhan; also Wiley to Hull, February 3, 1935, *FR: Soviet Union, 1933-39*, p. 175.

53. Bullitt to Roosevelt, August 5, 1934, PSF, 15; Bullitt to Kelley, May 12, 1934, 861.40634/5, National Archives. Bullitt requested moving pictures from the United States Polo Association in order to facilitate the teaching of Polo to the Red Army. Bullitt to Hull, October 2, 1934, 861.5017/Living Conditions/769no. 188, National Archives. Bullitt reported that he personally imported the polo balls and mallets and that a National Polo Championship Tournament would be held in Russia the next summer. See Thayer, chapter 8, "Polo for the Proletariat," for a hilarious account of Bullitt's efforts.

54. Bullitt to Roosevelt, August 5, 1934, PSF, 15, Roosevelt papers.

55. Ibid. Bullitt paid approximately $800 to equip four baseball teams. Bullitt to Kelley, April 20, 1934, E/tfv 861.40634/1, National Archives.

56. Thayer, p. 156.

57. Bullitt to Roosevelt, May 1, 1935, PSF, 15, Roosevelt papers.

58. Thayer, p. 160.

59. Although Bullitt was delighted with his party, it was later used as an example of what an ambassador should *not* do. See Graham Stuart, *American Diplomatic and Consular Practice* (New York, 1952), p. 213-14. Stuart refers to Bullitt's "opulent extravagance" as earning him notoriety. Certainly it did in Moscow where one Russian lady declared that Bullitt had evidently not decided whether being an ambassador was a job or a charade.

60. Maxim Litvinov, *Notes for a Journal* (New York, 1955) is believed to be largely a forgery. See introduction to the volume by E. H. Carr.

61. Dirksen, p. 81.

62. *Vneshniaia Politika, SSSR* (Moscow, 1937), pp. 74-96 as cited in Henry L. Roberts, "Maxim Litvinov," in Gordon A. Craig and Felix Gilbert, eds., *The Diplomats, 1919-1939* (Princeton, 1953), p. 352.

63. Maxim Litvinov, *Against Aggression* (New York, 1939), pp. 35-45.

64. Roberts, p. 364.

65. F. P. Walters, *A History of the League of Nations* (London, 1952), II, 712.

66. Roberts, p. 370.

67. Dirksen, p. 81.

68. Merle Fainsod, *How Russia is Ruled* (Massachusetts, 1953), p. 282. Julian Towster writes that because of the sensitiveness attached to foreign policy decisions there came to be a "particularly close, direct, and continual relationship . . . between the Politburo and the Narkomindel in the conduct and control of foreign affairs." Julian Towster, *Political Power in the USSR, 1917-1947* (New York, 1948), p. 162. Of interest is an article written by Max Beloff in 1950 revising certain assumptions presented in his history of Soviet foreign policy. Beloff contends that he did not lay enough stress on the essentially subordinate nature of Litvinov's role. But he points out that this does not mean that there was no time during which Russia was prepared to cooperate to stave off Germany. Max Beloff, "Soviet Foreign Policy, 1929-1941: Some Notes," *Soviet Studies* (Oxford), II (October, 1950), 125-27.

69. Roberts, p. 372; French scholar, R. Girardet contends that Soviet diplomacy always had several irons in the fire and that Litvinov's policy was one of those irons. R. Girardet, "Litvinov et ses Enigmes," in Jean-Baptiste Duroselle, ed., *Les Relations Germano-Soviétiques de 1933 à 1939* (Paris, 1954), pp. 133-34.

70. Ambassador Bingham to Hull, July 10, 1934, *FR: 1934* (Washing-

ton, 1951), I, 494-95; Campbell to Sir R. Vansittart, July 26, 1934, *Documents on British Foreign Policy* (London, 1957), Second Series, VI, 875-76.

71. Gustav Hilger and A. G. Meyer, *The Incompatible Allies* (New York, 1953), p. 267.

72. Georges Castellan, "Reichswehr et Armée Rouge, 1920-1939," in *Les Relations Germano-Soviétiques de 1933 à 1939*, p. 219. Ambassador Dirksen, who had preceded Nadolny as ambassador, had also urged Soviet friendship, stressing that "collaboration with Germany is the most logical and the most coveted combination for the Soviet Union." Dirksen to the foreign ministry, February 20, 1933, *Documents on German Foreign Policy, 1918-1945* (Washington, 1957), Series C, I, 63.

73. Hilger and Meyer, p. 267.

74. Hilger and Meyer, p. 270; Dirksen to foreign ministry, May 14, 1933, *German Documents*, Series C, I, 422. See also Castellan, "Reichswehr et Armée Rouge," pp. 219-20.

75. Hilger and Meyer, p. 270. To Dirksen, Voroshilov stated that he was a good friend of Germany and had not changed in his attitude. The Soviet government, he added, also desired a continuation of Rapallo. Dirksen to foreign ministry, May 14, 1933, *German Documents*, Series C, I, 422.

76. The thesis that it was Hitler, not Stalin, who was responsible for the rupture in relations is born out by General Helm Speidel of the German air force, who recalls that in the summer of 1933 Hitler ordered all military relations with Russia liquidated. Castellan, "Reichswehr et Armée Rouge," p. 41. Castellan further reports that General Koestring in a 1948 interview corroborated the Speidel contention. Ibid., p. 206. In a conversation with Polish Ambassador Lipski in May, 1935, Hitler boasted that he had revoked the "former negative Rapallo policy towards Poland, represented by the Reichswehr with Groner and Schleicher at its head." Lipski to Beck, May 23, 1935, *Official Documents concerning Polish-German and Polish-Soviet Relations, 1933-1939* (London, 1940), p. 29.

77. Roberts, p. 369. In the opinion of George Kennan, Stalin was "playing desperately" for the Rapallo line. Stalin's flirtations with the Western powers and the League of Nations—through Litvinov—probably represented in his mind a means of putting pressure on Hitler to continue the Rapallo policy. Rapallo gave to Stalin at one and the same time access to the German military and economic strength and a coun-

terbalance to the influence of the German Communist Party in the world Communist movement. Letter of George Kennan to the writer, February 27, 1957. See also Dirksen, p. 116; Castellan, "Reichswehr et Armée Rouge," p. 252; and Hilger and Meyer, p. 269.

78. Grew to Hull, July 2, 1934, *FR: 1934*, III, 204. Grew expressed the opinion that likelihood of a Soviet-Japanese war in 1934 seemed to have passed. Bullitt to Hull, July 30, 1934, 761.94/766, National Archives. Bullitt reported Litvinov's statement that he was no longer "in the least worried" in regard to the possibility of Japanese attack. Radek had expressed similar optimism.

79. Roberts, p. 352.

80. See above p. 114 and Bullitt to Hull, June 14, 1934, *FR: Soviet Union, 1933-39*, p. 107. A revealing conversation took place between Bullitt and Litvinov on July 20, 1934. Bullitt writes that he discussed with Litvinov the status of the Eastern Locarno negotiations. Litvinov "expressed the hope more or less as a joke that the Government of the United States would follow the example of the British Government and give its public endorsement to the Eastern Locarno proposal. In reply I merely smiled." Bullitt to Hull, July 20, 1934, *FR: 1934*, I, 497. A year later, in May, 1935, Bullitt wrote to Roosevelt saying, "I see no way that we can achieve anything by attempting to stop the march of events—horrible as it is—except by our own involvement in war and I hope that you will turn a very deaf ear to the songs of the sirens who must be keeping you awake nights with their music. I saw that Stimson had donned the mermaid's tail and there must be a thousand others whose hearts are better than their heads." Bullitt to Roosevelt, May 1, 1935, PSF, 15, Roosevelt papers.

81. Hull to Bullitt, September 17, 1934, *FR: Soviet Union 1933-39*, p. 148.

82. Morgenthau, *Diaries*, p. 73.

83. Bullitt to Hull, March 14, 1934, *FR: 1934*, III, p. 74.

84. Bullitt to Hull, March 14, 1934, 761.00/239, National Archives.

85. At a conference attended by FDR, Moffat, Admiral Standley, and Norman Davis, on October 3, 1934, Nancy Hooker, ed., *The Moffat Papers* (Cambridge, Massachusetts, 1956), p. 117.

86. Phillips to Moffat, October 22, 1934, 500.A15A4/2600⅓, National Archives. These were the terms FDR envisaged: 1) the signatory powers agree that over a period of ten years they will not allow any armed forces to cross the frontier of any neighbor nation or of any

other nation and that such an act is declared to be the act of an aggressor; 2) every signatory power agrees that, in the event of an act of aggression, as defined above, it will decline to trade with aggressor; 3) at the end of five years, the League of Nations will call a disarmament conference, in view of this agreement, to discuss limitation of arms and also extension and strengthening of the agreement itself.

87. Moffat to Phillips, October 23, 1934, 500.A15A4/2600⅔, National Archives.

88. Bullitt to Hull, January 4, 1934, 761.62/296, National Archives.

89. Bullitt interview, September 19, 1955; also see Joseph Alsop and Robert Kintner, *American White Paper* (New York, 1940), p. 52.

VII. THE EDUCATION

1. William E. Dodd, Jr., and Martha Dodd, eds., *Ambassador Dodd's Diary, 1933-1938* (New York, 1941), pp. 277-78.

2. Bullitt to Hull, May 9 1934, 120.36/206, National Archives. Bullitt pointed out that clerks were threatening to resign because they had been unable to bring their wives due to lack of space. But Bullitt observed that since life was so "abnormal and unpleasant," he believed the wives would be most unhappy in Russia. He was convinced that "discontented wives will not produce the contentment of discontented husbands," but nevertheless felt it was *"contra bonos mores"* to attempt to convince any staff member that the presence of his wife would make him more miserable. Bullitt to Hull, May 21, 1934, 124.611/153, National Archives.

3. Bullitt to Hull, July 12, 1934, 123 William C. Bullitt/74, National Archives.

4. Eugene Lyons, *Assignment in Utopia* (New York, 1937), pp. 500-501.

5. Undated memorandum written by Bullitt sometime in 1918, Bullitt papers at Yale University.

6. Bullitt to Hull, October 2, 1934, 861.5017 Living Conditions/769, National Archives. In May, 1935, Bullitt wrote to FDR that the terror had risen to such a pitch that the least of the Muscovites, as well as the greatest, was in fear. "Almost no one dares have any contact with foreigners and this is not unbased fear but a proper sense of reality." The "only real friend" of the embassy, George Andreychine, was in

prison awaiting either death or exile. Bullitt wrote that even the dentists who had treated the foreigners had been exiled "leaving members of the American Embassy hanging on to temporary fillings!" "I can, of course, do nothing to save anyone. In fact, *strictly between ourselves*," Bullitt wrote, "I got a message from Andreychine, sent grapevine from the OGPU . . . prison asking me for God's sake to do nothing to try to save him, if I should he would certainly be shot." Bullitt to Roosevelt, May 1, 1935, PSF, 15, Franklin D. Roosevelt papers.

7. Point 4 of propaganda pledge of November 16, 1933, *Foreign Relations of the United States: The Soviet Union, 1933-39* (Washington, 1952), p. 29.

8. 861.00 Congress of Communist International VII/38;99;119. National Archives.

9. Bullitt followed the Russian speeches in translation. He did not know the language although he had begun studying it when he arrived in Moscow.

10. Bullitt has been criticized by W. A. Williams and L. Fischer for taking this point of view. Both Williams and Fischer contend that the popular front policy, if fully developed, might have prevented war. William A. Williams, *American-Russian Relations: 1781-1947* (New York, 1952), p. 241; Louis Fischer, *Men and Politics* (New York, 1941), pp. 307-308.

11. Bullitt to Hull, July 14, 1935, 861.00 Congress Communist International VII/19, National Archives.

12. Bullitt accepted this thesis although he noted that certain observers close to the Kremlin contended that the postponement of the Congress from the autumn of 1934 did not mean that indefinite postponement would follow. The delay, they claimed, was for the purpose of attempting to persuade the left wing Socialists of all countries to join with the Communists in the forthcoming Comintern Congress.. The Congress when held would therefore be of extreme importance. This we know now was the case since the Comintern meeting in 1935 proclaimed the popular front. Bullitt, however, considered those who held to the view of indefinite postponement "better informed" than those who predicted a meeting of importance in 1935. Bullitt believed that activities of the Third International had been subordinated completely to the interests of the Soviet Union as a national state. Bullitt to Hull, October 2, 1934, 861.00 Congress Communist International VII/6, National Archives.

13. The negotiations for an Eastern Security Pact in the years 1934-35 broke against the resistance of Germany to any multilateral arrangement which might act to curb her eastern ambitions. Poland's refusal to enter into a system in which Germany would have no part prevented even a more modest measure. The only tangible results of Litvinov's efforts were the Russian pacts of 1935 with France and Czechoslovakia.

14. Bullitt to Hull, October 2, 1934, 861.5017 Living Conditions/769, National Archives.

15. Bullitt to Hull, July 8, 1935, *FR: Soviet Union, 1933-39*, p. 222.

16. Bullitt to Hull, July 9, 1935, ibid., p. 223.

17. Although Litvinov's "collective security" and the "popular front" are often identified, the change in Comintern line at the Congress of 1935 did not really eradicate the difference between the two policies. Litvinov continued to be embarrassed by activities of his comrades. In 1936, for example, Coulondre pointed out to him that the interference of the Comintern in French internal affairs was imperiling the Franco-Soviet pact. In response, Litvinov could only fall back on his old claim that the Comintern had nothing to do with the foreign policy of his government. Henry L. Roberts, "Maxim Litvinov," in Gordon A. Craig and Felix Gilbert, eds., *The Diplomats, 1919-1939* (Princeton, 1953), p. 368.

18. Bullitt to Hull, August 21, 1935. 861.00 Congress Communist International, VII/56-62, National Archives.

19. Bullitt to Hull, August 25, 1935, *FR: Soviet Union, 1933-39*, p. 250.

20. Although Litvinov would himself have preferred that the Comintern Congress did not meet in Moscow, he insisted afterward that his conscience was clear; that he had said to the President that he could not be responsible for the Third International; and that the President had replied that he would hold the Soviet Union to its pledge only in case of important injury to the United States. Bullitt replied that his memory was entirely different: he recalled Litvinov saying that he could make no promises about the Comintern but that the President told him that he would hold him to strict accountability and that he, Litvinov, had subsequently signed the pledge. Litvinov replied that he had made his statement to FDR after signing the pledge. This statement, Bullitt believed, made Litvinov's position even weaker. Bullitt to Hull, November 9, 1935, *FR: Soviet Union, 1933-39*, pp. 264-65.

21. Bullitt to Hull, August 29, 1935, 711.61/541, National Archives.

22. Hull to Bullitt, August 30, 1935, 711.61/542B, National Archives. A statement was released to the press on September 1, 1935. On September 6, Ickes noted in his diary that at the last cabinet meeting there was discussion of the exchange of notes between Russia and the United States. FDR said he could not go on exchanging notes indefinitely and indicated that instead of sending another note a statement would probably be given to the press telling Russia to "be good or suffer the consequences." Ickes observed that later, however, another note was sent and there the episode seemed to rest. Harold L. Ickes, *The Secret Diary of Harold L. Ickes: The First Thousand Days* (New York, 1953), p. 430.

23. Bullitt to Hull, November 9, 1935, *FR: Soviet Union, 1933-39*, p. 265.

24. Richard H. Ullman, "The Davies Mission and United States-Soviet Relations, 1937-1941," *World Politics*, IX (January, 1957), p. 233.

25. Bullitt to Hull, March 19, 1936, 761.00/269, National Archives.

26. Bullitt to Hull, July 19, 1935, 761.00/260, National Archives. Excerpts from this dispatch appear in *FR: Soviet Union, 1933-39*, pp. 224-27. Attached to this dispatch is a memorandum by Robert Kelley to Hull, Phillips, and Moore praising Bullitt's insight and pointing out that his conclusions were in agreement with those arrived at by experts studying the subject.

27. Bullitt to Hull, March 19, 1936, 761.00/269, National Archives.

28. Bullitt to Hull, April 20, 1936, *FR: Soviet Union, 1933-39*, pp. 294-96.

29. Bullitt interview, September 19, 1955. Bullitt's outrage in this instance recalls the remark of Felix Frankfurter, Harvard law professor, upon meeting Bullitt again in 1933. Remembering Bullitt from the Wilson days, Frankfurter asked, " 'Well, Bill, have you learned to keep your shirt on yet?' " " 'Absolutely,' " Bullitt laughed, " 'it is nailed down this time.' " Raymond Moley, *After Seven Years* (New York, 1939), p. 136.

30. Fischer, *Men and Politics*, p. 308.

31. Roosevelt to Bullitt, April 21, 1936, Elliott Roosevelt, ed., *F.D.R. His Personal Letters, 1928-1945* (New York, 1950), I, 583.

32. Bullitt to M. de Kalb Brogley, December 5, 1947, in M. de Kalb Brogley, "William C. Bullitt and American-Russian Relations," unpublished master's thesis, University of Wisconsin, 1949, pp. 62-63.

33. *New York Times*, August 2, 1936.

34. Harold L. Ickes, *The Secret Diary of Harold Ickes: The Lowering Clouds* (New York, 1955), p. 124.

35. Bullitt interview, September 19, 1955.

36. William W. Kaufmann, "Two American Ambassadors: Bullitt and Kennedy," in Craig and Gilbert, *The Diplomats*, (Princeton, 1953), p. 654.

37. Bullitt to Hull, May 31, 1937, 852.00/5567, National Archives.

38. Bullitt to Hull, April 20, 1936, 861.01/2120, National Archives.

39. Dodd, pp. 309, 372.

40. Bullitt to Brogley, December 5, 1947, in Brogley, pp. 62-63.

41. The loan was never granted. Dodd, p. 309.

42. Bullitt to Hull, February 11, 1937, 751.6111/185, National Archives.

43. Bullitt to Hull, February 23, 1937, 740.00/118, National Archives.

44. Bullitt to Hull, September 30, 1937, 751.6111/196; February 7, 1938, 740.00/287, National Archives.

45. Bullitt to Hull, September 24, 1937, 852.00/6545; January 25, 1938, 740.00/277; February 18, 1938, 740.00/298, National Archives.

46. But Bullitt suspected that the British were working behind the scenes to prevent rapproachement. Donald F. Whitehead, "The Making of Foreign Policy during President Roosevelt's First Term, 1933-1937," unpublished doctoral dissertation, University of Chicago, 1952, pp. 178-79.

47. Bullitt to Hull, December 16, 1936, as cited in Charles C. Tansill, *Back Door to War: The Roosevelt Foreign Policy, 1933-1941* (Chicago, 1952), p. 321. Probably Schacht wanted these conversations largely in reference to the Tripartite Monetary Pact.

48. Bullitt to Hull, February 20, 1937, 740.00/117, National Archives.

49. Tansill, p. 321.

50. It is a point of interest that the phrase "I hate war," which Roosevelt used so effectively in his Chautauqua speech, was one that Bullitt had carried in his memory since 1917. During a private talk with President Wilson soon after America's declaration of war, Wilson, with tears in his eyes, had seized Bullitt's hands and, with great emotion, had used the expression. Bullitt related this story to Sam Rosenman. Samuel I. Rosenman, *Working with Roosevelt* (New York, 1952), p. 108.

51. Bullitt to Hull, December 16, 1936, 751.62/380, National Archives. Until the ground had been prepared by direct conversation between French and Germans, however, he believed that such a pro-

nouncement should be avoided. In December, 1936, Bullitt sent Marcel Knech, editor of *Le Matin*, to Dodd with a message asking Dodd to urge FDR to take a hand in working for a Franco-German alliance. Dodd, p. 372.

52. Phipps to Foreign Office, June 13, 1934, *Documents on British Foreign Policy* (London, 1957), Second Series, VI, 751.

53. Phipps to Dodd, February 12, 1936, Dodd, p. 310.

54. Dodd, p. 372.

55. Bullitt to Hull, April 30, 1937, 740.00/156, National Archives.

56. Dodd, p. 310.

57. F. L. Ford and C. Schorske, "The Voice in the Wilderness: Robert Coulondre" in Craig and Gilbert, *The Diplomats*, pp. 555, 570, 577.

58. Bullitt to Hull, April 30, 1937, 740.00/158, National Archives.

59. Winston S. Churchill, *The Second World War: The Gathering Storm* (Boston, 1948), pp. 118-19.

60. Kaufmann, p. 656.

61. *Foreign Relations, 1938* (Washington, 1955), I, 601.

62. As late as September, 1938, Bullitt urged Washington to avoid encouraging the French to go to war in order to keep 3,200,000 Sudetens under the rule of 7,000,000 Czechs. To the French Bullitt made it clear that the United States would not contemplate sending troops overseas to safeguard provisions of Versailles. Gordon Wright, "Ambassador Bullitt and the Fall of France," *World Politics*, X (October, 1957), 70.

63. Georges Bonnet, *Défense de la Paix* (Geneva, 1946), I, 294. Beneš has accused Bullitt of maintaining a wholly negative attitude toward the Czechs during the September, 1938 crisis. Bullitt did not hide his feelings according to Beneš, who records that Daladier clearly hinted that Bullitt supported his policy of appeasement. Bullitt made it clear that in his view Prague was not behaving with sufficient circumspection toward the German minority and that President Beneš was an anti-German chauvinist whose policy was endangering European peace. Eduard Beneš, *Memoirs: From Munich to New War and New Victory* (London, 1954; trans. Godfrey Lies), p. 173.

64. William L. Langer and S. Everett Gleason, *The World Crisis and American Foreign Policy: The Challenge to Isolation, 1937-1940* (New York, 1952), p. 37.

65. On September 24 Bullitt cabled Washington urging that if the

British and French decided to reject the German demands of September 23, Roosevelt should appeal for an International Hague Conference with American participation to discuss means of preserving peace. Langer and Gleason, *Challenge to Isolation*, p. 37.

66. Fischer, *Men and Politics*, p. 591.

67. Bullitt to Hull, March 18, 1939, 740.00/632, National Archives. Bullitt advocated his new position with a vigor customary to himself but confusing to contemporaries. The liberal Dodd continued to suspect Bullitt of being pro-Nazi. Dodd, pp. 371-72. The appeasement-minded ambassador to London, Joseph Kennedy, and later the isolationist historian, Charles Tansill, assigned to William C. Bullitt considerable blame both for drawing America into war and for igniting the general European conflict. Walter Millis, ed., *The Forrestal Diaries* (New York, 1951), pp. 121-22; Charles C. Tansill, *Back Door to War: The Roosevelt Foreign Policy, 1933-1941* (Chicago, 1952), pp. 556-57.

68. As early as October, 1938—after Munich—Bullitt had urged expanded plane production on FDR. He also made successful efforts at supplying France with American-made airplanes; in December, 1938, the first of the French purchasing missions had slipped into New York. Plane production remained a source of concern to Bullitt and it was he who was largely responsible for convincing Roosevelt of the need to expand America's output. Langer and Gleason, *Challenge to Isolation*, p. 481.

69. The President rejected this proposal for fear of seeming to align the country irrevocably against the Axis. Ibid., p. 82.

70. Basil Rauch, *Roosevelt from Munich to Pearl Harbor: A Study in the Creation of a Foreign Policy* (New York, 1950), p. 117.

71. The fleet was not sent because Washington felt that as long as the main fleet was in the Pacific there was not enough force in the Atlantic to risk a major demonstration. Cordell Hull, *Memoirs* (New York, 1948), I, 780-81.

72. William L. Langer and S. Everett Gleason, *The World Crisis and American Foreign Policy: The Undeclared War, 1940-1941* (New York, 1953), p. 270.

73. Conversation of May 14, 1941, as cited in Langer and Gleason, *Undeclared War*, pp. 455-56.

74. *New York Times*, October 24, 1941.

75. See dispatches from Bullitt to Hull for February and March, 1939, 852.01/469; 498; 500; 506; 525, National Archives. Hull has defended recognition of Franco as an action by which the American

government hoped to prevent the war in Spain from erupting into a general European war. Hull, I, 483. American Ambassador to Spain Claude Bowers opposed Hull's position. According to Bowers, Roosevelt was aware by March, 1939, that he had made a mistake in Spain regarding the embargo. He quotes the President as saying to him: " 'We have made a mistake; you have been right all along.' " Claude Bowers, *My Mission to Spain: Watching the Rehearsal for World War II* (New York, 1954), pp. 416-18. However, the United States subsequently recognized the Franco regime. Robert Bendiner has accused Bullitt of being one of those responsible for Roosevelt's "mistake." According to Bendiner, Bullitt, like Kennedy in London, repeatedly telephoned the President urging him to retain the embargo so as not to embarrass the British and French. When Bowers arrived in Paris to arrange help for the starving Spaniards and to urge on the President once more the importance of aiding the Loyalists, he thought it best, according to Bendiner, to keep his visit a secret from Bullitt. Bendiner does not document these allegations. Robert Bendiner, *The Riddle of the State Department* (New York, 1942), pp. 59-60.

76. Ickes, *Diary*, I, 658, conversation of August 10, 1936. Louis Fischer learned from Lord Lothian that Bullitt, in April, 1936, came to Lothian and told him and other Britishers that the Bolsheviki were preparing a revolution in Spain. Fischer accuses Bullitt of making ample contribution to the Fascist victory in Spain by informing responsible persons in England that Moscow was preparing trouble in Spain. When the trouble came, the British appeasers naturally concluded it was this which Bullitt had foreseen. Fischer points out that the Spanish war was started by Franco and not the Communists. Fischer, *Men and Politics*, p. 586. Bullitt reported in 1936 that the French were convinced the Soviets intended to push the conflict in Spain to the end. The French supposed that while Russia would suffer an initial defeat by the overthrow of the Madrid and Barcelona governments, the extensive ambitions of Germany and Italy in Spanish Morocco and the Balearic Isles would eventually result in war with England and France and the consequence would be the "bolshevization of the whole of Europe." Bullitt to Hull, November 25, 1936, 852.00/3886, National Archives.

77. Hull, I, 707. Bullitt has written that FDR had been "so angered by Stalin's aggressions against Finland that he had used his influence to have the Soviet Union expelled from the League of Nations." William C. Bullitt, "How We Won the War and Lost the Peace," *Life*, XXV (August 30, 1948), 91. Hull's recollections are different. He claims

that when the Russo-Finnish case was about to come before the League, Bullitt on December 1 asked FDR and Hull to urge Britain and France to take a strong stand against Russia at Geneva. Hull replied to Bullitt on December 4 that he could not urge Britain and France to pursue a certain course as League members since the United States was not a member. Also he and the President did not wish to offend strong isolationist sentiment in the United States. Hull, I, 707. There is no evidence in available documents in the National Archives or at Hyde Park to support Bullitt's recollection. FDR may simply have expressed personal anger to Bullitt and implied action which he did not take.

78. According to Leger, the British hoped for eventual Russian cooperation and feared driving the Russians further into the Nazi camp—an idea which Leger incorrectly considered "idiotic." Leger claimed that it was Daladier's insistence that convinced the British finally to back the move for Russian expulsion from the League. Bullitt to Hull, December 14, 1939, 740.0011 European War 1939/162, National Archives.

79. When the Germans arrived, Bullitt and General Henri Dentz, military governor, delivered Paris to the enemy—June 14. Bullitt remained in Paris until June 30 caring for Americans and stranded British and other Allied nationals.

80. Hull writes: "Had Bullitt, with his unequaled contacts with the leaders of the French Government, been able to represent us during those historic days, it is possible, if not probable, that the Government would have taken the fleet, gone to North Africa, and continued the fight from there." Hull, I, 789.

81. Bullitt's letter to the *Times* was prompted chiefly by Hull's implication that Bullitt disobeyed Department instructions by remaining in Paris. Bullitt writes that on May 27, 1940, Hull, in answer to Bullitt's request that he be allowed to remain in Paris, sent a telegram indicating Roosevelt's approval that Anthony Biddle should act as Bullitt's deputy to the French government. He implied that Bullitt could stay on in Paris. In accord with this telegram, Bullitt informed the French government that he would do so. After most of the government had left Paris, and the city was in panic produced in part by the approach of the German army, in part by the Communists, whose clandestine radio was calling for revolt, Roosevelt called on the telephone. " 'Bill,' " he said, " 'you'll be killed if you stay in Paris, and I don't want you killed. I want you back here. If the Communists don't get you before the Nazis come in, the Nazis will kill you. They hate you worse than any-

one.' " "I replied that the prospect did not disturb me." The President continued to talk about Bullitt's safety, referring to the Communist radio threats and anonymous threats of murder. Bullitt said he should have thought of all that, as he himself did, before having him commit himself to assume protection of French and Allied interests in Paris. FDR had no argument in reply. According to Bullitt, Roosevelt did not intimate that he thought any advantage could be gained by Bullitt's leaving with the government. After saying he would pray God to take care of Bullitt he hung up. Then he sent Bullitt a telegram countersigned by Hull concluding with, " 'On behalf of the Government of the United States I salute you in this hour of crisis, and personally you have my ever affectionate regard.' " Bullitt writes that he therefore considers it unreasonable, in view of Hull's May 27 answer and this later telegram, for Hull to have written that " 'as the Germans approached Paris, Bullitt communicated to the President direct that he knew the State Department would oppose the proposal he was about to make, hence he was approaching him personally. He then proposed staying in Paris, instead of going with the French Government.' " *New York Times*, February 19, 1948. In this case one is inclined to accept Bullitt's recollections. They have the support of FDR, who, on June 20, 1940, sent Hull a *New York Times* and a Washington *Post* clipping, both of which indicated Hull's annoyance that Bullitt had remained in Paris. FDR wrote: "Don't you think, in fairness to Bullitt, that you should say something, calling the newspapers by their right names. It is, after all, only fair to Bullitt." Roosevelt to Hull, June 20, 1940, OF, 799, Roosevelt papers.

82. Bullitt to Hull, June 11, 1940: June 12, 1940, 740.0011 European War, 1939/3658 and 3691³/14 as cited in Wright, p. 86.

83. Wright, pp. 86-87.

84. Hull, I, 772.

85. William L. Langer, *Our Vichy Gamble* (New York, 1947), pp. 21-22.

86. Ibid., p. 22. This is also the opinion of Wright, p. 90.

VIII. CONCLUSION: THE DECLINE

1. William L. Langer, *Our Vichy Gamble* (New York, 1947), p. 76. Because of his advocacy of American diplomatic relations with Vichy, Bullitt was accused of "roaming around the country pleading

the cause of the . . . Nazi-controlled Petain government," and "advocating dictatorship." *Congressional Record*, August 19, 1940, pp. 10478-80, 15010. Such charges were gross distortions. In July, 1941, Bullitt wrote FDR suggesting that since the Free French forces were fighting Hitler and since the United States had declared its willingness to help all forces fighting Hitler, FDR ought to announce that the country would supply the Free French in Equatorial Africa. "It is in our interest to go on trying to stiffen Petain, energize Weygand, and support de Gaulle. And it is not beyond the wit of man to do all three without breaking relations with Vichy." Bullitt to Roosevelt, July 1, 1941, PPF, 1124, Franklin D. Roosevelt papers.

2. Howe died in 1936.

3. William L. Langer and S. Everett Gleason, *The World Crisis and American Foreign Policy: The Challenge to Isolation, 1937-1940* (New York, 1952), p. 509.

4. Ibid., p. 510.

5. Harold L. Ickes, *The Secret Diary of Harold Ickes: The Lowering Clouds* (New York, 1955), III, 343-44. Probably at Bullitt's behest, his secretary and good friend, Carmel Offie, had phoned Mrs. Ickes asking her to speak to Ickes on Bullitt's behalf. Offie explained that Bullitt was becoming restless and unhappy over his awkward status to the degree that he was not going around and seeing people. Ibid.

6. Grace Tully, *F.D.R. My Boss* (New York, 1949), p. 242.

7. See the Bullitt-Roosevelt letters at Hyde Park.

8. Ickes, *Diary*, III, 278, 487.

9. Ibid., 520.

10. Ibid., 538.

11. William L. Langer and S. Everett Gleason, *The World Crisis and American Foreign Policy: The Undeclared War, 1940-1941* (New York, 1953), p. 798.

12. See above, p. 3.

13. Langer and Gleason, *Challenge to Isolation*, p. 126.

14. Joseph E. Davies, *Mission to Moscow* (New York, 1941), p. 511.

15. Davies, p. 496.

16. It is the view of Langer and Gleason that Davies' arguments may well have been the ones that influenced the President. *Undeclared War*, p. 540.

17. According to Bullitt, Roosevelt broke the news to him of Davies' appointment to Moscow in 1936 by saying that he knew Davies was not

capable but that Mrs. Davies had just given $10,000 to the campaign and wanted to be Mrs. Ambassador. Bullitt interview, September 19, 1955. Richard H. Ullman, "The Davies Mission and United States Soviet Relations, 1937-1941," *World Politics*, IX (January, 1957), 239, expresses the view that, although Davies was right about Russia's military power, he totally lacked comprehension of the realities of the Soviet regime.

18. Ickes, *Diary*, III, 615. Ickes noted that when Bullitt came in with the news, it was a "Bill Bullitt in distress." Bullitt was "terribly hurt" by his exclusion.

19. Ickes, *Diary*, III, 616. Bullitt remarked to Ickes that it seemed that the President had to have someone near him who was dependent upon him and who was pale and sick and gaunt. He had had such a person in Louis Howe, and now another in Hopkins. Ibid.

20. Robert E. Sherwood to Margaret L. Coit, in Coit, *Mr. Baruch* (Boston, 1957), p. 448.

21. Grace Tully memorandum, April 13, 1942, PPF, 1124, Roosevelt papers.

22. Roosevelt memorandum for Elmer Davis, June 23, 1942, OF, 799, Roosevelt papers.

23. In 1939 some Pennsylvania Democrats had tried to start a Presidential boom for Bullitt, aiming at the 1940 election. *New York Times*, March 23, 1939. Whether Bullitt's own ambitions soared that high is not known.

24. Bullitt to Roosevelt, June 18, 1942, PPF, 1124, Roosevelt papers.

25. Bullitt to Roosevelt, June 18, 1942, OF, 799, Roosevelt papers.

26. Roosevelt to Bullitt, June 22, 1942, OF, 799, Roosevelt papers. "Don't worry any more about Bill Bullitt," FDR wrote Elmer Davis. "He has just been given an appointment as an Assistant to the Secretary of the Navy." Roosevelt to Davis, June 23, 1942, OF, 799. In 1942 and 1943 Bullitt was still asking if he might see the President "urgently for 5 minutes." Usually his requests were discouraged. In 1943, Bullitt, still seeking a position in the administration, was involved in a State Department intrigue which so outraged the President that Bullitt's chances of obtaining a top government position, if they existed, were permanently ruined.

27. A *Life* article featured Bullitt as a man who talked with the President by transatlantic phone almost daily. During his recent visit to the United States, the article indicated, Bullitt was requested three

times by the President to postpone his return to France. "His Excellency, Bill Bullitt," *Life*, VI (March 27, 1939), 61. This was the kind of self-praise of which Bullitt was often guilty.

28. Mrs. Roosevelt has expressed doubt that Bullitt ever meant a great deal to the President. Eleanor Roosevelt, *This I Remember* (New York, 1949), p. 170.

29. Ambassador Robert Murphy contends that it was the misunderstanding and ill-feelings between Bullitt and Undersecretary of State Sumner Welles that caused both men to be sidelined at a critical moment in American history. Ambassador Bullitt felt he had an understanding with Roosevelt which made him principal White House adviser on European affairs, while Welles, also close to the President, was the principal adviser for other areas. When Roosevelt sent Welles to Europe in February, 1940, without even informing Bullitt, the latter concluded that Welles had "violated an agreed division of functions." A bitterness developed which Murphy regards as a severe blow to American wartime policy-making. Murphy suggests that Roosevelt's postwar policies would have been shaped more realistically had he kept these two brilliant advisers. Robert Murphy, *Diplomat Among Warriors* (New York, 1964), pp. 35-36.

30. Marquis Childs, "Trouble Maker," Washington *Post*, September 9, 1944.

31. The article "The Bankrupt Spy" by K. Demidov was reprinted from *Pravda* in *Life*, XVII (September 25, 1944), 4.

32. New York *Herald-Tribune*, August 11, 1954.

33. William C. Bullitt, "Should We Support an Attack on Red China?" *Look*, XVIII (August 24, 1954), 32-33.

34. His remarks in a *Life* article were typical. Roosevelt, he claimed, had entered a state of mental deterioration by the time of Yalta, hence the Russians were able to win a diplomatic victory. In this same article Bullitt attacked FDR for his "charm-school foreign policy," his efforts to win Stalin over by good-fellowship. This attack seems uncalled-for since Bullitt was the original exponent in Roosevelt's circle of such a Russian policy. William C. Bullitt, "How We Won the War and Lost the Peace," *Life*, XXV (September 6, 1948), 86. In a more recent article Bullitt has castigated George Kennan as a "discredited guide," a man whose "emotional involvement in Russia was so great that he could not bear the idea of standing up to the communists with force. . . ." William C. Bullitt, "What Should We Do About Russia," *US*

News and World Report, XL (June 29, 1956), 69, 71. These remarks are an example of Bullitt's sweeping condemnations.

35. Bullitt also wrote a book, *The Great Globe Itself: A Preface to World Affairs* (New York, 1946), in which he reiterated his warning that the Soviet aim remained the conquest of the world for Communism.

36. Ernest Sutherland Bates, "Unusual Talent," *Saturday Review of Literature*, II (May 1, 1926), 754.